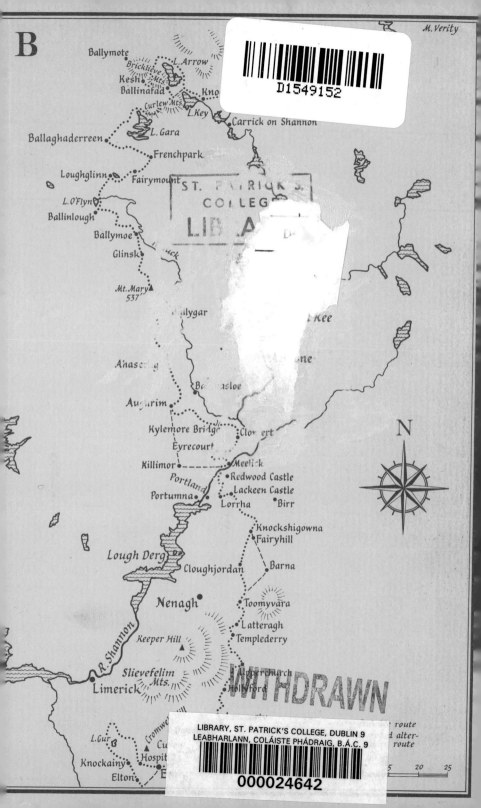

B

M. Verity

Ballymote
Bricklieve
Kesh Mts.
Ballinafad
Curlew Mts.
L. Arrow
Kno...
L. Key
Carrick on Shannon
Ballaghaderreen
L. Gara
Frenchpark
Loughglinn
Fairymount
L. O'Flyn
Ballinlough
Ballymoe
Glinsk
Mt. Mary
537'
...lygar
...Ree
A'nasc...g
B...asloe
Aughrim
Kylemore Bridge
Clon...ert
Eyrecourt
Killimor
Meelick
Portland
Redwood Castle
Portumna
Lackeen Castle
Lorrha
Birr
Knockshigowna
Fairyhill
Lough Derg
Cloughjordan
Barna
Nenagh
Toomyvara
Latteragh
Keeper Hill
Templederry
R. Shannon
Slievefelim
Mts.
...church
Limerick
Holyford
L. Gur
Cu...
Knockainy
Hospit...
Elton

N

...route
...d alter-
...route

FROM BANTRY BAY TO LEITRIM

SVLLEVANVS BEARRVS BEARRÆ ET BEAN·TRIÆ COMES
·TATIS SVÆ · LIII·CHRISTI VERO DOMINI M· DC· XIII·ANNO

Donal Cam O'Sullivan Beare

FROM BANTRY BAY
TO LEITRIM

A journey in search of O'Sullivan Beare

by

PETER SOMERVILLE-LARGE

LONDON
VICTOR GOLLANCZ LTD
1974

Printed in Great Britain by
The Camelot Press Ltd, London and Southampton

CONTENTS

LIST OF ILLUSTRATIONS

LIST OF PARTICIPANTS

The Irish Side

Donal Cam O'Sullivan Beare (1560–1618): Chieftain of
Beare and Bantry.

Dermot O'Sullivan of Dursey: Donal Cam's uncle, who
accompanied him on the retreat from Glengarriff to Leitrim
and survived.

O'Connor Kerry: A Kerry chieftain who survived the retreat.

Hugh O'Neill, Earl of Tyrone (1540–1616): "The best man
of war of his nation." Member of an illustrious Irish family that
once held the High Kingship. Partly educated in England
and brought up as an English gentleman. Returned to
Ireland in 1567 at the age of seventeen, and from that time
until the defeat of Kinsale in December, 1601, was the greatest threat to the English crown. In April, 1603, he submitted
to Mountjoy at Mellifont. Four years later, on 14th September, 1607, together with Rory O'Donnell and ninety-seven
followers, boarded a ship at Lough Swilly and sailed into
exile. This was the "Flight of the Earls", marking the end of
Gaelic rule in Ireland. He died in Rome.

Hugh Roe O'Donnell (1571–1602): The other great sixteenth century leader of Irish revolt against English rule. A
much younger man than O'Neill, he was a brilliant general,
but inclined to be too impetuous—his tactics at Kinsale are
said to have cost the battle. Immediately afterwards he went
to Spain seeking further assistance for the Irish cause, but
died suddenly there. He was buried in the chapter monastery
of St. Francis, Valladolid, "in the most solemn manner any
Gael ever had before been interred".

Rory O'Donnell (1575–1607): Hugh Roe's brother. Led the
army back to the north after Kinsale. Took over the chieftaincy. Submitted to Mountjoy at Athlone in December, 1602,
and became Earl of Tyrconnell. In 1607 joined Hugh O'Neill
in the Flight of the Earls. Died in Rome.

Philip O'Sullivan (born 1590): Son of Dermot O'Sullivan
and first cousin of Donal Cam. In 1602 he was sent to Spain

and educated there. Became a soldier and sailor, and then turned to writing. His most important work was *Historiae Catholicae Compendium*, published in 1621, which contains a detailed account of O'Sullivan Beare's retreat.

PHILIP III: Became King of Spain in 1598. Irish chieftains in revolt acknowledged him as their sovereign, although he had lost interest in Irish affairs after the Battle of Kinsale.

The English Side

SIR GEORGE CAREW (1555–1629): Able military commander, adept at psychological warfare, organized a spy network. As Lord President of Munster, subdued the province in a series of brilliant military campaigns. Took part in the Battle of Kinsale and was responsible for the successful siege of O'Sullivan Beare's fortress of Dunboy. Retired from military command in 1603; created Earl of Totnes.

LORD MOUNTJOY (1558–1603): Reluctantly pressed into Irish affairs. Informed Cecil that "he coveted no mortal fortune more than to be fairly rid of the part played on so dangerous a stage". A capable ruthless commander who fought in the Netherlands and captained an English ship against the Armada. Became Lord Deputy of Ireland in 1601 and within two years had utterly defeated the Irish. Tactics included winter campaigns and inducing famine by burning crops. A man of few words and great personal bravery. After a tempestuous love affair, married Penelope Rich to whom Sir Philip Sydney wrote his sonnets. Created Earl of Devonshire. In spite of wearing four pairs of stockings at a time, and smoking tobacco as a protection against the damp climate, he died of inflammation of the lungs resulting from his Irish experiences.

SIR CHARLES WILMOT (1570–1644): Commander who assisted Carew at the siege of Dunboy. Afterwards early in 1603, his troops invaded the Beare peninsula "destroying all that they could find meet for the relief of men". Later became President of Connacht and was created Viscount Wilmot of Athlone.

SIR OWEN O'SULLIVAN (died 1594): Donal Cam's uncle who was dispossessed.

OWEN O'SULLIVAN (died 1618): Son of the above, who sided with the English when they came to capture the fortress of Dunboy. Lord of Bantry, 1594–1603. Lord of Beare and Bantry, 1603–1618.

FYNES MORYSON (1566–1630): Secretary to Lord Mountjoy. Wrote an account of his experiences which is perhaps the best description of the country by a contemporary Englishman. Took part in the siege of Kinsale beside Mountjoy. More observant than Spenser, he had all Spenser's prejudices and a few of his own. Travelled widely in Europe before coming to Ireland. Disliked slovenly lodgings and ill-cooked meals. Irish historians consider him biased. Fellow of Peterhouse, Cambridge.

THOMAS STAFFORD: A soldier who served under Carew, he wrote *Pacata Hibernia*, a history of the Irish campaigns of the late sixteenth century. Accurate and beautifully written, though inevitably bloody minded. His fighting experiences included Kinsale and Dunboy.

QUEEN ELIZABETH (1533–1603): Her forty-five year reign saw the overthrow of Gaelic society in Ireland. She hated Irish wars because of their expense. She died in the year of O'Sullivan Beare's retreat and O'Neill's submission to Lord Mountjoy at Mellifont.

FOREWORD

ON 31ST DECEMBER, 1602, Donal Cam O'Sullivan Beare set out with a thousand followers from Glengarriff in the far south-west of Ireland on a flight to the north. His territory in Beare and Bantry had been invaded by the soldiers of the Lord President of Munster, and there was a reward for his capture. His castle of Dunboy had been razed after a grim siege, and all its defenders killed. He made the decision to go north to the shores of Lough Neagh, where he hoped to link up with Hugh O'Neill who also held out against the English. Fifteen days after he left Glengarriff he reached Leitrim, where he took refuge with Brian Oge O'Rourke. He had marched over two-hundred miles, crossed the swollen Shannon in midwinter, fought countless skirmishes and lost the great majority of his people during the hardships of the journey. When he arrived at Leitrim Castle, only thirty-five remained of the thousand people who had set out with him. Nearly all the rest had died on the way.

We know from contemporary sources where O'Sullivan camped during that fortnight, where he found food, where his horse drowned, the sites of the battles he fought and how and where he crossed the Shannon. From the story, O'Sullivan Beare's character emerges—ruthless, practical, devious, with a stubborn bravery and optimism bolstered by piety which helped him survive the journey.

This terrible retreat by a fugitive outlaw possesses an epic quality which Irishmen have recognized for hundreds of years. Perhaps in England and Scotland the flight of Bonnie Prince Charlie has something of the same heroic appeal. The episode has had an obsessive fascination for me and I have become familiar with most of its details. It was suggested to me that one way of getting a clearer understanding of the extent of O'Sullivan's achievement was by following the route that he and his followers took. The more I thought about this idea the more interested I became in carrying it out. I planned to walk it in midwinter, setting out on the last day of the year, stopping at the places he did, seeking out traditions about his flight. This I managed to do during January, 1972.

At first I thought that I would try to stick to his exact time-table, making night marches through Connacht and camping in the places where he stopped. But his schedule was un-pleasantly arduous; he covered over thirty miles the first day, and then, unless impeded by having to fight, moved as rapidly as possible, starting before sunrise each day. On a number of occasions his people had to march by night—once for more than fifty miles without stopping. I did some walking during the night, but I felt that to attempt over two hundred miles in a fortnight would have given me little time to absorb the atmos-phere of places on the route. The idea of camping in deserted churchyards on cold January nights was unappealing, although, when I did come to sleep out, it was far less uncomfortable than I thought it would be. Most evenings I sought out conventional accommodation. My pace lacked urgency so that my journey became twice as long as O'Sullivan's. I took liberties in follow-ing his traditional route, which at many points is speculative. It seemed wrong to be passing within ten miles of Spenser's country and not to make a detour to visit it; or to miss out the mysteries of Lough Gur and Keshcorran just because O'Sullivan did not go very near them. My plans became less and less rigid, since inevitably the phantom I followed receded as I became absorbed in my own experiences. I did not find out anything new about O'Sullivan, and this is in no way a historian's account. But I found the places associated with him and many of the traditions about him that have lingered for four-hundred years. I have tried to clarify the episodes of the flight by bringing in contemporary detail about Ireland during this terrible period of defeat. It has seemed best to begin with an account of his early life, the siege of Dunboy and the circumstances leading up to the march.

In the account of my walk a number of themes dominate. One is the weather: it rained a lot. Another is pubs: my journey may read as one long pubcrawl, but it would be just the same if I were to do it again. This is merely because the warmth and feeling of community in any town or hamlet rested in the pubs, and there was limited comfort and entertainment outside them. I walked through winter landscapes of subdued smoky colours, big skies, bogs and mountains. Ruins are a good part of it as well. There were times, especially when it was raining hard, when austerity and depression dominated; but more often I felt exhilaration in crossing wild and beautiful country. The route of the march is across a part of Ireland that is largely off the tourist beat. The other theme that I have tried to convey is the pleasure of meeting infinitely kind, patient and hospitable people who had to deal with the problems of someone wholly unexpected—a traveller walking in midwinter.

Captain Sean Feehan suggested the idea to me. Among others who have given me the benefit of their specialized knowledge, I would like to thank Colonel Cyril Mattimoe and Commandant Barry O'Brien of the Irish Military History Society, Dr E. M. Fahy of University College, Cork, Mr Michael FitzRyan of the National Museum, and Captain Kevin Danaher of University College, Dublin. On my walk I was helped at every stage by people like Mr William O'Donnell at Annacarty, Mr Denis Collins at Liscarroll, Mr and Mrs Ryan-Purcell, Colonel Galloway, Mr Joyce at Aughrim, The MacDermot and Madam MacDermot. The Royal Irish Academy has allowed me to use its library, and Miss Boyd of the photographic section of Bord Fáilte advised me on the selection of photographs. I am also grateful to the trustess of Maynooth College for permission to reproduce O'Sullivan Beare's portrait. My wife did not make the walk with me, but after it was finished worked with me at every stage of writing this book.

The translations from Irish poems on pages 89, 141 and 147 are taken from Frank O'Connor's *Kings, Lords & Commons*. The lines on page 209 are from Philip Larkin's *Churchgoing*.

P. S.-L.

INTRODUCTION

Donall O'Sullivan Beare was the most formidable opponent
of the English amongst the chiefs of Munster. Indeed he was
almost the only important "mere Irishman" who in
Elizabethan times resisted the crown in Munster.

W. Butler. *Gleanings from Irish History*

1 DONAL CAM

THE SIEGE OF Dunboy ended on 22nd June, 1602, when the
castle was blown to pieces. The defenders were all killed in the
fighting or executed after they surrendered. The English
victors, with their immense superiority in men and arms, had at
least eighty casualties as a result of the furious fighting. (Six
months before at Kinsale, the battle that had changed Irish
history, they lost about a dozen men.) The siege was not very
important militarily, being merely the reduction of a rebel
stronghold in Munster, a postscript to the Battle of Kinsale that
helped to discourage Spain from taking further direct part in
Irish affairs. But it was fought with a ferocity that was remarkable, even by the savage standards of the day.

The ruins of Dunboy lie on the southern shore of the Beare
peninsula in a corner of West Cork that has retained a feeling of
remoteness, if not inaccessibility. They overlook the narrow
entrance to Bearhaven harbour; across the sound rises the
squat bulbous shape of Bear Island, and behind the island
stretches the line of the Caha mountains, dominated by the
high rounded dome of Hungry Hill. Nothing much remains of
the original castle; part of a tower is to be seen, and a fragment
of staircase. Recent excavations have revealed that after it was
destroyed the site was used again. A starshaped enclosure has
been retraced, marking a fort built by the Cromwellians half a
century after the siege. Later this fort was transformed into a
two-storey house, all trace of which has vanished. Of the original
fortress the foundations of the inside curtain wall have been
discovered. The castle was built right beside this wall, and
against it was erected the famous sod bank which was thrown
up as a fortification just before the siege began. On its south side

the curtain wall bestrode a cistern or tank, a very unusual feature in an Irish castle, and a valuable asset during a siege. Water could be drawn from it from both outside and in.

I camped on a quiet summer evening beside the ruins of Dunboy. The knob of land overlooking Bantry Bay on which it stood lies only a few hundred yards from another ruin—the vast nineteenth-century Italianate mansion built by the Puxley family and burnt down by the I.R.A. in 1921. The Puxleys settled here at the end of the seventeenth century, first living over the castle ruin, then building up their great folly, still impressive in its setting of luxuriant rhododendron and scrub trees that cover much of the ground on which the siege took place. All around Dunboy itself they planted evergreen oaks to romanticize the view, and these trees still flourish.

During the day the sea and the clouds had created a particular brilliance of light which changed restlessly every few minutes. A portion of the grey silky water would become a patch of Mediterranean blue; bars of light would cut through the rain on a distant mountain coloured like a chameleon's skin with succeeding blues, greens, browns and greys. In the evening the wind died; the sea relaxed into a mirror, absorbing images of trees and rocks and doubling the belt of seaweed left by the tide. The slightest sound magnified like a gunshot . . . a slap of an oar, the chug of a trawler's engine returning to Bearhaven with its catch. I sat outside my tent, watching the light fade slowly from the sky until all that remained was the dark red beam from the lighthouse on the island that marks the entrance to the sound. As the dusk thickened, a heron got up and went home, flying lazily, the slow beat of its wings just keeping its heavy body from touching its reflection. At the point of darkness, a colony of rooks arrived and settled in the trees, breaking the silence with their querulous cawing and flapping of wings. As they jostled to find themselves places to roost, their movements seemed to recreate some of the urgency of the past; they evoked the background of the battle for me, and I thought of the Irish and Elizabethan soldiers who had died before the ruined walls. The broken stairs which we see today lead down to what was called "the cellar", where the defenders were trapped in a fog of gunpowder smoke and masonry dust; a few

feet from my tent was the place where they had made their
final submission, knowing that they would be hanged.

Dunboy was the chief fortress of O'Sullivan Beare. Its
defence was the responsibility of Donal Cam O'Sullivan Beare,
chieftain of Beare and Bantry, who was just past forty at the
time of the siege. He belonged to a sept, or clan, that came
originally from the country around Tipperary that stretches from
Clonmel to the great fortress mound which overlooks the Suir
at Knockgraffan. After the Norman invasion the O'Sullivans
were driven southwards, eventually to West Cork and Kerry.
The land they took over stretched round the indented coast
from Bantry Bay to Dingle Bay. Shortly after settling these
shores the clan divided into two great branches, O'Sullivan
Mor and O'Sullivan Beare. The territory of O'Sullivan Beare
was south of the Kenmare river and included most of the Bearhaven peninsula, Dursey Island and Bantry.

Donal Cam's father, Donal, was chieftain. On his death, in
1563, "slain by a bad man named MacGillicuddy", the succession passed to his uncle, Owen O'Sullivan, because Donal
Cam was a child. The traditional Gaelic system of inheritance
did not acknowledge primogeniture, but allowed for the chieftaincy to go to the strongest man in the sept. Another uncle,
Philip, was appointed *tanaiste*, or successor to Owen, and given
the family castle of Ardea on the Kenmare river. It seemed that
Donal Cam had little chance of receiving any great portion of
the land over which his father had ruled.

His name is said to be derived from *Domhnaill Cam*—crooked
Donal—indicating that he had one shoulder higher than the
other. It is not known whether this was true throughout his life;
certainly there is no sign of any physical disability in the existing
portrait of him which was painted when he was in exile in
Spain. This used to hang in the Irish college at Salamanca, but
after the college closed in 1954 it was brought to Ireland and is
now in Maynooth. It shows a strikingly handsome middle-aged
man dressed as a Spanish grandee. He wears a high starched
ruff, armour, and round the back of his neck the gold order of
St. Iago Compostella of which he was made a knight by Philip
III. A helmet rests on the table beside him. The Latin inscription
translates as "O'Sullivan Beare, Count of Beare and Bantry, in the

53rd year of his age, but in the 1613th year of Christ our Lord".

Like other sons of chieftains he received an Anglicized education. After a childhood spent in Eyeries on the south side of the Kenmare river, he was sent to school in Waterford where he learnt Latin and English. Knowledge of Latin was essential to an Irish gentleman; English was increasingly useful in view of the changing circumstances of Ireland's history.

Stories survive of his youthful exploits. The writers of the *Annals of the Four Masters* describe how at the age of eighteen he led a force against a raiding party consisting of an Englishman named Captain Zouch, an O'Donovan and a McSwiney, who came to plunder Bantry Abbey. He had less than fifty men, but killed 300 of the enemy. This may be the same occasion when he is said to have pursued and captured a cattle raider, also named O'Donovan; the oak tree on which the thief was hanged and under which he was buried used to be pointed out as *Dairchin Dhiarmada*, Diarmuid's grave. Cattle raiding provided an initiation into manhood for a young warrior, whether he was protecting the *creaght*, the great herd belonging to the clan, or rustling a neighbour's. But otherwise Donal Cam does not seem to have been involved in the violence of the times; he took no part in the later sequences of the Desmond rebellion, although he must have grown to manhood during its last phases. Perhaps he was already considering the possibility of obtaining his father's lands and titles by invoking Roman law at the expense of the laws of tanistry which had given the chieftaincy to his uncle.

The O'Sullivan Beare were subject to the MacCarthy's of Carbery and Muskerry, and had to undertake tiresome duties such as "coshering", putting up the MacCarthy lords and their dependants every so often for two days and two nights of "entertainment" at Dunboy. They had to pay MacCarthy Mor's out-of-hand expenses, like travel and marrying off his daughters, building his houses and being responsible for his debts. Other obligations imposed by MacCarthy Mor included a levy of two shillings and sixpence on every ship that entered O'Sullivan Beare's harbours, regular recruitment of gallowglass and kern to fight for him, and provisions for his greyhounds, hounds and horses.

In 1565 MacCarthy Mor had acknowledged the English crown under the system of surrender and regrant, and had been created Earl of Clancarthy. His subsidiary chieftain, Donal Cam's uncle followed suit and became a knight, Sir Owen O'Sullivan. He was confirmed in his rights by the Queen, at the same time acknowledging his continued list of services to the new Lord Clancarthy.

But in spite of his subservience to the MacCarthys, Sir Owen O'Sullivan was lord of his own territory. Although this consisted largely of mountain land, "scabby country", it more than made up for its lack of good pasture by the importance of the fishing off its shores. Somewhere near the Skellig rocks the Atlantic currents divide around a vast bed of plankton that spreads about the south-west coast of Ireland. As a result, the fish feeding in these waters have always been abundant enough to attract the fleets of Europe to the coasts of West Cork. In the sixteenth century the waters off Beare teemed with pilchards; pilchards were not only eaten, but oil was obtained from them which was used in industrial processes like making saddlery and harness. They were an important factor in medieval economy.

The chieftain known in poetry as *Ua Súileabháin na gcaolbharc*, O'Sullivan of the Slender Ships, controlled a large section of these fishing grounds. Remote from any central government, he could exact rents for fishing which the authorities in Cork might consider to be theirs, and dispose of pirates and trespassers a good deal more ruthlessly than modern Icelandic gunboats. The ships from France and Spain which had come in search of the pilchards and herring shoals had to find harbours to refit and obtain provisions and water. Of all the harbours on the south-west coast Bearhaven was the most attractive. "Bearhaven is an excellent harbourage," considered Thomas Stafford, "a narrow entry, slack tides, good anchorage, places fit to ground ships, deep and evermore smooth waters—of capacities sufficient to contain all the ships of Europe . . . the coast yields such abundance of sea fish as few places in Christendom . . . the fishing dues, though light, brought £500 per annum to O'Sullivan . . .".

Donal Cam's uncle had followed the lead of the clan's

overlord in adopting an English title and acknowledging the jurisdiction of the crown. It was understandable that Donal Cam himself should consider that English law should be adopted in respect of his own position. By that law he could claim his uncle's position as head of the sept. Throughout Ireland there was a gradual adherence to the new system, undermining the more complicated legal etiquette of Gaelic law. Often the countryman welcomed the changes; in theory, at least, his chieftain became his landlord, and controlled rents were introduced instead of the old levies which could be exorbitant. Tanistry (the laws relating to inheritance) and gavelkind (the word English lawyers gave to the traditional form of land tenure, which meant periodical redistribution of land) were being replaced as the policy of surrender and regrant became general. Local jurisdiction was abolished in the face of acknow-ledgement of English legal practice. A great deal of injustice was suffered in individual cases, but it seemed that for a short time tenants were protected because security of tenure was to be guaranteed. The new system was designed to absorb local and national customs smoothly. The old Gaelic society had scarcely been democratic; Sean O'Faolain has considered that "the native upper classes . . . were liked little better than nineteenth-century landlords". But the changes were accom-panied by systematic and ruthless colonization; the wars of the Elizabethan era were followed by a long series of land distur-bances during the seventeenth century. Gaelic nobility was eclipsed and destroyed, and with it most aspects of Gaelic culture.

The tanist system was one of the first casualties brought about by the new innovations of law. Its decline was inevitable. It had always demanded too much good will and co-operation in families of warriors who tended to dispute with the too flexible rights of succession. Inheritance by lineal descent had the advantage of being simple and clear, and unless the heirs were minors, gave less opportunity for dissent. Disputes over succession were increasingly common. "The chiefest occasion of dissension," wrote Nicholas Browne, "is still between them that challenge by tanistry."

Thus in 1587 Donal Cam was following a trend when he felt himself in a strong enough position to challenge his uncle's right to the chieftaincy of Beare, claiming the title under English lineal law. His case, which lasted for two years, became an unedifying family quarrel. Commissioners were appointed to visit Beare and Bantry, pedigrees were produced and examined, witnesses called. "Sir Owen declares Donnell's witnesses are murderers, thieves, drunkards, beggars. Donnell retorts that two of them are Lords of great countries, one an Alderman of Cork . . . Sir Owen describes the lands in dispute as barbarous and uncivil, and the people unacquainted with civil government until his time . . ." The report of the Commissioners made plain the real value of the inheritance. "The standing rent due to O'Sullivan out or upon the country [is] but £40, and that itself was ever allotted the lady for the time being towards her idle expenses, the country being no good for land, but all valleys, cragged rocks and hills . . . and therefore O'Sullivan for time being liveth only by the sea and the commodity thereof, as the fishing, his wrecks and such like. . . ."

The Commissioners decided in favour of Donal Cam; it suited the English to change the succession. Not only was the imposition of lineal inheritance part of a pattern to break up the great Irish lordships; but, as it happened, Sir Owen O'Sullivan had been implicated in the Desmond rebellion. Sometime during 1593–94 at Mallow, the title of Chieftain was awarded to Donal Cam; he was now O'Sullivan Beare, and he was granted the greater part of his father's territory. Sir Owen had to be content with Whiddy Island and part of Bantry, which was in fact the richer portion of the land. But he had been deprived of the most important part of the patrimony, the harbour of Bearhaven with its rich fishing dues, and the chief castle of Dunboy nearby. Donal Cam's other uncle, Philip the *Tanaiste*, was confirmed in the ownership of Ardea.

Sir Owen died the same year, and was succeeded by his son, a second Sir Owen. Seven years later this dispossessed son was to fight on the side of the English and to aid them considerably in his efforts to demonstrate his loyalty. He saw a chance of getting back his patrimony which Donal Cam had taken from him. Almost all the important families of the time were divided in this way, some acknowledging the Crown, others going into rebellion. There was a Queen's O'Rourke and an Irish

O'Rourke, a Queen's Maguire and an Irish Maguire, and so on. Donal Cam O'Sullivan Beare, in spite of having his inheritance restored by English law, chose to become one of the most formidable of the enemies of the Queen.

In Munster the new English settlers were an increasing threat. They had been encouraged to take over the coastline as a precaution against possible invasion from Spain. Thirty years earlier Sir Humphry Gilbert and his associates from the west country had applied to the Queen to form a chartered corporation to exploit the fishing of West Cork . . . "to have of her highness in fee fearme the havens of Baltimore and Beere haven . . . and the Ilandes belonging to Beere haven . . . to make a Corporat Towne and to fortiffy the same . . . at Beere haven or upon eny of the Ilandes aforesaid . . .". Nothing of the sort had happened yet. Berehaven was remote, but it must have seemed only a matter of time before O'Sullivan Beare's newly acquired inheritance and livelihood was claimed by force. After the Desmond rebellion in 1580 more than 574,000 acres of land in Munster had been confiscated. Recently in 1596 his great neighbour, the first and last Earl of Clancarthy, had died, and now his estates were in dispute, eventually to pass into the possession of settlers.

In 1600 Munster flared in rebellion. The violence which destroyed towns and castles throughout the province and made Spenser into a refugee brought about the collapse of the plantation system which had been built up during the previous thirty years. The Munster rebels were briskly defeated by Sir George Carew, but these defeats were paralleled in the north by the brilliantly successful campaigns of Hugh O'Neill and Hugh O'Donnell. Their victories gave new encouragement to uncommitted chieftains like O'Sullivan Beare to whom the political and military situation began to look auspicious. The prospect of driving out the English permanently seemed even brighter when Spain finally sent aid to her Catholic ally.

Spain had always been a threat to English rule in Ireland. Throughout the reign of Elizabeth the English had an exaggerated fear that their hold of the country would be wrested from them by Spanish interference, much as nineteenth-century English imperialists continued to be convinced that India would be invaded by Russia. This fear had stimulated some of the greatest cruelties of the Irish wars. Foreign soldiers taken in arms at Smerwick and exhausted survivors of the Armada had died in their hundreds in order to discourage the King of Spain from acting on that much-quoted proverb: "He that will England win, let him in Ireland begin." Prevailing winds could bring Spanish fleets swiftly to the south-west shores at any season of the year; Spanish sailors and fishermen had been familiar with Irish waters for centuries. Now twelve years after the Armada the Spanish were sending another fleet to land an army on Ireland's south coast.

The fleet set out from Cadiz in the early autumn of 1601 with over four thousand foot soldiers, six pieces of artillery and arms and ammunition for the Irish. As usual, the weather was unkind to Spanish ships invading these islands. The fleet was caught in a storm and forced to divide into two sections. In September, 1601, the larger force of ships made Kinsale and landed the army under Don Juan del Aguila, who proceeded to fortify the little town. Immediately, O'Sullivan Beare, who was not long in receipt of his new title from the English commissioners, sent del Aguila notice that he was prepared to offer him two thousand soldiers, a thousand armed and a thousand to be armed at Spanish expense. They would be used to block the advance of Lord Mountjoy towards Kinsale. This offer was refused by the Spanish commander.

The smaller portion of the divided fleet, under the command of Don Pedro de Zuibar, which had put back to Cadiz, set out once again. Six ships made a landfall at Castlehaven, thirty miles west of Kinsale, on 1st December, 1601. This second Spanish landing coincided with the arrival of Hugh O'Neill and his army at Kinsale, and finally persuaded O'Sullivan Beare and other Munster chieftains to commit themselves irrevocably to rebellion. The O'Driscolls at Castlehaven delivered their castle to the Spaniards at once; Sir Fineen O'Driscoll of Baltimore, who had been a loyalist all his life, yielded the two castles that covered the entrance to the port of Baltimore. And further to the west, O'Sullivan Beare also delivered up the castle of Dunboy by formal treaty to the Spanish in the name of the King of Spain.

He had marched over from Bantry to Castlehaven where he
assisted de Zuibar in driving off the English admiral, Leveson,
who had hurried over to Castlehaven from Cork. After Leveson
had sailed his battered ships away, O'Sullivan Beare arranged
for his uncle, Dermot O'Sullivan, to guide a subordinate of de
Zuibar, a young captain named Saavedra, to Dunboy. On 20th
December, 1602, Saavedra was installed there, having been
supplied by O'Sullivan Beare with beasts of burden and two
months' provisions. He had sixty soldiers and eight pieces of
cannon; his orders were to "keep open for the Spanish fleet
access to the harbour which is a safe and much frequented one,
and to keep out of the enemy therefrom".

Meanwhile, O'Sullivan Beare, who had assembled an army
of a thousand men, set about marching to Kinsale to the support
of O'Neill and O'Donnell. On the same day that Captain
Saavedra was settled in Dunboy, O'Sullivan wrote to the King
of Spain, pledging him his entire support in the united battle to
destroy the heretic enemy. He acknowledged King Philip III
as his commander in chief. "I bequeath and offer in humbleness
of mind and with all my heart, my own person with all my
forces perpetually to serve your majesty. I commit also my wife,
my children, my manors, towns, country and lands, and my
haven of Dunboy, called Bearhaven (next under God) to the
protection, keeping and defence or commercie to your majesty,
to be and remain in your hands and at your disposition. . . ."
This letter was captured by Carew's agents, and could not
have helped O'Sullivan's cause when he came to sue for
pardon.

2 THE SIEGE OF DUNBOY

The whole number of the ward consisted of one hundred
and forty fighting men, being the best choice of all their
forces, of which not one escaped, but were either slain,
executed or buried in the ruins, and so obstinate a defence
had not been seen within the Kingdom.

Pacata Hibernia

O'Sullivan Beare was present at Kinsale, the final battle which
is said to have marked the death knell of Gaelic Ireland. During

the wild thunderous night of 23rd December, 1601, lightning flamed on spearheads like lamps. The English army, under the command of the Lord Deputy, Mountjoy, was short of supplies, its horses weak from want of food, its men sick and dying from some unspecified disease—dysentery or typhus, which was known as the Irish Ague, or perhaps a severe form of Spanish flu. It represented the centre of a dismal sandwich, between the Spanish garrison, more or less comfortably installed in fortified Kinsale, and the combined forces of the Irish gathering to attack. Before dawn on the 24th, the English—who had somehow been warned of the impending Irish advance, perhaps by Carew's friend, Brian MacHugh Oge McMahon—crawled out of their flooded trenches and moved over the miry ground to meet the oncoming Irish. An hour later they had won an overwhelming victory, having suffered an absurdly small amount of casualties—Graeme's Cornet killed, Sir Henry Danvers, Sir William Godolphin, Captain Henry Crofts, the Scout Master, wounded and about half a dozen common soldiers dead. In view of the army's depressed state, the triumph came as a surprise. "No man," said Sir George Carew, "can yield reasons for this miraculous victory."

The shattered Irish left twelve hundred dead on the battlefield. O'Neill led his broken forces northward back to Tyrone over the same route they had passed on their triumphant way south through Ireland a short time before. O'Donnell handed the command of his surviving soldiers over to his brother, Rory, to take back to the north. He himself had made the decision to go to Spain and personally seek further help from King Philip. "When the resolution was heard by all in general," wrote the Four Masters, "it was pitiful and mournful to hear the loud wailing and lamentation that prevailed through O'Donnell's camp at the time, for never afterwards did they behold as a ruler over them, him who was then their leader and earthly prince in all the land of Erin."

O'Sullivan Beare, who had not had much field experience, nevertheless distinguished himself at this melancholy defeat. He demonstrated that he was a cautious strategist by siding with O'Neill against the more impetuous O'Donnell, whose orders to attack had been so disastrous. He proved himself an

enterprising field commander, one of the few who kept his head
and managed to extricate his forces intact.

Before they departed his superiors promoted him. According
to the Four Masters, "After Kinsale, these high Irishmen,
namely O'Neill and O'Donnell, ordered that the chief command and leadership shall be given to O'Sullivan Beare, the
son of Donal, son of Dermot, for he was at this time the best
commander among their allies in Munster." In the chaotic
conditions it was not altogether a welcome promotion, and at
first O'Sullivan Beare preferred to sue Mountjoy for pardon.
He was refused. There is a story, quoted by Standish O'Grady,
that this refusal was partly the result of a letter he wrote which
contained some malicious remarks about the Queen. It is more
likely that he was considered outside pardon because he still
had a dangerously well equipped army at his disposal and had
done nothing to disband it. In addition, he was a prominent
chieftain who had shown sudden and unexpected disloyalty
after living in obscurity the whole of his life. His distant fortress
at Dunboy could become a focus for waning Irish hopes.

Other soldiers and chieftains joined him. They included
Daniel MacCarthy, son of the lately deceased Earl of Clancarthy, O'Connor Kerry, who was to continue to be his comrade
throughout all the difficult events of the next year, the Knight
of Glin, the Knight of Kerry, and so on. In addition he enlisted
for pay two famous and energetic mercenary captains, William
Burke, a Connacht man, and Richard Tyrell, a ruthless Anglo-
Irish *condottiere* who had been considered the best professional
commander in O'Neill's army. Along with their gallowglasses
and his own soldiers from Beare and Bantry, his force numbered
two thousand picked men, which was a large army by Irish
standards. He sent a message to del Aguila, the Spanish general
besieged in Kinsale, to try to convince him that he was strong
enough to hold the English in check for a while until further
help came. But del Aguila was already preparing to
surrender.

During the débâcle the Spanish had sat in the walled town of
Kinsale unaware of what was taking place. They sallied forth
only when they heard the volley that Mountjoy ordered to
be fired in celebration of the victory; they found the English

army there to meet them and they saw no sign of the Irish. Co-operation between del Aguila and O'Neill and O'Donnell had been negligible. The Spanish made a few more efforts to engage the enfeebled English forces, who were still dying of sickness at a terrible rate, but their hearts were not in the work, and it was plain that del Aguila considered his mission was over. When he sued for peace, he found that he got along much better with his enemies than he had with his allies, for he seems to have shared some of the current English views about "mere" Irish. During the parley he told the intermediary, Godolphin, that he thought the Irish were weak and barbarous, if not perfidious. By the time he left for Spain, congratulating himself on the terms he had received, he and Mountjoy, and Sir George Carew, Mountjoy's subordinate, were all good friends. (Before he was disgraced by King Philip and died under house arrest after a plaint from Irish exiles, there was time for an exchange of gifts. Carew sent del Aguila "a small bark laden with Irish commodities and in it a choice Irish horse with a rich pad". Del Aguila sent back some wine and lemons and oranges; unfortunately they arrived sour and rotten.)

On 2nd January, 1602, following many stately courtesies between del Aguila and Mountjoy, terms of surrender were drawn up in English, Spanish, Latin and Italian. The Spanish forces were to be shipped back to Spain; they were permitted to take with them their colours, artillery, money and other possessions. The castles at Castlehaven, Baltimore and Dunboy, which the Irish chieftains had given over by treaty to the Spanish command, and which were garrisoned with Spanish soldiers and guns, were to be handed over to the English.

The programme of organizing the surrender of these castles began on 9th January, when Lord Mountjoy directed Captain Roger Harvey and Captain George Flower to go by sea with several companies and take over Castlehaven, Baltimore and Dunboy. Their progress was delayed by strong westerly winds, so that it was not until 12th February that Captain Harvey reached his first objective, and entered the harbour of Castlehaven. There he found the Spanish commander, Pedro Lopez de Soto, in the act of besieging the castle which he had charge of. The O'Driscolls had retaken their own stronghold by a ruse, and now the Spaniards were trying to get it back in order to surrender it formally to the English.

When they saw Captain Harvey's fleet appear, the O'Driscolls capitulated immediately, and the surrender of Castlehaven was effected. Captain Harvey then took de Soto across to Baltimore to arrange for the surrender of the two castles there. From Baltimore he set sail for Dunboy with two companies. But contrary winds again assailed him on the difficult winter journey as he tacked towards Mizen Head; he lost no fewer than fifty men from sickness during a sea voyage that must have been frightful to endure. At last he was driven back, leaving Dunboy still in the hands of the Spaniards.

O'Sullivan Beare had meanwhile returned to the Beare peninsula, where he stormed and captured Carriganass, a castle belonging to his cousin and enemy, Sir Owen O'Sullivan. When he heard of the surrender of Castlehaven, he decided to retake his own castle of Dunboy which was next on the list to be delivered up to the English. He marched a thousand men down from Carriganass to Dunboy, a distance of about twenty-five miles, and stationed them outside the fortress; then "in the dead of the night when the Spaniards were soundly sleeping and the key to the castle in the Captain's custody, O'Sullivan caused his men, amongst them some masons, to break a hole in the wall." He crept inside with a force of two hundred; before Saavedra and the angry Spaniards, aroused from sleep, were persuaded to surrender, they put up some resistance and discharged their muskets among the Irish. Three of O'Sullivan's best gentlemen were killed.

He wrote testily to King Philip, justifying his actions. He had initially delivered up his castle to his Spanish allies for the purpose of making war on his enemies, and felt that he had every right to retake "the only key of mine inheritance, whereupon the living of many thousand persons doth rest", rather than hand it over to English heretics.

The subjection of Dunboy, now the main rebel fortress in Munster that held out against the English, had become a supremely important objective. It was the responsibility of Sir George Carew, the Lord President of Munster, who was determined to make an example of it in order to break the back of the rebellion in the south. Carew was an experienced veteran, who in thirty years' fighting in Ireland had taken many castles. He had served in the Desmond and Baltinglass rebellions, and had rounded up survivors of the Armada. More recently, in 1596, he had gone abroad to Cadiz with Essex's triumphant expedition. He was one of a number of Elizabethan soldier-statesmen who thrived in the chaos of Ireland, where his brilliant military tactics, superior organization and unscrupulous system of playing off one Irish chieftain against another had brought him continued success. His ruthless campaign after the Munster rising in 1598 had quietened the province. He had taken a decisive part in Kinsale, and indeed, he hinted more than once that he, rather than Mountjoy, was responsible for that victory.

He was a man of obsessions. There was the curious obsession inherited from his uncle, Sir Peter Carew, that he was entitled to vast estates in Cork which had been granted by Henry II to his ancestor, Robert FitzStephen, four centuries before. Sir Peter had stirred up the Desmond rebellion trying to obtain his mythical possessions; he died in 1575, but his nephew still pursued this ancient claim a quarter of a century later. And Dunboy, too, had become an obsession. "If I can take the castle of Dunboy," he wrote to Cecil on 19th April, "I will soon send them packing and end the rebellion in Munster." Experienced soldiers and friends, among them the Earl of Ormonde, who knew the terrain, considered the castle inaccessible, and even if it were reached across the mountains of Beare, it might well prove impregnable in its natural defensive position, strengthened by Spanish artillery. Carew's problem was to get his own artillery there. Massive guns were necessary to batter the place down. This problem was by no means unusual; cannon had been used in Ireland as early as 1492 during the siege of Waterford, and henceforth made the strongest castles open to attack. If, however, they were at all remote, the forests, bad roads and bogs that lay around them made the transport of guns impracticable. But Carew knew that however impenetrable Dunboy might seem by land, it was accessible by sea. When the fine weather came, with the right kind of organization, heavy cannon could be brought around by ship into Bantry Bay.

Since he did not set out for Dunboy until late in April, O'Sullivan Beare had a respite. He sent Saavedra to Baltimore with most of his men for shipment to Spain, keeping with him the artillery and three gunners to man it. The Irish were always short of guns, ammunition and skilled instructors, and Donal Cam was no exception. For this reason these men were important. During the siege they were specifically offered pardon by Carew, but they refused it and perished with the rest. Now they gave O'Sullivan their professional advice as to how Dunboy could best be defended against the coming attack. Unfortunately their ideas appear to have been worse than useless. Under their direction the curtain wall of the castle was faced with sods to a depth of eighteen feet. The purpose of this sod bank, strengthened with wood and faggots, was to absorb as much as possible of the cannon shot that would be directed against the castle walls. But the mountain of earth also managed to cover the slits of the curtain wall, so that the garrison within was largely unable to see out or to return the enemy's fire except from the top of the castle. Also, if the enemy succeeded in knocking down enough of the fabric of the building into the narrow space between its outer wall and the curtain wall, the slopes of the sod reinforcement would provide an easy climb to a storming party trying to enter the breach.

During the lull before the attack O'Sullivan wrote letters in Latin to his Spanish allies. To the King he said: "I have taken upon me with the help of God to keep my castle and haven from the hands of my enemies. I have sent my son and heir, being of the age of five years, as a pledge for accomplishing your will on this behalf." The child was dispatched to the Governor of Galicia, a faithful supporter of the Irish cause, who kept him in his care until O'Sullivan went into exile. Now Donal Cam wrote to him that "all of us who took the part of the king are on the verge of ruins in consequence of the agreement made by Don Juan del Aguila with the Lord Deputy" . . . "I, by God's grace, can serve his majesty anywhere with a thousand men armed in our Irish fashion, and will muster them at my own expense from my twenty leagues of protected coast." If and when the worst came, he begged the Spaniards "to send a small ship towards the coast to relieve me and the rest of my family . . . to be carried into Spain for the saving of our lives out of the hands of these merciless heretical enemies." The "small ship" did eventually arrive with a different purpose which was to prove fatal to his fortunes.

In early March Carew directed his subordinate, the Earl of Thomond, to reconnoitre the Beare peninsula with four thousand men. The Earl's instructions were to "burn the rebels' corn in Carbery, Beare and Bantry, take their cows and to use all hostile prosecution upon the persons of the people as in such cases of rebellion is accustomed . . . the capital rebels that are to resist you are O'Sullivan and Tirrel . . . Your Lordship must leave no means unessayed to get them alive or dead." Thomond had no specific instructions to attack Dunboy at this stage; with his large force he was merely to carry out a massive job of reconnaissance. But the weather was against him. In bitter cold and howling wind he marched to Bantry Abbey, where he established himself, stationing seven hundred of his men on Whiddy Island opposite. Most of his force consisted of Irish levies; scarcely five hundred were English. The rest were Irish and Anglo-Irish who, in the words of Philip O'Sullivan, "in the desperate circumstances thought it would be unsafe and dangerous to disown the Queen".

At Bantry Thomond's spies brought him news of Dunboy's fortifications, and he made one or two essays into the snow-covered mountains that lay between him and the castle. Then he gave up, and returned to Cork to report to Carew, leaving behind a garrison consisting of eight companies on Whiddy Island.

Carew set out from Cork on 23rd March to take Dunboy. On the way he stopped at Timoleague and hanged three rebels; then he made a detour along the coast via Rosscarberry to inspect the garrisons of Castlehaven and Baltimore, where he received some supplies before marching on to Bantry. In crossing the mountains between Skibbereen and Bantry he met with some slight resistance from O'Driscolls and O'Sullivans, but not enough to deter him from reaching the head of Bantry Bay by the last day of the month. He made his headquarters at O'Sullivan Beare's castle of Dunnamark, the Fort of the Ships, which he immediately renamed Castle Carew in honour of an ancestor

whom he fancied had built it. Here the dispossessed Owen
O'Sullivan came to meet him and acknowledge himself a
useful ally.

At Dunnamark, wrote Thomas Stafford, who accompanied
the expedition, "we sat down as well as to give annoyance to
the rebels as to tarry the coming of the shipping with victuals,
munitions and ordinance". O'Sullivan Beare's forces were
camped only half a mile away and there must have been
numerous skirmishes. Carew was awaiting supplies on ships
which had been collected from Cork, Waterford and as far
away as England. He was also expecting reinforcements from
Sir Charles Wilmot, who had been successfully subduing
Kerry, and was now marching across to Bantry. The ships with
food and munitions arrived on 11th May, and Wilmot rode in
on the same day, having brought his forces over by Killarney
and across Mangerton, "a most hideous and uncouth mountain". On the next day, 12th May, a hoy bearing the cannon
sailed down Bantry Bay.

Carew now held a council of war in which it was decided
that the only practical way of reaching Dunboy was to ferry
the attacking force by sea. This would obviate the necessity of
fighting a way down the peninsula through pathless rebel-held
mountains. Like Mountjoy and most Elizabethan warriors,
Carew had naval experience. But to move his troops by sea he
needed good weather, and the weather that month was frightful. Wind and rain swept continually down the bay, and in his
new castle, counting the daily increase of the sick list, he
declared that the country of Beare was full of witches.

The fine weather did not return until 31st May. Leaving his
sick under guard on Whiddy Island, Carew broke camp and
marched his forces down the shorter Sheep's Head peninsula on
the south side of Bantry Bay to a point opposite Dursey Island.
Studded with pinnaces and galleons, the water stretching to a
western horizon touched with light, Bantry Bay must have
resembled a landscape painted by Claude. The view from
Sheep's Head to the line of mountains across the wide girth of
the bay cannot have changed very much, for even the scummy
line of hotels and villas at Glengarriff and the unsuccessfully
camouflaged oil storage tanks on Whiddy Island are reduced

by the splendid arrangement of scenery. Not that Carew's mind was on scenery. On 1st June Thomond's regiment was ferried over to Bear Island. Wilmot's men followed, then Sir Richard Percy's and finally Carew's, under his own command. They camped at the east end of the island where a Martello tower now stands. At the west end their scouts could look across a slip of deep water directly towards Dunboy.

Having seen shipload after shipload of enemy soldiers approach the land on Bear Island, the Constable of Dunboy, Captain Richard MacGeoghegan, rowed over from the castle to have an interview with Thomond. Thomond was an Irishman who could speak Irish, and an easier intermediary than any of Carew's English officers. He informed MacGeoghegan that this was the last chance for the besieged men to surrender with a hope of having their lives spared. MacGeoghegan answered that he had only come over out of the affection he felt towards him, and to warn him that the crossing from Bear Island to Dunboy must be the occasion for unnecessary bloodshed. "I know that you must land at yonder sandy bay, where before your coming, the place will be so trenched and gabioned as you must run upon assured death."

He spoke with every confidence and then returned to Dunboy to await events. It is plain that when he came over to parley with Thomond he had no idea of surrender, although his small garrison was facing an opposing force of over four thousand, and he had seen the shipping of the cannon across the bay. His confidence did not only arise from the good defensive position of the castle, but also from the expectation of impending Spanish help. The hopes of the besieged had been aroused by definite news that a Spanish ship had arrived at Ardea Castle on the Kenmare river just across Slieve Miskish mountains to the north, just a day's march away.

This news, which seemed to offer the first tangible evidence that the Spanish were returning with more reinforcements, actually ensured the doom of the defenders. The patache *Santiguillo*, which had only sailed from Cadiz after many delays, arrived in Ireland just at the wrong time. The money it carried had come too late to buy more recruits to defend the castle. At the same time it encouraged the besieged with false hopes, especially since it brought assurances, both verbal and written, that more practical Spanish aid in the form of soldiers would follow very shortly. After its arrival, the garrison waited without trying to cut its way out until in the end there was no escape and it had to fight to the death. The defenders of Dunboy had also to fight Carew without their proper leader. O'Sullivan Beare had gone across the Caha mountains to Ardea to meet the Spanish ship himself.

At a time when his castle was facing destruction, O'Sullivan Beare was not inside it; he was at Ardea personally greeting the fatal vessel with its disappointing load—food, ammunition and 20,000 ducats of gold. There were three weeks of June, in which he could return and fight with the trapped men or make a stand against Carew. He must have had well over a thousand men with him, and could have marched back with Tyrell and Burke and their experienced mercenaries who were in his employ. But he did not. People still feel passionately angry about his non-appearance at Dunboy. His apologists have affirmed that it was necessary for him to stay at Ardea and meet the boat personally. Some have suggested that since Dunboy was technically held for the King of Spain, and the Spanish had instructions to formally surrender it to the English, O'Sullivan decided that it would be illegal for him to defend his own castle. This unsatisfactory theory is disproved by his explanatory letter to the King of Spain.

His detractors have implied quite simply that he was a coward. But his behaviour on countless other occasions was the reverse of cowardly. It is possible, because he was a ruthless man, that when he learned Carew had managed to land his guns and was in the process of establishing them within firing distance of the castle, O'Sullivan decided quite cold bloodedly to sacrifice Dunboy and its defenders and so avoid a direct confrontation. After the siege was over and Carew and the bulk of his forces had retired, he would be in a strong position to organize a mobile guerrilla campaign, which is what in fact he did. But it may also be that torn with his desire to receive the new Spanish reinforcements, and lead them directly to the scene of the siege, he lingered on in Ardea, not realizing in the muddle of difficult communications that Dunboy was in imminent peril. He was, after all, expecting the Spanish soldiers hourly, reinforced by the promises of the two priests who had landed from the *Santiguillo* and were waiting with him. One was Father Archer and the other was Bishop MacEgan.

Father Archer, a Jesuit, had been at Kinsale and joined with O'Sullivan after the battle was over. When O'Sullivan captured Dunboy from the Spaniards, it had been Father Archer's task to inform Saavedra of his position. He was experienced in negotiation; before Kinsale he had various interviews as an intermediary with the English, including one with Carew and Thomond which almost ended in blows. His contemporaries either admired or execrated him. Philip O'Sullivan wrote that "he was held not merely in awe by the heretics, but even in a kind of superstitious terror, and they believed him able to walk dry footed over the sea . . . arguing that he ought to be called the Arch devil rather than Archer". Now after helping O'Sullivan recapture Dunboy, he had made a lightning trip to Spain and was returning.

The Jesuits, in particular, had done much to foster the counter-reformation and to incite the rebellious Irish. The English authorities detested them. "Sermons and prayer they never have—the alehouse is their church—the text Spanish sack. . . ." Two years after Dunboy they were banished by decree. "As all the evils that afflicted the province of Munster during the recent rebellion was due to the influence of Jesuits and priests . . . it has been decided to decree capital punishment against all priests. . . ."

Certainly Father Archer's influence over O'Sullivan Beare seems to have been very strong. But what finally decided his behaviour was the advice of another cleric. Among the passengers aboard the *Santiguillo* was the fierce titular Bishop of Ross, Owen MacEgan. It was the eloquence of Bishop Mac-Egan that persuaded everyone concerned that Spanish reinforcements would arrive at any moment. He wrote to Richard MacGeoghegan, "within a few days you shall have relief of men coming to help you thither out of Spain. The great army of fourteen thousand is coming." Father Archer believed it. MacGeoghegan believed it. Everyone believed it. The only word of caution seems to have come from another passenger, also a priest, John Ania, who wrote to Brother Dominic Collins at Dunboy advising him to hold out for as long as possible. "Although we expect speedy relief out of Spain yet be you wise to preserve the store of victuals discreetly. Devise yourself all the invention possible to hold out this siege. . . ."

Some of the ducats were divided up at Ardea, a transaction witnessed by Owen O'Sullivan's captured wife. Then O'Sullivan Beare, his clerical friends, and his army settled down and waited for the Spanish to arrive. But the truth was that they would never come. Originally, and this was the reason that Bishop MacEgan had been so confident, there were actual plans to prepare a fleet for Ireland, and two galleons and twelve transports were marked out at Corunna as being vessels for the Irish relief force. But King Philip decided to cut his losses; he was less keen than his father had been to help his co-religionists. After Kinsale his interest in involving his country directly in Irish affairs steadily dwindled. "The king grows weary of the Irish who flock thither, and incessantly suing for recompense for their losses (as they allege) sustained in his majesties service whom they and all the rebels in Ireland call their king and master."

In the absence of its leader, the events leading to the destruction of the garrison have a grisly inevitability. Carew could have shelled Dunboy from Bear Island—his guns were powerful enough. But the defenders would have had a chance to escape, and he wanted to annihilate them. He was a military strategist of genius, and he neatly established an attacking force on the mainland below the castle. During his parley with Thomond on 2nd June, MacGeoghegan had revealed that the Irish intended to fortify the sandy bay and make a stand there. Carew absorbed this gratuitous piece of information while he reconnoitred the coast in a pinnace, observing another point where landing was feasible, a place concealed from the sandy bay by high ground.

On Sunday, 6th June, he landed two guns and two regiments on the little islet of Dinish between Bear Island and Dunboy. These were a feint; their orders were to keep the defenders on the sandy bay under fire so that they would think that a landing was planned there. But the next two regiments who embarked from Beare Island were not landed on Dinish or on the sandy bay. The transports veered onward and took them to the point further up the east that Carew had selected during his reconnaissance. There they landed safely, to be followed up as quickly as possible by reinforcements. By the time the Irish were aware of their presence they had established a beach-head. When MacGeoghegan's soldiers tried to drive them back into the sea, they were beaten off and forced to retire into Dunboy. Richard Tyrell, O'Sullivan Beare's mercenary captain, was wounded in this fighting but, probably summing up the position, managed to slip away with many of his soldiers and join O'Sullivan at Ardea. He must have brought news of what had happened—that now the defenders could only get away by abandoning the castle and trying to cut their way out of the siege. Even the sea was constantly patrolled by boats to prevent anyone escaping by swimming, while in the deep waters of Beare Sound and in Bantry itself, warships watched for Spaniards.

Carew's military tactics had been smart, although as usual he acted against advice, since Owen O'Sullivan considered such a landing impossible. Now he was able to bring over his guns within easy distance and establish them somewhere about the site of the present ruin of the Puxley mansion. Setting them up was a cumbersome business which would take about two weeks.

After Tyrell's escape the unenviable task of defending the castle was left to a hundred and forty picked men. They included the three Spanish gunners, one Italian who had come over with the Spanish force at Kinsale, two Englishmen and another cleric. This was Brother Dominic Collins, also a tireless apostle of the counter-reformation, and, in addition, a fighting man. Originally from Cork, he went to the continent as a young man to enlist as a soldier, but instead became a Jesuit lay-brother in Santiago. He had come over from Castlehaven with de Zuibar as bearer of letters to the Irish princes, and had been with O'Sullivan Beare at Kinsale. Inside Dunboy he waited for deliverance. Father Archer had written to him from Ardea: "Out of Spain are we in vehement expectation, and for powder, lead and money furnished . . . now to come to more

practical matters, understand that there are two ways to
attempt you, that is scaling with ladders and with battery. For
scaling I doubt not but your wits need no direction, and for
battery you may make up the breach in the night. . . ." It was
advice that Brother Collins must have received rather dubiously
as he looked out on to the platform Carew was building for his
massive siege guns. The fact that these urgent letters were
smuggled in during the siege, to be found after the surrender,
indicates that for a time there may have been means of escape
for the garrison before the castle was cut off on its headland.

Meanwhile other pockets of resistance in the area were
broken. A force made a surprise landing on the mainland and
secured Castle Dermod, another small O'Sullivan fortress on
the site of the present town of Castletown Bearhaven. Earlier,
before Carew had set out from Dunnamark, Owen O'Sullivan
and his two brothers went with a small force to capture the
O'Mahoney castle of Dunmanus guarding the next bay. While
the guns were in the process of being entrenched before Dunboy,
on 20th June an expedition set off from the main camp under
the command of John Bostock, again accompanied by Owen
O'Sullivan. Its objective was Dursey Island where O'Sullivan
Beare had planned to make a last stand in the event of Dunboy's
surrender. Dursey was considered virtually impregnable,
because, although it lies close to the mainland, for much of the
year it is cut off by currents that sweep through the narrow
sound. The difficulty of getting a force across its currents in
small open boats meant that in most circumstances it could be
cut off on landing. There was a castle, which had been built
fairly recently by O'Sullivan Beare's uncle, Dermot O'Sullivan,
on a point at the eastern edge of the island overlooking the exit
of the sound into the Atlantic and guarding the approach of any
enemy coming over from the mainland. Here O'Sullivan
Beare had stationed a small garrison of forty picked men under
the command of Connor, son of Sir Fineen O'Driscoll of
Baltimore. They had three small Spanish cannon with which
they hoped to defend themselves and the scores of refugees who
had flocked over to Dursey from the mainland. They were
probably not looking for trouble until after Dunboy had fallen.
On 12th June the treacherous sea was calm and when Bostock

and Owen O'Sullivan slipped easily over the sound, the garrison
was caught by surprise.

Islands are not good places on which to take refuge, since
there is nowhere to escape to. It is possible that the attacker
may be feeling merciful, but he will find it tiresome to ferry
prisoners and hysterical women and children back to the mainland, across a tricky piece of water like Dursey Sound. Owen
O'Sullivan may have been incensed at the sight of his wife, who
had finally been brought over to Dursey Castle after her
capture at Carriganass.

First of all the attackers dismantled the fort and set fire to
the ancient little church of St. Michael whose ruins are still to
be seen. Then, wrote Philip O'Sullivan, "they shot down,
hacked with swords and ran through with their spears the now
disarmed garrison and others, old men, women and children,
whom they had driven in one heap. Some ran their swords up to
the hilt through the babe and mother who was carrying it at her
breast, others paraded before their comrades little children
writhing and convulsed on their spears, and finally, binding all
the survivors, they threw them into the sea over jagged and
sharp rocks, showering on them shots and stones."

The day continued fine, and the sea calm, and the attackers
were able to drive back over the sound five hundred milch cows
which had been collected on the island from all over the
countryside.

At Dunboy the work of entrenching the guns continued. The
garrison with its substitute leader tried to beat off the enemy
who surrounded it; there were skirmishes, sallies and counter-
attacks. Once a sniper nearly hit Carew from the battlements,
but he reined his horse in time and escaped spattered with
earth. The much vaunted "Spanish ordinance" was unable to
find the range of the working parties; the small cannon installed
by Saavedra and manned by the Spanish gunners only proved
effective during the final stages of the siege.

On the 16th the "gabions, trenches and platforms" were
finished and during the night the guns were drawn up and
ranged within a hundred and forty yards from the castle.
Carew wasted no more time.

"About four o'clock in the morning." wrote Thomas

Stafford, "our battery, consisting of one demi-cannon, two whole culverins and one demi-culverin, began to play which continued without intrusion till towards nine in the forenoon, at which a turret annexed to the castle was beaten down." This was the south-west turret, in which one of the Spanish guns, known as a falcon, had been mounted. Many of the defenders died when they were buried under the tower's masonry, and its collapse brought about a crisis within Dunboy, as the survivors realized that the castle could only stand up to the guns for a few more hours. In the confusion a messenger came out to the English offering to surrender if the garrison was allowed honourable terms and permitted to march out with their arms. But behind him was the noise of firearms, as some of his comrades continued to discharge their weapons towards the guns. Carew promptly hanged him.

Carew had anticipated that the fabric of the castle would hold out for seven days against the pounding of his cannonade. But much to his satisfaction it took less than a day before a breach was made, four hours after the collapse of the turret. Dice were thrown among his officers, to select who should lead the assault, and the luck fell to Captain Doddington and Lieutenant Francis Kirton. They led their soldiers to a furious and desperate fight. A tower flanked the newly opened breach, and in this the defenders still had a Spanish gun which at last proved its worth. It was fired into the thick of the attacking troops, mowing down scores of them, until at last a chance shot from the English side killed the gunner. The besieged continued to rain down shot and stone until at last pressure from the numbers of the attackers began to drive them inside. Eventually the whole garrison was driven down into the cellars while the enemy overran the battered castle above it. Forty of the defenders managed to break away from the battle and run down to the water where they threw themselves into the sea to try to avoid capture by swimming. But Carew's patrol of boats, positioned precisely to prevent them doing so, rowed about firing at each swimmer, picking them off one by one so that they were shot or drowned to a man. Among those watching from the boats was Thomas Stafford, the author of *Pacata Hibernia*.

The survivors, now reduced to seventy-seven, grouped in the

cellar which was a small semi-underground room, the remnants
of whose walls still survive. Again they offered to surrender on a
promise of their lives, but they were refused. Dusk was falling
and the assaulting regiments put a strong guard on the trapped
men and retired to wait for the dawn.

After a night spent in crowded darkness among groaning,
wounded and dying, twenty-six of the men in the cellar surrendered unconditionally next morning. They included the
two surviving Spaniards and the Italian. They came up to the
daylight from a wild scene beneath them where "there lay a
great heap of bodies and arms, the whole hall ran streams of
blood". Lying among the corpses and nine barrels of gunpowder
which had been stored there as ammunition for the guns, was
Richard MacGeoghegan, the Constable, who was too seriously
wounded to continue the command. The leadership of the
defenders was now given to Thomas Taylor, an Englishman
belonging to Tyrell's forces—he was actually married to
Tyrell's niece.

Carew resumed the bombardment, intending to bury the
survivors beneath the masonry. But rather than die in this
terrible way they compelled Taylor to arrange their surrender.
After negotiations a number of English officers went down into
the vaults. In the semi-darkness, MacGeoghegan, covered with
wounds, managed to stagger to his feet and make his way
towards an open barrel of gunpowder with a lighted candle in
his hand to destroy himself and his enemies as Samson did. He
was seized and held by Captain Power, who meant to make him
prisoner, but in the confusion and fear other soldiers rushed
forward and stabbed him to death. Then Taylor and the rest of
those who had surrendered were brought out.

Thomond hanged fifty-eight of them in pairs in the market
place in the camp. Taylor and fifteen others were reprieved for
the time being, because they were mercenaries employed by
Tyrell. Tyrell had been wavering in loyalty to O'Sullivan
Beare, and earlier in the campaign had had an interview with
Thomond about the possibility of going over to the English. It
seems that he had been prevented from doing so by the eloquence of Father Archer. Now, although some of his men were
hostages, he would not change sides in order to save their lives,

and later they too were executed. Taylor and Brother Collins were taken to Cork, where Taylor was hanged in chains; Collins was then brought to his native Youghal and executed there.

Given Carew's mood and the grim military etiquette of the time, there was nothing very unusual in contemporary eyes about this execution of brave men. It was perfectly standard practice. Throughout history there have been harsh military rules about sieges. If a town or castle resisted, it has to pay the penalty when it falls. The custom of hanging the defeated of a hard-won siege was long established throughout Europe; to give only one example among scores, King John hanged the defenders of Rochester in 1215, after a siege that was noted for the savagery of its hand-to-hand fighting. The remarkable point about the story of the burghers of Calais was that they were spared. In Ireland during the sixteenth century and afterwards the total destruction of a besieged garrison was too common to draw any special comment. The horrible massacre of Smerwick was not condemned even by Catholic sources, which merely considered that Lord Grey was taking the tough line. Carew, also, was taking the tough line; he wished to crush Munster, and the deaths of the men who defended Dunboy, the fact that no one was allowed to escape, was a warning to others who considered resistance. In Ireland today men have been hooded and shot for similar reasons.

On 22nd June the walls that were left standing were blown up with the Spanish gunpowder that MacGeoghegan had tried to ignite when they came to get him.

3 DEPARTURE

I am not only disappointed by all power, but also driven to run to the mountains, there to live like wolves for the safety of my life, and to leave to their merciless discretion all the poor men, women and children within the length of thirty leagues.

Letter from O'Sullivan Beare to Don Pedro de Zuibar, March, 1602

Carew considered his main task done. It was not necessary for him to march his troops across the Slieve Miskish in pursuit of

Plaque commemorating the Siege of Dunboy

Ruins of Dunboy Castle

Winter landscape, Glengarriff

O'Sullivan Beare. The chieftain was less important than his stronghold. Instead, an expedition was mounted against the O'Mahoney castle of Leamcon, situated on a remote spit of land off the southern coast of Carbery. Captain Roger Harvey was sent the thirty-odd miles over mountainous terrain to subdue it. Leamcon surrendered after putting up some resistance, since it had to be undermined by the besieging instrument known as "the sow", traces of whose action can still be seen at the base of the castle walls. Captain Harvey, a favourite of Carew, was less stern than his patron. Those who surrendered were spared and a list of men shipped to Spain on 7th July, 1602, included Conor O'Mahoney of Leamcon. Meanwhile Carew had set out for Cork on the last day of June, leaving six garrisons in Carbery to perform mopping-up operations.

But O'Sullivan Beare was not yet an insignificant fighting force. His *creaght*, his main herd of cattle, had not yet been captured. He had plenty of money, Spanish gold, with which he could pay his *bonnaghts*, the soldiers in his employ, and attract other dissident Irishmen to his side. He could command a force of over a thousand soldiers. He knew his country well, terrain perfectly suitable for the sort of guerrilla warfare in which the rebels were adept. "Wheresoever forces are conducted against the rebels," wrote Thomas Gainsford, who had fought at Kinsale, "they forthwith retire and hold themselves close in bush and bogs, without engaging in any fight, but upon advantage; and no sooner shall our camp move or dislodge, but they forthwith possess and overspread the ground we held . . ." The Munster coastline may have been in English hands, but much of the interior was still outside their control.

For a short time O'Sullivan Beare's forces had a limited success. They formed a flying column, not dissimilar in spirit to Tom Barry's three hundred years later, and swept through Muskerry retaking some of the more important castles—Carrignacurra and Dundareirke, which was in the hands of the Queen's MacCarthys, Macroom Castle which was held by the O'Donoghue of the Glens, and the high rock tower of Carrigaphooca, another MacCarthy stronghold. The men who defended these castles for the Queen changed sides. If Spanish help, ever expected, had arrived things might have been different.

On 18th July, Father Archer sailed yet again for Spain in a small ship captured from the English; his mission was yet another plea to King Philip for soldiers. But the Spanish treasury, strained with efforts to maintain armies to crush the rebellious Dutch, could afford no more costly Irish failures. Besides, "news had come to Spain from England that all the rebels in Munster were taken in as subjects, and had been put in security for their loyalty or been slain". Even so, in late August it was rumoured that a fleet of twenty-four Spanish ships had been sighted off the Old Head of Kinsale. "Hereupon you might see horsemen galloping this way and that way, to and fro with such signs of gladness and apparent joy as though the day of their deliverance was near at hand. ..." But the rumours proved false. Later there was news that Hugh O'Donnell had died on his way to another audience with the King at Valladolid. His death at the age of thirty at Simincas on 16th September, following a short illness, was sudden and unexpected. Carew believed that he had been successfully poisoned by his agent, James Blake, which is quite possible, although in those days of medical mysteries unexplained illness and death often led to diagnosis of poison.

The loss of Dunboy, now a heap of blackened stones, had not wholly destroyed the morale of O'Sullivan Beare's allies. But O'Donnell's death and the realization that "the Spanish come not this winter" wrecked any hopes of an Irish revival in Munster. The first of his allies to desert him were the wavering MacCarthys, so that he lost control of his new gains in Muskerry and was obliged to retreat to the area around Bantry. Then Tyrell left. Although he had managed to avoid being trapped at Dunboy, Tyrell had been badly shaken after a defeat by Sir Samuel Bagenal which took place while he was fighting in Muskerry during October. According to Stafford, "Tyrell had run away in his shirt, leaving both his garments and weapons behind him, and his wife followed no better clothed". Asked by O'Sullivan Beare to make a diversion into Kerry, he was offered a payment from the Spanish funds and a bonus in the form of cattle if he would stay for a further three months' service. But he was tired of fighting a losing war in the south and set off with his own small band of soldiers to march for Connacht. His defection must have been a bad blow, since all accounts of the period show him to be a most capable commander. The Four Masters commented that "it would be impossible to reckon, describe or innumerate the preys he made, the deaths he caused, the castles he took, the men he made prisoner".

The English forces had weakened over the summer through sickness and the steady natural drain of deaths that affected their troops any time they campaigned in Ireland. Now in early winter they were brought to full strength by a thousand new recruits gathered in Cork. Sir Charles Wilmot, the veteran of the Kerry campaign that previous spring, was detailed as Governor of Beare to assault O'Sullivan's bases on the peninsula. Once again he crossed from Kerry, marching over the mountains from his post at Dunkerron Castle near Kenmare. With his reinforcements he had good prospects for a quick and successful action. The Irish were at a natural disadvantage in winter, since supply became an increasing problem. Cattle were wasted by being driven to and fro; when stores of grain were burnt there was nothing to replace them. Rebels could be seen more easily through the leafless trees. Winter campaigns broke Irish hearts, wrote Fynes Moryson. They were an innovation of Mountjoy's, the first general to disregard the inclemency of the Irish weather.

Wilmot concentrated his force near Glengarriff, "on a plot of dry ground (environed with woods and bogs)", wrote Thomas Stafford, "of so small capacity that most of our guards and sentries were held either on the bog or the edge of the wood, and yet there was not so much firm ground within five miles of the place. Within two miles therof encamped Donnell O'Sulevan, William Burke with his bonaghts."

The Irish camp was soon spotted through the grey oak trees. Sometime late in December Wilmot engaged it and managed to capture the *creaght*, O'Sullivan Beare's cattle. Fighting for it was fierce; the struggle lasted six hours and there were heavy casualties on both sides. But from Wilmot's point of view the capture of two thousand cows and four thousand sheep was worth while. Not only did it ensure his army's rations, but it meant disaster for O'Sullivan Beare.

The first consequence of the loss of his essential supplies was a violent row between O'Sullivan Beare and William Burke, the chief commander of his remaining mercenaries. O'Sullivan Beare argued that he had been a fair employer and a good friend. Burke retorted that he had gained nothing in his service; he had lost not only all his possessions and any spoils of victory he had laid hands on, but his comrades and kinsmen whom he valued more than all the King of Spain's treasure. "And therefore with extreme passion (as was reported) cursing and damning himself for staying so long in Munster, in all haste with two hundred men (for the rest were either slain or protected) he fled and followed Captain Tirrell into O'Carroll's country."

Hemmed in by Wilmot's troops without enough soldiers to form an effective force, or supplies with which to feed them, O'Sullivan now made his decision to break out of the Beare peninsula and go north. Fighting in Beare had brought him nothing but misfortune. His allies had all gone north, where the chances of resistance appeared to be better. If he stayed trying to elude Wilmot, the chances were that his remaining forces would be slaughtered. Above all, now that his cattle had been captured he had an urgent supply problem. Beare, like the rest of Munster, was suffering from famine conditions, and although O'Sullivan had money, there was probably no food to buy.

His destination was the camp of O'Neill at Glenconkeine which is in modern Fermanagh by the shores of Lough Neagh. Here he could assume that there was still territory which held out against the English, and that the remnants of O'Neill's army had regrouped. His route, which veered on a slight south-west/north-east axis, cut across the western half of Ireland for three hundred miles, before turning eastward for a further hundred and fifty miles to Glenconkeine.

The speed and distance that he covered was striking, although by no means unique. In modern times the length of an average day's march under normal conditions is fifteen miles a day, averaging eighteen minutes to a mile with numerous halts. But this pace can be speeded up considerably; medieval foot soldiers were expected to cover thirty miles a day without difficulty. Under pressure they could do more; in 1200 King

John's army, marching to the relief of Mirabeau, covered eighty miles in two days. O'Donnell's soldiers completed many spectacular marches. In 1600 they went into Connacht to attack the Earl of Thomond, travelling as far as Loop Head in County Clare and back again in eight to ten days—a distance of thirty to forty miles a day. On O'Donnell's march south through Ireland to the relief of Kinsale, he had avoided Carew's army at Holycross in Tipperary, by making a spectacular crossing of the frozen Slieve Felim mountains in early November, covering thirty-two Irish miles (just over forty English) in virtually a single march over mountainous country. This earned Carew's grudging admiration; he said it was "the greatest march that had ever been made for a winter campaign". But on many occasions O'Sullivan Beare had to move just as quickly, impeded by his train of civilian camp followers, suffering from hunger and constantly having to fight as they went.

All along their route O'Sullivan and his people were attacked and harried by those through whose territory they passed. It was a time of universal terror when people had to struggle to keep alive—and this fugitive and his men were doubly unwelcome. The return northward of O'Neill's men exactly a year before had been just as terrible, when many of the retreating soldiers, who were dying of starvation, had had to fight off their fellow countrymen. "They that did kiss them in their going forward, did both strip them and shoot bullets at them on their return, and for their arms they did drown them and tread them down into every bog and soft place." O'Donnell's army, which had burned the country on its way down, covering it with smoke, suffered badly from those who sought revenge. In the end a troop of women, Carew said, might have beaten it.

But it is O'Sullivan Beare's march that survives in the popular imagination. The flight of a persecuted people fighting determined enemies along the way is more appealing than the fortunes of defeated armies. The story has an epic quality about it; Dunboy and O'Sullivan Beare might be said to echo the fortunes of Troy and Pious Aeneas. And much of the fascination of the march arises from the fact that its details have been meticulously preserved.

When O'Sullivan Beare's young son was shipped off to Spain as a refugee he was accompanied by another little boy, Philip, the son of Dermot of Dursey. Philip was one of seventeen children, thirteen of whom are said to have perished as a consequence of the wars. He received a Spanish education and became a soldier and a sailor, fighting for his namesake, King Philip III. He was also a writer, and he wrote *Historiae Catholicae Iberniae Compendium*, the Catholic History of Ireland, which he dedicated to the King. In this work he chronicled the Irish campaigns in detail, heightening the wickedness of the invading heretics. The climax of the story of the final wars is his vivid day-to-day account of O'Sullivan Beare's march. He heard it at first hand, since his father had taken part in it, and most probably he had discussed it with O'Sullivan Beare himself. His narrative is largely paralleled by another detailed contemporary source, written from the English point of view. This is the account of the Munster campaigns, *Pacata Hibernia*, by Thomas Stafford, a veteran of Carew's army who was present at Dunboy and fought with Wilmot at Glengarriff. His magnificent Elizabethan prose relates an Old Testament narrative of slaughter and retribution.

O'Sullivan Beare had left Glengarriff hurriedly, flying before Wilmot's army. He took with him a thousand people of whom thirteen were horsemen and about four hundred soldiers. The rest, an assortment of foot followers, horseboys, women, old men and servants, could only be described as refugees. They had one day's rations with them. They set off in bitter weather on the last day of the year to cross the cold mountain passes behind Glengarriff. Thomas Stafford described their predicament with cruel clarity: "O'Sullivan, finding his estate desperate, that either he must starve in Munster or beg in Ulster, made choice of the lesser evil." Even the wind helped to drive O'Sullivan Beare out of his country, which he would not see again.

CHAPTER ONE

Glengarriff—Gougane Barra

On the 31st of December in the year of our redeemer's birth, 1602, O'Sullivan set out from Glengarriff and at night pitched his tents twenty-six miles in Muskerry country at a place which the natives call Augeris.

Philip O'Sullivan

IN BANTRY RAIN hammered the car windows as we drove through the deserted market square past the statue of St Brendan, his arms raised blessing a patch of dirty water in the harbour. The day before had been clear and sunny. The weather will hold, people had said earnestly as if they had tied it up in a bag for me. They were right; twenty minutes later the clouds had gone and a pale golden light shone down on Glengarriff and its ring of mountains. Now the morning was mild as spring, full of the warmth that brings daffodils in West Cork to bloom in January.

According to tradition O'Sullivan Beare began his journey from a place called Dereenafalla, which is derived from *Doire na Fola*, meaning the Oakwood of Blood. The site is in the heart of the present state forest, where surviving oaks huddle in dusty grey squares among the new forestry plantations and the long brown cuttings of bog. We drove past an incongruous red-roofed bungalow and stopped at a bridge.

My wife looked on as I strapped on the rucksack and tottered before sitting down on a bank at the side of a road. The evening before she had watched me struggle to push cooking pots into it, the sleeping bag and stove, money, eight or nine maps, underwear and so on. For a couple of weeks before, when I had remembered, I rubbed my feet with surgical spirit to harden the soles and prevent blistering. This morning I put on woollen combinations, which were too warm for the day, some old clothes which I hoped to wear out, and a Japanese hunting cap with fur earflaps which I had bought the day before in

Ballydehob. Most essential of all, I carried a good umbrella.

"Only necessary things should be taken," wrote Fynes Moryson, in his *Discourse on Travelling*. As Mountjoy's secretary he had followed the Lord Deputy all over Ireland, besides visiting many countries in Europe. He was scornful of stay-at-homes: "Running water is sweet, but standing pools stink." He also wrote that "one should consider one's age, for neither the very young man nor the old man will profit—middle age is best". That was all right by me. Two centuries later Latocnaye, the young French aristocrat, who came to Ireland in 1798, brought with him "a powder bag made with a woman's glove, a razor, some pairs of silk stockings, a pair of breeches fine enough to be rolled into a lump as big as a man's fist; two very fine shirts, three handkerchiefs and my travelling dress. I put my three bundles in a handkerchief and carried them on top of my sword cane—on which I had an umbrella, which excited curiosity everywhere and made the girls laugh, though I do not know for what." In 1842 the American missionary, Asanath Nicholson, travelled here wearing a polka-dot mackintosh over her dress. Her portmanteau contained Bibles for distribution, and she, too, had an umbrella.

My wife drove off and I began to walk to Leitrim. I tried to imagine O'Sullivan Beare and his people breaking out from the encirclement of Wilmot's troops and travelling along this route. He had four hundred picked soldiers, experienced and well armed, a mixture of mercenaries and recruits from his own clan. The gallowglasses, originally of Scottish origin, had been bred to war for generations; but the distinction between them and the Irish soldiers who fought under a similar mercenary arrangement had long broken down. The kern, recruited originally as local levies or *bonnaghts*, fought under separate command. Many of O'Sullivan's soldiers were Connacht men. Veterans of Kinsale, they had been fighting almost ceaselessly since the fall of Dunboy, and had become an efficient integrated fighting force, a miniature version of O'Neill's army where the *bonnaghts* had been grouped in companies of a hundred under a constable or captain. By 1601 they were paid 3*d.* a day, exclusive of their keep, and O'Sullivan must have worked on a similar system.

View of Glengarriff

Ruins of
Carriganass
Castle

Pass of
Keimaneigh,
Co. Cork

Ruins of
Eachros
Church

Some wore pieces of armour and mail shirts; others may have had jerkins made of skins, helmets of bascinet type, and perhaps gambersons, which were quilted iron-reinforced tunics. There was no recognized uniform among Irish soldiers and their clothes ranged from relative finery to rags. Weapons would have been equally varied. O'Sullivan Beare himself would most probably have worn a more conventional style of military dress. He had been educated in an Anglicized atmosphere in Waterford, and had been brought up to emulate the more efficient aspects of English military organization. His clothes and armour may have made his appearance very similar to that of one of Carew's officers.

Only a few of his own officers and companions are named. They included his uncle, Dermot of Dursey, who was seventy years old, the veteran O'Connor Kerry, and Thomas Burke, another mercenary member of the Connacht clan, perhaps a near relative of that William Burke who had departed in a rage.

The small army was efficient and capable. It carried along with it six hundred civilians, old and young, non-combatants, women, baggage carriers, body servants and grooms. They had left at dawn and now were moving at top speed, a long column making swiftly for the mountains. They walked, or rather raced along, carrying their possessions and leading horses loaded with baggage, a straggling group placed between the divided force for protection, with a rearguard constantly on the look-out for trouble. When they came under attack, these civilians, constantly falling behind and unable to keep up with the column's speed, were the natural victims of harassment.

Like the soldiers they would have presented a motley, confused appearance, reflecting the changes in traditional clothing during the last half of the sixteenth century. Pictures of Irishmen "drawne from the quickie" in mid-century still showed them dressed in traditional knee-length tunics above bare legs and feet. But in John Derricke's *Image of Ireland*, published in 1581, the Irish soldiers are pictured wearing homespun trews and leather brogues. By 1610 "civil" or anglicized Irishmen could be described as "apparilled at all poynts like the English, only that they retain thyr mantle which is a garment not indecent. It differs nothing from the long cloke but to the fringe at the upper end which in cold weather they wear over their heads for warmth."

The majority of O'Sullivan's camp followers would have worn the mantle, the famous garment whose value in protection against the weather the English had recognized. It was issued to Mountjoy's troops. "Being never so wet [it] will with a little shaking and wringing be presently dry; for want of which the soldiers lying abroad, marching and keeping watch and ward in cold and wet in the winter time, die in the Irish ague and flux most pitifully." Fynes Moryson reported that among the Irish the cloak was often wetted at night before its owner settled down to sleep, "for they find that when their bodies have once warmed the wet mantles the smoke of them keeps their bodies in temperate heat all the night following". This extraordinary custom was also practised by the Scotch with their plaids. There would have still been those who wore their hair in heavy fringes known as glib. Glib hid the expression in a man's eyes; it infuriated Elizabethan observers almost as much as that other persistent Gaelic custom of ploughing by the tail.

The phantom army which I now began to follow had slipped away from this wilderness. Behind fields of winter grass which had dried to a deep orange the bowl of mountains rose in the direction of the Kerry border, grey-rocked scarred peaks tossed up to the sky. There was a burnt look about the hillsides; St Brendan may have remembered a winter Irish landscape when the Devil opened the door of hell and showed him "plains bare and burning, hills round and hairy, valleys crooked and wormy, bogs rough and prickly, woods dark and fiery, roads filthy and beast haunted . . .".

I asked the first man I met, a farmer attended by a couple of spotted dogs, if he knew about O'Sullivan Beare.

"Donal Cam? Why wouldn't I? If he had any head at all on him he would have fought the English before they ever reached Dunboy." He told me that there was a place in the neighbourhood called *Cúr na Fola*, the Froth of Blood, but that the men who knew all about these old things had died.

A signpost marked the turn-off for Youngfield, once *Gort-na-Caillighe*, where Wilmot had camped with his force of five

thousand men. The distance between the Irish and English
camps had been only about three miles; yet the forests then
were so thick that for some time the enemies had been unaware
of each other. In 1602 this valley was covered in trees. The old
richness and variety of the forest can be seen in the remnants
that have survived, patches of huge oaks garlanded in moss and
ivy with overhanging branches as thick as ships' spars. In fact
branches from this forest had been used for ships' spars. As
early as 1603 the great forests of Munster were supplying
wooden casks for wine and wood for galleys in Scotland, and
providing timber for the East India Company. But most of
them were cut for charcoal. Only a few years after O'Sullivan
Beare's departure Sir William Petty began iron works on the
Beare peninsula. Later the Whites of Bantry also used oak wood
for smelting—"a villainous furnace had been erected in the
vicinity, and its open and cupidinous throat had absorbed,
when turned into charcoal, all the ancient woods of Glengarriff
where the O'Sullivans hunted in prosperity and hid in adver-
sity". The forests were systematically destroyed so that later
travellers would exclaim at the barrenness of the Beare peninsula. In 1600 almost one-eighth of Ireland was forested; by 1800
this proportion was reduced to one-fiftieth as a result of commercial exploitation.

The forests consisted mainly of oak, arbutus and birch. The
arbutus has vanished and *rhododendron ponticum*, introduced in
the nineteenth century, some time after its appearance in 1812
as a rare exotic in Dr Thorton's beautiful flower book, *The
Temple of Flora*, has taken its place. It seeds itself all through the
forest, triumphantly pushing its way into fir plantations and
spreading towards the bleakest of hillsides. Rhododendron has
never been accepted as part of the Irish scene in the way that
fuchsia has—and yet fuchsia is more of an interloper, since it
did not come to Ireland until the beginning of this century.

The winter tones of the bare trees contrasted with the
dazzling green of the ivy twisted round their trunks. I wondered
why this little wood of ancient trees had survived at all;
probably because they had scenic appeal to Lord Bantry. There
were enough for Victorian tourists to admire them when
they came to Glengarriff to admire the felicitudes of nature

encouraged by the damp climate. The Prince of Wales, later Edward VII, came here as a boy of fifteen. After he left they named a scenic route after him which included the transport of visitors by steamer from Bantry down to admire such land-marks as Lady Bantry's Seat, "made or laid out under the direction of her Ladyship".

Past the rustic benches and picnic tables which the Forestry Department provide as a lure to get modern tourists to leave their cars was Lord Bantry's Lodge, built on an island which used to be approached by a bridge made from the mainmast of one of the French ships that invaded Bantry Bay in 1796. The river cut its way through the trees, its syrupy waters rumbling through the broken arches of Cromwell's bridge.

Glengarriff was deserted, the souvenir shops shuttered against the salt wind as I walked down the empty street, hoping to get a refreshment in Eccles Hotel. But Eccles was closed, its door bolted shut; a wintry sun played on the wrought-iron balcony and shone through the windows of the lounge on to the Shakespearian prints that lined the walls. My face peered back at me in the darkened glass, grey and vaguely menacing. The wind crackled through the palms and the peeled silver stems of eucalyptus and two swans craning their necks in the shallow sea on the other side of the road were the only living creatures to be seen. But someone had been in Glengarriff recently: *Happy Christmas to All* was written in cotton wool across a shop window.

There was no incentive to stop among the closed guesthouses with names like Mountain View and Arbutus Lodge. I hurried on past modern villas, fairly standard in pattern, mostly with roofs the colour of verdigris and black asphalt tongues sticking out at Bantry Bay. Overhead hovered the huge television aerial like a starved albatross, and beside each, the septic tank was dug deep as an Ethiopian church. The silence and smells of seaweed and mud followed me up the mountain road until I reached a point just beyond a sharp turn in the road marked Accident Black Spot. Close to here I took the inland road to Glaslough Lake and Coomhola.

I looked back at the bay for the last time, at the expanse of waterlit spokes of light and at Bantry and Glengarriff in their customary depression. In all the length of the bay there was one ship, one of the smaller versions of oil-tankers that carry oil to and fro from Whiddy Island. The British fleet used to anchor here, and its departure in 1921 seems as remote as that of O'Sullivan Beare. In his book *The British Empire*, James Morris beautifully evoked the old battleships in Bantry Bay whose presence filled this magnificent gloomy panorama with bustle and activity. "There the great ships lie, black, white and yellow, bow to stern in their anchorage, some with sails furled above their high funnels, some with barbette guns like forts above their decks. Steam pinnaces chug officiously across the bay, with gigantic ensigns preposterously out of scale at their sterns, and bearded sailors swanky with their landing poles. There are jolly boats rowing smartly down from Berehaven, and flags flying everywhere, and a tremendous sense of disciplined agitation, painting, polishing, saluting, swarming up steel ladders, officers alert on white scrubbed bridges, and over all a drift of black smoke from fifty yellow smoke stacks."

From here O'Sullivan Beare had his last view of the bay. It would probably have been as empty as I saw it now; the three-master and transports which Carew brought round from Cork with cannon and supplies would have long departed. The full subjugation of Munster would be the task of land forces. The Irish wars were invariably land wars; in spite of being brought up beside the sea the Munster chieftains took relatively little advantage of that element. They made no attempt to build up a navy, although some sea fights took place. The ship that O'Sullivan had anchored off Dursey at this moment, which he reserved for possible escape to Spain, had been captured from the English. But he himself never seems to have taken to the sea for fighting.

All round the south coast little shiploads of exiles and messengers had been departing regularly for Spain ever since Kinsale. It was not an easy voyage for landsmen in those small unsteady vessels. Captain Harvey had lost fifty men from sickness trying to round Mizen Head into Bantry Bay, although this was probably the illness that was dogging the English army and had killed so many in Kinsale—rather than mere sea-sickness. So distinguished an expatriate Irishman as Hugh O'Donnell arrived in the Asturias debilitated by his voyage; he was invited by the Earl of Caracena to spend the night in his house, "but he, being sea sicke, in good manner refused the courtesy". There were shipwrecks; Philip O'Sullivan's sister, Helen, was drowned on a voyage between Spain and Ireland. The prayer of another exile setting out for Spain was heartfelt:

> Bless my good ship, protecting Power of Grace,
> And over the winds, the waves, the destined coast,
> Breathe, benign spirit . . .

For O'Sullivan Beare the long voyage into exile was in the future. Over the tops of the forest he viewed for the last time Slieve Miskish and Hungry Hill which hid the charred remains of Dunboy. He turned off from the sea to cross at least 250 miles of forests, rivers and bogs all scattered with his enemies.

The road took the first little swoop into the hills, whose crumpled brown shape rose in tiers ahead of me. On the descent to Coomhola the first lonely farm changed the expanse of bog and bracken into a nest of green fields bordering winter hedgerows with clusters of red berries and the dried golden stalks of fuchsia. Coomhola had a church, a National School and an old stone bridge through which a smooth black current gurgled over boulders. Near here, where the cleft of the Borlin valley opens up a breach into the hills, O'Sullivan was faced with a choice of routes to Gougane Barra. The easiest way was by Carriganass Castle and the Ouvane river, up to the Pass of Keimaneigh. Although the alternative was slightly shorter, it was much more difficult; however, some people believe that he marched directly up the Borlin valley and, turning northwards, crossed the range of mountains to descend to Gougane Barra by way of Valleymount.

I had walked both routes, and I am sure he must have gone by Carriganass. I do not believe that the horses could have made Valleymount. I went that way in summer, crossing between the two small summits of Bealick (1,764 ft) and Foilastooken (1,698 ft), along a boggy slope which even in August was racked by a bitterly cold wind. Opposite me was the peak of Knockboy (2,321 ft) with the gap of the Priest's Leap invisible to me beside it; behind them a spine of mountains swept down the Beare peninsula. The Priest's Leap was named for that Brother Dominic Collins who was in Dunboy and who was afterwards hanged in Youghal. According to legend, before the siege he had been raising the country for the defence of Dunboy, and was pursued on his way by Irish kern. He managed to reach the Priest's Leap, and with the hand of an enemy on his shoulder and no possible means of escape, he said a prayer to the Virgin and jumped from the topmost crag. "Off he went, sailing like an eagle down the valley—soaring over lake and hill and river—floating on faith until he pounced on that rock which stands there, an incontestible witness of the truth of the transaction." The rock is about a mile from Bantry. (Another legend mentioned by the French traveller, Latocnaye, refers to a priest travelling by this method to visit a sick parishioner. After arriving at the rock he said a short prayer and then threw himself from the summit, to achieve more quickly his mission of mercy.)

Looking northward I had a bird's-eye view down into Gougane Barra with its man-made forest lining the U-shaped head of the glacial valley. I would have enjoyed following Brother Collins' example if I were more certain of spiritual assistance, because nearly every way down seemed to be quite impractical. Eventually I chose an almost vertical gulley which sped down through a stepladder of boulders. My own opinion was that if the devil was behind me I wouldn't have brought a mixed collection of people and animals down that gorge in midwinter. A column of men used it during the Civil War in 1921, but it could not have been easy for them either. When I took off my rucksack just above the forest road, somehow it rolled over and escaped me; gathering momentum, it began spewing its contents, tea, sugar, porridge, camping stove, on to the heads of a family of English tourists picknicking beside their car and sedately watching me make my descent.

Now in winter I took the more orthodox route to Keimaneigh. Only a mile or two from the coastline of gimcrack bungalows and guesthouses the road became wild, the country bleak, scattered with traces of small farms that had been wiped out and gone back to bracken. A bedhead thrown across a gap in a hedge, an abandoned cottage, a rusty barn—each announced

a defeated effort to make a living. Once, however, between the
folds of smooth grey rock and slopes of blackened heather I
passed a few brilliantly green fields rich and luxuriant with a
texture of velvet; a small herd of black Kerrys grazed on them,
cows which would give a splash of yellow milk as rich as Jerseys.
I was glad to catch up with another pedestrian carrying a sack,
a shrunken man in a suit which wallowed around his legs.

"Not many people walk now," I said.

"Only fools," he replied. Afterwards I read of a Victorian
traveller who came this way over a century ago, and struck up
a similar fatuous conversation. "My companion was astounded
at the information that I had walked from Glengarriff. He
said, so long as he had a shilling in his pocket he would not
walk."

We soon parted company, as he had to hobble off in the
direction of Kealkill. Before he went I asked him how much
further it was to Gougane Barra. "Blast you—you'll get there
before dark."

At Carriganass a tall fragment of ivy-coloured wall stands up
in a jungle of vegetation just above the bridge where the Ouvane
river, pounding by its keep, takes a sharp tumble through a
gorge in the rocks. There was a ball alley and a large white
religious statue labelled "Pray for Donor".

Only a short time before the siege of Dunboy O'Sullivan
Beare and his allies besieged Carriganass, which belonged to
his hated cousin, Owen O'Sullivan. After he had successfully
reduced the garrison he captured his cousin's unfortunate wife
and packed her off to Dursey. Philip the historian described
how the castle was reduced by "partly raising a rampart,
partly by towers, mantles, sows and gabions and partly by
battering it with brass cannon". Later it was once again
attacked by the English, and considering the pounding it took,
a good deal of wall survives.

The sow or mantelet was used by Roger Harvey to reduce the
O'Mahoney castle of Leamcon after Dunboy had fallen, and at
many previous sieges like that of Sligo Castle in 1595, when Sir
Richard Bingham actually demolished the fortress. It was a
contrivance on wheels covered with skins which were dampened so that they would not catch fire too easily from the brands

and burning timbers hurled down from the castle walls. The frame-work, "filled with heroes, warriors and artisans", was pushed as close to the walls as possible and under its somewhat flimsy protection the soldiers could mine away to make some sort of breach. A more elaborate sow used against Ballally Castle in 1641 was thirty-five feet long and nine feet broad; "it was made upon 4 wheels made of whole timber, bound aboitt hoopes of iron, there axell trees where on she run was great round bars of iron, the beames she was built upon being of timber".

O'Sullivan Beare's machine was probably much simpler. Whatever damage his people did to the walls, the castle was still in use when he came by nine months later on the first stage of his retreat. Presumably it was in the hands of his own people, since there is no account of any fighting taking place on this last day of December. He did not stop here, but continued his flight. Only six days after he passed by, this castle, together with the castle at Ardea, surrendered to Wilmot. "On the sixth day of the same month, despairing of their master O'Sulevan's return, [they] rendered both their castle and their lives to the Queen's mercy." If he returned to Beare, he would now have no fortress or haven in which to retire.

From Carriganass the road wound gently up through broken countryside where the occasional small mountainy farm survived, a few fields trailing off into gorse and heather.

"There's no good land here," a farmer leaning over a fence told me, "until you get to Ballingeary East."

Near Keimaneigh the forest spills over the hills in stripes of fir and larch, surmounted by Djouce mountain. At five o'clock it began to get dark as I reached the top of the pass with grey shadows covering the hills and a bow of pink clouds fading to the west. Keimaneigh is a long defile between rocks, whose name, meaning the Deer's Leap, recalls the time when the forests harboured herds of red deer, the largest land mammal in the British Isles. In Ireland they dwindled as the oaks were cut, but unlike the wolves, they managed to survive—the herds in the woods of Killarney are true native remnants and not park introductions. The ravine at Keimaneigh makes a natural boundary. Today it marks the official division between the small Irish-speaking area of the West Cork Gaeltacht and the rest; before it was the dividing line between O'Sullivan and O'Leary territory. O'Sullivan Beare, passing through here in the gathering dusk, was marching out of his own country where his family had established itself and ruled in the most generous and civilized traditions of Gaelic society. *"Nulla manus, tam liberalis et generalis atque universalis quam Sullivana."* Beyond Keimaneigh he was a stranger who could expect no help or mercy from those whose lands he crossed.

It was dark now and the wind blew down the defile into my face. I began to find that the preparations I had taken for walking had been inadequate, and the occasional outing with the dog and the vague régime of push-ups had done very little to strengthen my legs. Pains shot up and down my thighs and my feet were encased in bottles of melting glass. A car drove up and stopped.

"Lift?"

"No thanks." I watched the rear lights twist out of sight between Keimaneigh's high walls. With the prospects of a hot meal and a bed to keep me going I plodded on, my rucksack weighing down my shoulders and my feet blistering inside the prison of my boots. The weariness of those last few miles increased; I rested in the darkness on the edge of a bank and then made a few more yards before the wonderful relief of seeing the two hotels at Gougane Barra which looked extraordinarily inviting in that dark little valley because they were all lit up. They blazed like Las Vegas beside the shadows of the lake and Holy Island.

I dropped my rucksack and knocked at the door of the larger establishment. There was a long wait before a woman pushed it open and peered out.

"I'd like a bed and something to eat."

She looked at me doubtfully. "We're closed for the winter. You can try next door."

The lights were candles set in window-sills, which nodded and shone, scores of them glowing and beckoning. Next door the bar was open and the young barmaid moodily watched me drink a pint of Guinness. There was nothing for me to eat, she affirmed, not even a bag of crisps. It seemed that I would have

to subsist on a liquid dinner, but then all of a sudden quite
unexpectedly the hotel's owner, Mr. Walsh, arrived up from
Bantry. A friendly man, he took pity on me.

"We're closed, but come in anyway." Brisk directives were
given, and a few minutes later I found myself in a parlour with
its hearth and turf fire and fed on bacon and eggs. A chilly
bedroom was aired and warmed while Mr. Walsh explained a
local custom. Candles and lights were placed in every window
at Gougane on Christmas Eve, Christmas night, New Year's
Eve and New Year's night.

"I suppose they are in the nature of a welcoming sign. Of
course, no one's expecting tourists."

CHAPTER TWO

Gougane Barra—Ballingeary

Was there e'er such a plight for a chieftain to face?
But cowardice and fear were unknown to his race.
. . . .
Onward, right onward the fugitives hied
And Acheris they reached that same eventide
                                    Jeremiah O'Mahoney

GLACIERS BRUISED AND scarred Gougane Barra; it is a
place where one is very much aware of their colossal imprint.
Everywhere the earth has been scraped away and rocks bubble
to the surface. On a wet day it is a penance to be within the
small lakeside hollow under gloomy crags and dripping trees,
but at other times the horseshoe of tawny hills enclosing the
shiny black water has a special enchantment.

Gougane Barra seems to be a mini-Glendalough. They both
attracted anchorites seeking solitude and they share similar
mountain scenery dominating a lake. The atmosphere of
Glendalough, which is too near to Dublin, has been largely
eroded by tourism, and Gougane is not what it used to be
either. In the nineteenth century a tourist wrote that "the
Ethiopian valley that Johnson in all the richness of his language
describes as the abode of Rasselas, was scarcely more inap-
proachable on every side . . .". Today you can drive up there
easily enough and stay at one of the two hotels which continue
the ancient tradition of pilgrim accommodation by attracting
busloads of people in season. Although they had seemed
beautiful on New Year's Eve with all their welcoming candles, by
daylight they turned out to be startling eyesores. But they do not
manage to destroy the serenity that still pervades the valley.
Robert Gibbings thought it "the holiest place I know", and
its mood catches most people, so that looking at the small
island in the lake, they believe it was inevitable that a saint
should choose it for his hermitage.

On Gougane Sunday at the end of September people arrive to pray and make the old rounds. Finbarr, the fair-haired, founded the monastery in the sixth century, having come here to kill off the last Irish dragon. Like all early Irish saints, biographical details about him are unreliable, but he is said to have been born in AD 560 and to have left Gougane sometime around AD 600. A few miles south of the lake there is a rock where he is supposed to have stood and looked back for the last time on the scene of his labours. He is credited with many miraculous cures, and the holy well still happily keeps up his high reputation.

All trace of the monastery and oratory that he built has vanished; so has the old causeway which used to link the island to the northern side of the lake. The buildings which are on Holy Island now are imaginative reconstructions of what might once have stood there. The eight small cells surrounding the court with its dead tree studded with coins are fakes, though perhaps it would be too harsh to call them follies. (The cells of the early monks would have been wattle huts.) These ruins, dating back from the early eighteenth century, were noted by the Cork historian, Charles Smith, in 1750 as "a chapel, with some cells, a sacristy, chamber and kitchen erected by the late recluse, Father Denis O'Mahoney, who lived a hermit in this dreary spot for twenty-eight years". Father O'Mahoney, having timed his stay ten centuries too late to earn canonization, is buried in an enclosed grave facing the island.

The present oratory, designed at the turn of the nineteenth century by Samuel Hayes, was copied from Cormac's chapel on the rock of Cashel. The ruins of an older chapel lie nearby, and it was probably here that O'Sullivan Beare's band of followers paused in the late dusk of New Year's Eve, 1602. At that time the island and lake were enclosed by oaks, since the forest survived in these hills until the nineteenth century. The Forestry Department has made a brave stab at replacing a section of the old woods by its plantation at the head of the valley, where for once the carefully planted larches and firs, allowed to grow to their full height, look entirely at home among the rocks.

My own experiences at Gougane were dismal. After an

c

uncomfortable night my legs refused to function the next
morning. Standing upright produced pain and walking downstairs meant creeping down foot by foot like a crippled penitent
come to take the waters of the holy well. I hobbled to the island
and cemetery where the Tailor and Anstey are buried. When
Eric Cross wrote of them in 1942 and reproduced the Tailor's
wit and his mildly racy anecdotes, it was during the most
repressive period of Irish censorship. The book was banned as
being "in general tendency indecent", and the Tailor was
subjected to a macabre local boycott and persecution. On one
occasion three priests appeared at his cottage and made him
get to his knees and burn his own copy of the book. But now in
this quiet churchyard he has been remembered by his friends
for whom he epitomized a gentle society famous for story-telling
and just good plain-speaking. Seamus Murphy designed his
tombstone and Frank O'Connor chose an epitaph for him from
Much Ado about Nothing . . . "A Star danced and under that was
I born". To be so remembered in this quiet churchyard is
perhaps adequate and eases the other sour memories of his
persecution.

The hundred yards back to the hotel seemed longer than the
thirty miles I had walked the day before. I should have made
proper preparations for the journey and hardened my sloppy
muscles. Despondently I looked for the telephone in the hotel
lounge and rang my wife.

"It's my legs—I can't walk on them. You'll have to come and
fetch me."

But over a long breakfast I reasoned that athletes gripped by
agonizing pains often recover within a short space of time.
Perhaps the discomfort would ease and I would be spared the
humiliation of giving up so soon. Watched by the waitress, who
paused as she brought me a chrome-covered pot of tea, I took
some more trial steps over the floral carpet. They seemed a little
easier; I thought I might get over a short distance today, and
went back to the telephone to tell my wife I had changed my
mind.

Before leaving I ditched some of the more cumbersome
equipment, which I think is still in the hotel. The pack was a
lot lighter as I stepped out again into the cold morning. Heads

of clouds stooped round the hills and the lake shone black. On Holy Island the light flickered over holly and birch and the mass of rhododendron which in spring would be covered with candy-coloured flowers. People often describe this part of Ireland as tropical because of its heavy rainfall and the unusual luxuriance of undergrowth in sheltered places. It seems a careless comparison; there is seldom anything remotely tropical about the stuffy chill of Cork and Kerry gardens under their rainwashed skies and mountains.

Above the valley the sun caught at a corner of a cloud, and its rays hitting the lake were not unlike the golden ladder that was seen to rise from St Finbarr's church up to the gate of heaven for twelve days after his death. Perhaps he exerted himself to push me on my way; I began to forget the state of my legs as I followed the road into the wet lead-coloured hills where O'Sullivan spent his first night on the march. I crossed a bridge over the Lee, a bubbling mountain stream that had just spilled out of the lake. Eastward the river slowed down and took its time through the long water meadows outside Cork, reluctant to wind below the hills near Shandon covered with their bright new suburbs, and carry the mailboat out into the harbour. Here it was a furious little torrent rushing between leafless alders, wreaths of soft brown moss and the dead tufts of fern which would uncurl in the sun when the spring came.

A couple of rabbits sprang for the safety of the hedge. Rabbits seem to be re-establishing themselves and I had seen others the evening before as I approached Keimaneigh. But it would be a long time before they approached the density of the rabbit population of my boyhood, when they came out at dusk and covered the fields like lice. Conolly, the rabbit-catcher, with his dogs, iron bar and bag of ferrets, would put his ear to a rabbit hole and estimate the number of the community within. After myxo he took his ferrets to Australia where there was still work for him.

I asked a farmer leading a small flock of black-faced sheep how far it was to Eachros.

"About four miles by our estimation. But by yours it would be a little farther." Seemingly the old rule still applied here: "The further from Dublin, the longer the mile." Jonah Barrington had a theory that the Irishman never computed distance "from where you then are, but from his cabin, so that if you asked twenty, in all probability you would have as many different answers, and not one of them correct". When it was in use, the Irish statute mile was longer than the English by a proportion of fourteen to eleven. I went on, wondering whether the farmer meant to addle a tourist, and how far it actually was to Eachros.

At midday it began to drizzle, and at the same time the country changed, receding into bogs and fields of rushes, a lowering empty landscape dominated by whirling black clouds. I rested in a dripping copse of birch and holly, easing my feet for a time until the rain ceased. I walked on slowly to the place off the crossroads at Gortenkilla, where O'Sullivan Beare and his weary followers made their first stop and camped beside the church at Eachros, "a very rude and ancient church", according to an early traveller. It stands on the land of people named Cronin. Their farmhouse is typical of the area, a substantial two-storey building with outhouses and the yard behind, the whole place comfortably protected from the weather by walls and thick hedges. When I told Mrs Cronin, a matriarchal lady, that I had walked from Glengarriff, she said that that was nothing by the standards of the old days. Her neighbour used to walk to Bantry and back in a day for a shilling's work. I said that he had better legs than mine, and watching me limp around the yard, she agreed. She thought modern people weak; and the next generation would be weaker still. The children had never been the same since the school buses were brought in and they stopped walking four miles to Ballingeary and back each day to school.

She knew all about O'Sullivan Beare who had camped on this land, which had been forested then—the Cronins frequently found buried oak when they dug for turf. She also knew about his horse which was drowned in a boghole up beyond Ballingeary. Eachros was down towards the stream; following her directions I walked over the fields to its ruins above the little Bunsheelin river, some broken walls surrounding an elm tree. The first of many holy places where O'Sullivan chose to camp, its origins are at least as old as the oratory of Gougane Barra, and it was most probably in ruins when the column made its first night's rest. It was ringed by a *cillín*, one of many ancient burial places where the dead with odd souls are buried, mainly unbaptized children. All round the ruin small stones pushed out of the dank grass, and it was tempting to speculate how many had been there to trip up weary campers 370 years ago. Mrs Cronin had said that her own baby sister was buried in Eachros, and later the last to be interned there was a travelling man.

Before saying goodbye I asked her about the prospects of accommodation locally. "Ballingeary is only a village," she said, "and Millstreet a scattering of houses." She added rather illogically, considering her former remarks, "And why haven't you a car?"

I walked fifty yards down the lane to view a grave of Finn MacCool on the neighbouring farm, a great wedge-shaped megalithic tomb stuck over the yard wall. Then I set out for Ballingeary. Originally I had thoughts of camping at Eachros, following as closely as possible the movements of O'Sullivan Beare, but even at this early stage I had given up all efforts at keeping pace with him and sharing his discomforts.

I fell in with a man riding a scooter, whom I stopped to enquire about places for the night.

"You don't look the type who has to walk. If I were you I'd invest my money in a bike." He told me that Mrs Connor, a countrywoman who had the misfortune to live in the village, would most likely look after me.

He didn't know about O'Sullivan Beare, but he could tell me all about the tithe war. In the old days the people had to pay a tenth of everything they produced to the Protestant clergyman, and it was in this very townland of Gortnakilla that they decided to take the law into their own hands. A battle was fought at the Pass of Keimaneigh between the local people and the forces of Lord Bantry.

"Are you with me?" he asked, and launched into *Caith Cheim an Fhia*, which is a long poem about the incident by Maire Brui Ni Laoghaire who had been born in the shadow of the glen of Gougane Barra, and had lived there all her life until her death in 1849. He recited, translating line by line from Irish into English, while I held the umbrella over our heads to keep the rain off. It was a good battle, he said, because no one was killed. Then after telling me that the people of Ballingeary were nice decent ordinary folk and never went to law, he started up his scooter and drove away ahead of me into the rain.

When I reached the long scribble of grey houses, I found that he had warned Mrs Connor of my impending arrival, and a few minutes after I had knocked on her door I was sitting down to a good meal. Robert Gibbings wrote that Ballingeary is the friendliest village in the world. "Everyone knows everyone and all about everyone. For anything you want there is always someone who knows someone who can manage it for you."

It was a crooked little village built around a crooked main street. There was a dark chapel filled with windows of Irish saints and the noise of a loud ticking clock. It had a garage, a post office, two pubs, houses with deep overhanging eaves, and plastic flowers in the windows, shops, and Irish college, some abandoned cars and a half-built laundry which, I was told, would deal with dirty linen all over West Cork. It was bounded by two rivers. At one end the Bunsheelin travelled behind some houses which used it as an overspill for garbage; at the other, near the Youth Hostel, the Lee turned up again with a fine old arched bridge thrown across its banks. In the four miles since leaving Gougane Barra on its way to the lakes at Inchigeela, it had dropped 269 feet and turned into a rippling brown stream streaked with crowfoot.

At this time of year the village was withdrawn, waiting for warmth to bring it to life. Under the rain the line of grey roof tops overshadowed curtained windows hiding interiors pervaded with winter languor—what Mary Lavin described in a marvellous phrase as "the curfew of lethargy". But it was only a seasonal pause; Ballingeary was in hibernation, relaxing after the hectic activities of its summer season.

Ballingeary is situated in the heart of the tiny West Muskerry Gaeltacht, which covers an area bounded by the Pass of Keimaneigh, Coolea and Ballyvourney. From June to August a rush of people from all over the country descends on the village to learn Irish—what the Tailor called the Boiling Programme, the intensive cultivation of the language. The majority of those who come are children, whose ages range from ten to eighteen. They stay with local families and bring a splash of colour to the area. In the main street houses advertise LEABAR-BREICFEAST. "We speak Irish in summer and English in winter," a woman told me cynically. But it was the best Irish in Ireland.

Before the Famine 90 per cent of the people of County Cork were Irish speaking, and twenty years later a traveller could write of this part of Muskerry . . . "Irish is the general language of the population, not only here, but throughout the district which we are now traversing, while English is as yet hardly known." By 1883 native speakers in West Cork had shrunk to 35 per cent. Today two tiny, carefully fostered communities, the one grouped around Ballingeary, the other on Cape Clear, still speak Irish. What particular spirit of pride and community or accident of location kept the language alive in these two small places alone in all Cork is difficult to identify. There are other isolated mountain areas, other islands, like Dursey, for example, where English has driven out Irish inexorably. In Ballingeary Irish survived against enormous odds, especially during the forties and fifties when so many people emigrated. Today there are more jobs, and the situation is said to be improving slightly. One recent survey of a class in the National School found that out of nineteen children enrolled, eight spoke nothing but Irish, three nothing but English and the rest were bilingual.

For four hundred years English was encouraged in Ireland until it almost won out. In 1537 a law was passed— "be it enacted that every person or persons, the King's true subjects, inhabiting the land of Ireland . . . to the uttermost of their power, cunning and knowledge, shall use and speak commonly the English tongue and language . . . and shall bring up his children in such places where they shall or may have the occasion to learn the English tongue, language, order and condition." Fynes Moryson, ever consistent in his prejudices, wrote that Irish "is a peculiar language; not derived from any other radical tongue (that I ever could hear, for myself neither have nor ever sought to have any skill therein). But all I have said thereof might well be spared, as if no other tongue were in the world, I think it would never be missed, either for pleasure or necessity." Many of the Anglo-Irish of that period were bilingual, speaking according to one observer, "a mingle mangle, a gallmanfrie of both languages, neither good English nor good Irish".

The strong antipathy felt by the English towards the Irish language meant that there was less pressure on Irish people to change their religion. The seventeenth-century clergyman, John Richardson, who sought in vain to utilize Irish as a means of converting the Papists, wrote that English people in Ireland "have a dislike to the nation, and this draweth them insensibly into a dislike of the language, for which no other reason can be given than that it is Irish".

O'Sullivan Beare was proud of his education which had taught him other languages. We know that when he was making his claim for the chieftaincy, he felt that he had a strong point when he stated that his uncle, Sir Owen O'Sullivan, only spoke Irish, while he himself "had been brought up in learning and civility, and could speak English and the Latin tongue". His spoken Latin would have been colloquial, while his written Latin was fluent; his letters to his Spanish contacts were in that useful *lingua franca* in which the men of Europe could communicate a lot more easily than they can today. (Later, during fourteen years of exile, he would have learned Spanish.) Latin was widely spoken in Ireland well up to the beginning of the nineteenth century, not only among the educated, but among more rustic speakers of "bog Latin". In 1588 Don Cuellar, the Spanish survivor of one of the shipwrecked vessels of the Armada, who had to make his way through Ireland as a fugitive, was able to make himself understood on a number of occasions through Latin alone.

Standards of culture among educated Irishmen in the sixteenth century were high. Not everyone, however, strove to better himself by learning English, and others probably felt like Shane O'Neill: "One demanded why Oneile . . . would not frame himself to speak English. 'What,' quoth the other in a rage, 'thinkest thou that it standeth with Oneile his honour to writhe his mouth in clattering English?'" His kinsman, Conn O'Neill, is said to have cursed "any of his pedigree who should learn English, build houses or sow corn".

left:
Gougane
Barra,
Co. Cork

right:
Tomb of
St Gobnat

Mountain view near Millstreet

Stone Circle, Musherabeg

From early times Irish was used almost as a test of Nationality. When Hugh O'Donnell attacked Connacht in 1595, he slaughtered all the English settlers between fifteen and sixty who could not speak Irish.

At Mrs Connor's a candle shone in the window, for this was New Year's Day, and the same custom applied here as at Gougane Barra. Under pictures of saints, three popes and a framed Memory of Irish Freedom I ate a massive fry with slabs of thick country bacon, sausages and eggs. In the kitchen Mrs Connor and her family, sitting around the range, enticed me into the circle of heat with cups of tea. Was I an Englishman? How far had I travelled? It was a bad time to be on the road. They chanted their fine West Cork English with its cadences and idiosyncrasies that derived from another language . . . Sullivan to rhyme with soothe, any direction prefixed by a compass bearing, and so on. Later, I said goodnight and went upstairs to scatter my clothes and climb into the double bed. I lay for a time listening to the patter of rain on the gabled window announcing the close of a long slow winter's day.

CHAPTER THREE

Ballingeary—Ballyvourney

On the next day, the first of January, 1603, starting off in the early morning, he reached before midday the populous village of Ballyvourney, dedicated to Saint Gobnata. There the soldiers paid such vows as each one list, gave vent to unaccustomed prayers and made offerings beseeching the saint for a happy journey.

Philip O'Sullivan

OUTSIDE MY WINDOW the sky wore its habitual grey covering. The reedy fields bordered with willows ran into the hills on whose slopes spread a red-tinged puff of larch trees. In the street a couple of hens stepped out and a man passed dressed in an overcoat down to his heels, smoking an old-fashioned pipe with a tin cover. Mrs Connor was at work in the kitchen, filling the house with rich scents of fried pork products.

Today was Sunday and I walked past the first trickle of people on their way to church. I passed two men joking as the bell rang. "Go and get to Mass, you old Protestant," one called out to the other as he lit a fugitive cigarette. This was the best of moments, this beginning of a new day. The rain had cleared and my legs were better. "I think variety to be the most pleasing thing in the world," wrote Fynes Moryson, "and the best thing to be neither contemplative alone nor active altogether, but mixed of both." The road climbed up behind the village leaving behind the spirals of turf smoke rising from the chimneys. A couple of dogs snapping at my legs were driven off by some small boys with a football, and a virgin looked down from her grotto holding out her hands to show that they were empty.

A few miles along I met another man walking alone, going to church in blue suit, baggy trousers, cloth cap and mackintosh. "You're dangerous looking," he said, eyeing my khaki anorak and leather hunting cap, "like one of those fellows in the North." When I told him of my journey his eyes lit up.

Did I know the church at Eachros where O'Sullivan had camped his first night? I had been there the day before? Did I know that in old times Eachros had moved from Beana Tempaill, the place where we were standing, across to the other side of the little valley to its present site? If I did not believe him he would prove it to me. He led me a few steps down the road to a place which overlooked the blanched ruin of Eachros that stood out in the distance on the opposite hill.

"Here you are," he said. "Can you tell me the reason for that?" Wedged in the rocks, almost entirely hidden, was a stone-cut font.

It seems probable that from Eachros O'Sullivan Beare followed the route along the Bunsheelin river at the bottom of the valley. The next man I met, a stocky old farmer with a drooping tobacco-stained Zapata moustache, told me that Donal Cam went off to the North like a bullet in the morning. And why anybody should wish to go up there, God knew. His horse's name was *An Cearc*, and he wrote it down for me in a wavering hand. Did I know what that meant? It meant the hen. It would have been like a pet name . . . perhaps the horse strutted like a hen. Did I know that it was drowned near here? I did? It was drowned in a place called *Poll na Circe* which means the Hole of the Hen. Where was it? He pointed towards the end of the valley. "You see the mountain and the sky? You see the green field below the farm? It's near there that he went down."

O'Sullivan Beare must have had a great number of horses at his disposal, even though since the wars there was a general shortage of them. "Whosoever will undertake for the rescue and recovery of this kingdom, must necessarily finish and provide a good stock of horses; for the horses of the kingdom are destroyed between the enemy and us." The death and destruction of horses is very much a feature of this whole march. Before he set out O'Sullivan had lost a hundred garrons— small rough horses—to Wilmot along with the rest of the *creaght*. He took with him thirteen mounted cavalry as well as a number of other baggage animals. These garrons would have been workhorses "bred in the fenny soft ground of Ireland"; they were unusually hardy and could "carry burdens of greatness whereof would startle any man's belief". Fynes Moryson did not think much of Irish hobbeys, but another commentator named Stanihurst disagreed. "The nag or hackenie is verie good for travelling, albeit others report the contrarie. And if he be broken accordinglie, you shall have a little tit that will travel a whole day without anie bait . . ." In good times horses had been so common that "the meanest Irishmen distained to ride on a mare". *An Cearc*, in spite of his unflattering name, was probably a superior animal; O'Sullivan Beare was very fond of him, and his loss must have contributed somewhat to his personal tragedy.

The farmhouse stood in a lozenge of fields below the road among stacks of turf thatched with straw, a hay barn, a few shivering cattle and dried fuchsia hedges. The farmer, without comment or surprise, brought me over to the boggy piece of ground, still called *Poll na Circe*, close to a waterfall. The fugitives must have arrived here in the early hours of 1st January. *An Cearc* would not have been carrying his master, but would have been burdened with baggage and in the charge of one of the horseboys whose duty it was to look after the horses and load them up. Picking his way over the bog in the uncertain misty light of dawn, he tumbled into the hidden watery hole and plunged to his death.

The road curved off through the Gortnabinnia Pass, a hollow in the mountains patched with brown bog and surrounded with hills of a red seaweed colour which the least touch of sun turned to flame. I took a track off it, originally made during the Emergency, just for the pleasure of leaving the tarmac. In a country so full of empty space this is a surprisingly difficult thing for the walker to do. The most obscure public lanes in the wildest places are neatly tarmac'd by County Councils, and it is difficult to get off them, since, for historical reasons, there is a lack of any system of rights of way in Ireland. England is webbed with foot-paths, zealously protected, over which you can walk along the spine of the Pennines up to Scotland or dodge the countryside in a way you cannot easily do here.

Over the brow of the hill ranges of mountains sprang into view—Mullaganish with its TV mast stuck in its head, the Derrynasaggart range and behind it what are starkly called

The Paps, twin peaks near Killarney; behind them again on the far horizon the sawedged sickle of the Reeks.

O'Sullivan Beare had moved down into the Sullane valley, where the rich vein of green beside the banks of the river contrasts with the poor land above, as the banks of the Nile with the desert. I strode among the heather slopes, away from traffic, receiving glares from black-faced sheep and a mud-encrusted pig browsing along the track, a ringed snout between his huge shaggy ears. Farms were poor up here, widely scattered, their barns full of abandoned carts and rusted machinery. An old lady in black, cleaning out a pot in a muddy yard beside a field of cabbages run wild, seemed to represent a final phase in the long tradition of poverty. After she died and the old farmers gave up the struggle to scratch a living from rocks and reeds, this place would become deserted and the fir plantations would move in.

The old church of St Gobnat where O'Sullivan Beare had prayed was above Ballyvourney.

"You can put away your maps," said the man from whom I asked directions. "You take the first road on the right, the *Bothar Ban*, and it's not far from there." This White Road had magical origins. Three magical cows emerged from the sea at Imokelly one May eve. The first cow was white, the second red and the third black. They kept company for about a mile, and then the White Cow went northwards from Glanmire eating her way in the direction of County Limerick. The Red Cow went to the west and the Black Cow went north-east towards Tipperary. The roads over which the cows roamed are still called after their colour.

Mist was plucking at the edges of the mountains when I saw before me the wooded slope above the Sullane where St Gobnat, a princess of Connacht, founded her nunnery. She selected a site which had already been in use for centuries, where a great deal of evidence of pre-Christian man has recently been discovered. Near the spot where her nunnery stood there is an ancient cooking place, known as a *fulacht fiadh*, or deer roast. Such cooking places have been associated with the Fianna, who were supposed to use them during the summer months when they went on hunting expeditions. There are many scattered throughout Munster and Waterford and they are found in other selected parts of Ireland. The occur in England and, more plentifully, in Wales. They do not have much appeal to archaeologists, as they reveal little material of datable interest. Skimpy evidence has set a few of them at different times during the Bronze Age. The cooking site at Ballyvourney was the first to be properly excavated and dis-coveries included a woodlined pit for boiling, a stonelined pit for roasting and the remains of a wigwam-like structure for storing meat. Typically brittle cooking stones were found nearby; they had been heated and then plunged into hissing pits of water in which food simmered. If you wrap a piece of meat in straw and throw it into somewhat muddy semi-boiling water, it will cook quite well without too much of a taste of ashes, mud or smoke.

Other remains at Ballyvourney, including St Gobnat's house or kitchen, a small circular stone-walled hut in which a crucible was found, reveal that this was an area where smelters in iron and workers in bronze carried out their trade. The circular hut was preceded by rectangular timber houses used for the same purpose. So that when St Gobnat came to the Sullane full of missionary zeal some time during the sixth or seventh century, she must have found an active community engaged in long-established industry, although this is hardly suggested by the charming legend that she chose the site because she saw nine white deer grazing together.

Before settling down she demolished a nearby pagan fort with a round polished stone the size of a croquet ball. This stone, known as *an bulla*, the bowl, which had special curative powers, was lost for centuries; rediscovered at the beginning of the eighteenth century, it was placed in a hole in the outside wall of the ruined medieval church, the *Tempaill Ghobnatum*, where it still lies. While her convent was being built, she lent one of her masons her grey mare. This mare, loaded with building tools, was stolen by a fellow mason, who rode away with it all one night, only to find at dawn that he had been galloping round and round the church. His head, or a replica of it, set in the church wall for all to know the likeness of the thief, is actually the carved keystone of a Romanesque arch. On the south wall, oddly contrasting with the traditional

Gothic window beside it, is a *sheila-na-gig*, a grotesque carving in relief of a boy's torso, his arms crossed over his stomach, his legs shrunk and shortened. No one has been able to make much of *sheila-na-gigs*, except to acknowledge that their origins are very ancient and that they have a disconcerting power of jolting tranquil Christian patterns of meditation and prayer.

A gravedigger cleaning up the graveyard pointed out the place to the south-west of the church where the saint herself is supposed to be buried under a circular mound with a slab on top surrounded by three small ballauns. These are three small rocks with hollows in them, thought to have been used either as fonts or as mortars in which the priest ground corn. The water which collects in them cures warts and is beneficial for diseases of the eye. On the slab and scattered around were pennies old and new, pieces of comb, a crucifix, a pencil and an old golf ball. While Spanish pilgrims may leave silver hearts or plaster replicas of afflicted limbs as ex-voto offerings, an Irishman will merely empty his pockets. In the act of depositing these simple objects, pilgrims transfer a measure of their worry and pain.

St Gobnat had both curative and destructive powers. When she threw *an bulla* at her enemies, they vanished. She was renowned as one of Ireland's first beekeepers, and her bees not only produced honey; on her command they blinded an intruder to her convent. If you pray to her she will blind your enemies as well. Robert Gibbings quotes a clerk who told him: "Every time the inspector comes into the office, I whisper to St Gobnat, and he never sees a wrong entry."

But her real fame has rested on her ability to cure the sick. In her lifetime she blessed a field during a plague, and the plague advanced no further. From this story came her attribution of miraculous healing.

The focal point of the cult of St Gobnat is a small wooden figure with a few traces of paint still adhering to it. Dating from the thirteenth century, it is twenty-seven inches in length and resides in the parish church of Ballyvourney, where the caretaker brought me to the sacristy to see it. She reached up to the cupboard and brought down a cardboard box. "It's so old we don't take any notice of it any more." The most prominent feature of the battered little oaken image is still that observed by the eighteenth-century bigot, John Richardson, "one large and archaic eye". It is worn from veneration; the sick used to rub their afflicted limbs against it and the handkerchiefs round its neck which were afterwards worn as prophylactics.

St Gobnat is one of the five surviving wooden cult statues of Irish saints. The others are St Maolruan, Bishop of Tallaght, St Molma of Killaloe, St Mo-Cheallog and St Molaise, the Abbot of Inishmurray. (St Molaise's image, now in the National Museum, was visited in 1588 by Don Cuellar, the Armada survivor, who, like O'Sullivan Beare, was to seek refuge with the O'Rourkes of Breffni.) Each of these images has been rediscovered near the place where the living saint lived and worked. That as many as five survive may be considered miraculous. Protestants held such images in particular odium from very early times. In 1539 letters patent under the Privy Seal were first issued "for the suppression of the Irish religious houses and for the destruction of statues that were special centres of devotion". St Molaise's statue survived a drowning by a zealot who threw him out of a boat. For hundreds of years Protestant churchmen and writers thundered against places like Ballyvourney.

"An image of wood, about two feet high and painted like a woman," John Richardson described St Gobnat in 1727 in *The Great Folly, Superstition and Idolatry of Pilgrimages in Ireland.* "The pilgrims resort to it twice a year . . . they conclude with kissing the idol and making an offering to it, every one to his chatters. The image is kept by one of the O'Herlihys, and when anyone is sick of the smallpox they send for it to sacrifice a sheep to it and wrap the skin about the sick person, and the family eat the sheep. But this idol has now lost its reputation, because two of the O'Herlihys died lately with the small pox. The Lord Bishop of Cloyne was pleased to favour me with the narrative of this rank idolatry, to suppress which he hath taken very proper and effectual steps . . ."

The Lord Bishop never succeeded in his purpose and Ballyvourney is still a place of pilgrimage and healing. It used to be known as "the beggars' university", from the crowds of beggars who flocked here, who were given the privilege of keeping the statue during the pattern day. They were called "Gobnat's Clergy". About 1840 the saint's image was handed over by a representative of the O'Herlihys to the parish priest of Ballyvourney—in whose care and cardboard box she still survives.

Plently of people still come to make the complicated pattern, whose rounds included the medieval church, holy well and St Gobnat's kitchen, and to "take the measure" of St Gobnat. Instead of actual physical contact with the ancient statue, modern pilgrims place a piece of wool or a ribbon along the length of it and wear that for a cure. I watched a man drive up, get out of his car and choose a sharp stone from the road. He would use this as he did the rounds of the pattern, nicking a scratch on various prescribed stony points that he came to, following a ritual trail-blazing which was established very soon after the saint died.

In spite of the antiquity of the site, written records only go back to the seventeenth century. On 12th July, 1601, Pope Clement VIII imparted a special indulgence to the faithful who would visit the parish church of St Gobnat on her feast day, could confess and receive holy communion. They were to pray for peace among Christian people, for the expulsion of heresy and for the exaltation of Holy Mother Church. This official recognition of St Gobnat's popularity was probably inspired in part by the political situation of the time—a brief blast of the counter-reformation. It had only been announced for eighteen months when O'Sullivan Beare made the church the second stop of his march. His people would not have benefited directly from the indulgence, but the shrine at which they prayed was famous; St Gobnat's cult was popular all over Ireland and even had adherents in Scotland. They were addressing a saint with particular traditional powers to strike down enemies. Perhaps in their "unaccustomed prayers" they imagined Carew and Wilmot pursued by clouds of bees. The Four Masters said they arrived at Ballyvourney on 1st January before noon, "where they left gifts and prayed to St Gubenata that they might have a prosperous journey".

At that time the little medieval church which had replaced St Gobnat's original creation still had a roof on it. This **was**

taken off fifty years later, according to tradition, to avoid its
falling into Cromwellian hands. The site, which was on the
hereditary lands of the O'Herlihys, who had been chiefs of the
area before St Gobnat came here, passed into the hands of a
man named John Colthurst. From then on the meagre records
reflect cold Protestant opinions. By the mid-eighteenth century
Ballyvourney consisted of "one masshouse, one popish priest, no
friary, no reputed nunnery, no popish school". Even so, "this
parish is remarkable for the superstition paid to St Gobinet's
image on Gobinet's day".

The site of the old nunnery was duly protestantized, and in
keeping with the irritable assertive attitude of the Church of
Ireland towards the cult, the small early-nineteenth-century
Protestant church was built only a few yards away. Below the
church and the graveyard, the rectory, a beautiful little house
in Strawberry Hill Gothic, lingers on, but it is now very dilapidated. Almost in the garden, surrounded by a grove of trees, is
St Gobnat's well, one of the landmarks of the pattern, with
steps leading down and a line of cups for drinking the water. A
pilgrim was filling up a couple of bottles with water before
driving off. It was a cure for anything and everything, he said,
"and you could be the lucky one."

I spent the night in Ballyvourney. There are two villages,
Ballyvourney and Ballymakeery, linked by a strip of houses
along the main Killarney–Macroom road, so that it is hard to
tell where one begins and the other ends. The Sullane river is
spanned by arched stone bridges at both places. They are
dominated by the vast Irish college of the de la Salle Brothers,
for Ballyvourney is also in the West Cork Gaeltacht. Also, by a
mill from which issued a piercing sound of machinery. "But
you wouldn't pay any attention to it after a few days."

The Colthursts had a great house here and a castle which was
modelled on Blarney Castle. (They had intermarried with the
people of Blarney.) Arthur Young met a Colthurst in 1776 ...
"Sir John was so obliging as to send half a dozen labourers with
me to help my chaise up a mountain side of which he gave a
formidable account."

The castle was lived in until shortly before the First World
War, when a caretaker was put in, although Sir George still

came up for the duck-shooting. It was burnt during the troubles with the excuse that the Black and Tans were about to take over. Part of the tower remains and the woodland.

After walking all day my legs seized up again. Vigorous rubbing with the ointment and a hot bath managed to persuade them to carry me round the hotel in my socks. I managed to make the bar to listen to a bit of farmers' talk. Bad prices were expected for sheep and foxes were knocking off the winter lambs; all farmers were slaves and made a life out of misery. They discussed the weather with passion, which brought them to asking what I might be doing in Ballyvourney at this time of the year? When I mentioned O'Sullivan Beare they looked blank, except for one man who had heard some stories about him, but didn't know if they were true. "Still, we must believe them that they came here." Some pints later an old farmer with the squeaky voice of a record played too fast told me that he had been cured by Gobnat of partial deafness. "A bit of stuff fell out of my ear." Before that he had been to doctors and they hadn't done a thing. He seemed a happy man.

CHAPTER FOUR

Ballyvourney—Millstreet

> They were pursued by the sons of Thady MacCarthy
> with a band of natives, harassing their rear ranks with
> missiles, and again and again returning to the skirmish
> after being driven off by O'Sullivan's wings of marks-
> men. . . . At last O'Sullivan, by making an attack with his
> whole column and killing some, put the enemy to flight.
>
> Philip O'Sullivan

"WHEN WOULD YOU like your breakfast?" the landlady asked.
"We get up at half-past nine, if that's not too early?"

The civilized programme would have been to breakfast at
ten and make a leisurely appearance on the road sometime
around midday, a course of action in keeping with the soporific
atmosphere of the winter countryside. But darkness fell a little
after five, and the short hours of daylight urged me to begin the
day's walk as early as possible. The problem, which was to
beset me every evening, was to suggest an hour for breakfast
which would not cause offence. Here in Ballyvourney, as in
almost every place I stopped, I was the only guest at the hotel. I
could demand and receive rather special treatment, but I could
not ask people to get up in the dark and prepare a meal for me.
Eight o'clock was indecent; half-past eight seemed almost as
bad, at nine o'clock one might reach the primary level of consciousness, but only by nine-thirty could one guiltily permit
oneself to surface, pull the curtains and gaze out on the misty
morning. The rest of the house was still utterly silent.

I started about an hour later and tried to quicken my pace a
little down the empty waterlogged street. A wet ball of sun
struggled to break up the mist as I came to the outskirts of the
village where a man in a horsedrawn cart on his way to the
creamery shouted down:

"Where do you come from?"

"Wicklow."

"Well, they've no sense up there."

I took the back road from Ballyvourney over the side of
Mullaganish which eventually comes down to Millstreet and
the Blackwater valley. The road sloped up through a little
wood with the Bohill river tumbling on one side and the birds,
in keeping with everyone else, singing their dawn chorus rather
late. I tried to distinguish the chortling of fat thrushes and the
angry tick of a startled robin. A little blackheaded bird made
a noise like snow chains on tyres; I thought it could be a stone-
chat. Fir trees stirred and squeaked as a flock of long-tailed
tits floated through them. Pigeons rose with a rusty whirr of
wings and a couple of crows delicately laced their beaks in a
pool of excrement. Soon I had left the settled oasis of the Sullane
valley and its rich green fields to climb up the back of Mullaganish. Ice crackled under my boots; a little snow had fallen
during the night leaving white chippings on the gorse and heather.

Near here O'Sullivan Beare was attacked by a force of Mac-
Carthys, and his soldiers had to fight their first engagement
since leaving Glengarriff almost two days before. From this
point onwards he could expect fighting all the way to Leitrim.
His opponents were the same MacCarthys who became his
allies after the siege of Dunboy and then went over to the
English. The method of trying to secure loyalty by payment is
very old, and not always successful. After the fall of Dunboy
Thady MacCarthy was given a substantial sum in Spanish gold
from the funds that O'Sullivan had received at Ardea, but
decided that not only would he keep the money, but he would
turn Queen's man as well. O'Sullivan attacked his castle at
Carrigaphooca, a fourteenth-century stronghold which still
stands above a high rock face overlooking the Sullane river on
the road to Macroom. Only after a difficult siege—the place
was too isolated to bring cannon and besieging instruments—
did the castle surrender, and the gold was recovered.

As a result of this the MacCarthys, still loyal to the English,
were his irrevocable enemies. They may also have been
tempted by the reward. "And it is also proclaymed that if any
psn or psons of what degree or qualitie soever that shall into the
Lo. President bring the live body of that wicked and unnatural
traitor, Donnell O'Sullyvane, als O'Sullyvane Beare, shall have

sum of three hundred pounds ster . . .". Carew was a great believer in rewards. In 1601 the Sugan Earl had been captured by the White Knight for £400 head money, and at the same time up to £1,000 was offered to anyone who killed the Ulster leaders. If Hugh O'Donnell was indeed poisoned in Spain, Carew's agent may have earned this payment in secret.

Now the MacCarthys came streaming out of Carrigaphooca up to this point above the Sullane and attacked the rear of the column. For four hours they used the wolf-pack technique of harassment, firing into a straggling line of unarmed refugees, retreating, dashing in again to aim another blow. On this occasion the rearguard would have kept the civilians successfully on the move, since there is no mention of fatal casualties. Both sides would have been armed with a medley of weapons, broadswords, claymores, axes, spears and pikes. The pike was gradually taking over from the traditional double-headed axe of the gallowglass; throughout Europe it remained as a key infantry weapon well into the seventeenth century, and its popularity lasted among irregular forces long afterwards. The Portuguese guerrillas of 1812, resisting the French with old blunderbusses, pikes, pruning knives and quince poles, must have been armed in rather similar fashion to O'Sullivan's men. The pike, of course, was used by Irishmen during the rebellion of 1798. "Pike" is a fairly general term to describe a number of spear-like weapons, varying in length from sixteen feet to the short half-length pikes which are probably what these soldiers carried on the march.

One or two of the fighters may have had long bows or crossbows, although they are not mentioned. There was no military training for bowmen; by 1600 bows and arrows had largely been replaced by firearms, and most of O'Sullivan's soldiers seem to have carried muskets. Musketeers originated as kern, or light infantry, who had exchanged their spears for guns. They would also have had to carry secondary weapons, as the musket took so long to load. There were two types; the smaller calivers of twelve pounds having a range of 150 yards and the twenty-pound muskets with a range of 100 yards. They were very cumbersome, requiring accessories of powder horn, lead pellets and fuse to be near at hand and kept dry. If a gunner

wished for accuracy, he also carried a tripod on which to rest
his musket. This was a refinement, although at a range of a
hundred yards the weapon was wildly inaccurate. It took a well-
trained soldier to get off forty shots in an hour; each shot
required about twenty movements in preparing and firing, and
it must have been rather like setting a charge of dynamite each
time. Musketeers generally carried twelve rounds of ammunition with them. Even so, muskets were valuable—the going
price for one was in the region of six cows.

The caliver was fairly accurate up to about sixty yards, but
in general these weapons were really only effective when they
were fired in volleys at point-blank range. On a running fight
of this nature, perhaps in adverse wind conditions, they did
very little harm. But O'Sullivan, hampered by his followers,
had no chance to shake off the MacCarthys or choose a favourable terrain to fight them. It was best to suddenly turn and
bring his vanguard round to the rear to attack. This bold
course of turning to face the enemy proved the most favourable,
and the MacCarthys were driven off after suffering a number of
fatal casualties. They hurried back to the safety of their castle
above the rock of Pooca.

Pacata Hibernia says that they took a quantity of the refugees'
baggage with them, although this is not mentioned by Philip
O'Sullivan. The baggage would have consisted of supplies
carried by non-combatants. The best equipped of the highly
mobile Irish forces marched with only essential provisions.
When O'Neill brought his army down from Dungannon the
year before, "he saw his men marching with their food on their
backs, only meal and butter, and a spare pair of shoes". But
O'Sullivan, leaving Glengarriff in haste, was less well organized; by the time he met the MacCarthys his followers were
without food. It seems probable that the six hundred civilians
in the train, like many refugees, overburdened themselves with
possessions and abandoned some of them at this point. The
baggage horses would certainly have been loaded with a large
quantity of ammunition; there must have been some household
goods, wolfskins, perhaps, even a small amount of jewellery.
O'Sullivan brought what was left of the Spanish gold with him,
which must have made a considerable weight. If they wanted to

make their escape more easily, they would have ripped a number of the less essential bundles off the horses' backs, and these would have fallen into the hands of the MacCarthys.

The road twisted up the bare slopes of Mullaganish. At the top of the pass the surface became icy, and the fields to either side merged in a white patchwork where cattle and sheep moved restlessly over the frost looking for forage. Behind me were the ranges of mountains I had already crossed; mist rose behind the higher peaks, while to the south-west the sky was blotted out by storm clouds. The rain over Gougane Barra was beating on the black water, and all the rocks were glistening. It was raining in Bantry and Glengarriff, lashing down on the lines of shiny rooftops and deserted squares.

On the other side of the pass the forestry plantation of Glendav fell away and rose again towards the violet shoulder of Musheramore (2,188 ft) and the Boggeragh mountains. Some-where above the treeline was a cromlech where those ubiquitous layabouts, Dermot and Grania, paused to rest. It was well out of my way, and instead I took one of the forest trails along a floor of red pine needles between the neat trees. Probably there were oakwoods here for O'Sullivan Beare; and although none of the accounts of the march mention wild animals, they must have been an added source of danger. Wolves, which had always been common, increased in numbers because of the uncertain conditions of rural life. Irish wolves, considered to be a ferocious breed, were said to grow as big as young horses. According to modern naturalists, wolves do not normally attack men except in extreme circumstances; however, the circumstances of the winter of 1601–2 were extreme. The extermination of wolves followed the destruction of forests, but before that they were considered a serious menace. In 1552 the Commissioners of Revenue were offering a bounty for each head, and in the same year an order was made forbidding the export of wolf dogs from Ireland. O'Sullivan would have been well used to hunting with wolfhounds; he would have had his own, and also handled those of his sept's overlord, MacCarthy Mor, the Earl of Clan-carthy. One of the tributary duties of the O'Sullivans of Beare was "to find throughout the year upon the territories of Bantry and Dunboy the hunte and huntes of the said Earl with con-

Cromlech near Millstreet

Standing stone made into gatepost near Millstreet

Bones in
Ardpatrick
Cemetery

Ardpatrick Cemetery,
Co. Limerick

venient sustenance for his greyhounds, hounds and spaniels".

A typical dog was offered for sale in the London Gazette of 27th March, 1604 . . . "a great Irish wolfhound, all his back of a sallow colour, his belly white". They were in demand for their hunting abilities throughout Europe and even further afield. Richard Hawkins, an English sailor of the famous Devon family, held prisoner in Panama in 1593, wrote home that his noble captor, Don Beltram de Castro, spent much time in that colonial pursuit of hunting. He considered that if de Castro had any say in determining his ransom, he would be satisfied with "nothing else but horses, hawks and hounds of Ireland".

The present forest of Glendav was planted about thirty-seven years ago, a commercial undertaking for making chipboard and sending larger pieces of wood to sawmills. Occasionally I passed the remains of farmhouses taken over by trees and glimpsed pieces of grey walls indented with ruined hearths exposed under the branches. After the ceaseless struggle to make a living the families who lived here were removed to the rich country around Midleton in East Cork. Theirs was an early defeat—it seemed only a matter of time before the farms I had seen the day before would be similarly lost beneath trees.

The Glendav valley was the scene of much of the writing of Canon Peter O'Leary (1839–1920), who spent his life endeavouring to revive the Irish language, using the colloquial Irish of North Cork as a literary medium. The house where he was born is at Carriganimy a few miles away. In his time this whole country consisted of hill farms, whose wrecks I was passing. "Small poor hard fields they were," he wrote in his autobiography, "the whole place was bad land. Yet before the blight came on them, the potatoes would grow well in any kind of land—and fine, sound abundant food they made, for people or cattle or horses or for any living thing that could eat food at all."

Carriganimy was where Art O'Leary was ambushed and killed.

> Swept last night to nothing,
> Here in Carriganimma
> Perish it, name and people!

Arthur O'Leary had a wife and a horse, both of exceptional

quality, but he was shot for his horse. He had retired back to
Ireland from Austria, where he served as Captain of Hungarian
Hussars in Marie Thérèse's army. When his white-nosed mare,
a charger he used when he was an officer, and afterwards
shipped back to Cork, took the brush at the local hunt, Morris,
the Protestant magistrate of the district, claimed the animal for
five pounds, as he was entitled to do under the Penal Laws.
O'Leary, refusing the money with the remark that he would
sooner part with his life, started a quarrel which ended with
him whipping Morris with his riding crop. Morris and his
fellow magistrates had him outlawed, and later a party of
soldiers shot him. He was twenty-six years old. His wife's
lament for him, *Caoine Airt Ui Laoghaire*, is an outstanding landmark of Irish poetry. According to tradition, this passionate
widow, a mourner of Hebraic intensity (and also Daniel
O'Connell's aunt), pursued his murderers as she said she would,
and had the soldiers who killed him transported. Morris, "the
black-blooded rogue", was shot at Hammond's Marsh outside
Cork city by O'Leary's brother.

At midday I got out of the trees and could look across the
valley towards the long rolling summit of Musheramore. The
weather had cleared into sparkling winter brightness; after a
few biscuits and coffee from my thermos I lay down in a bank
of heather, waking an hour later, still in sunshine, to the rattle
of a grouse breaking cover. I moved on, making my way to
where the wild peaceful country was sharply interrupted by the
Macroom—Millstreet road with its charging cars and milk
lorries. But above the road I knew that there were clusters of
stone circles and standing stones around Musheramore.

My first enquiry was at a farmhouse.

"You head east for Cork. There's a rise, but you don't pay
any attention to it. Then there's another rise, then a flat piece—
and it is somewhere around there."

In fact the first circle I discovered was in a neighbour's yard,
ten small upright stones, surrounded by a belt of trees and
invisible even from a helicopter. The farmer brought me into
the small living-room of his cottage with its ancient dresser and
wooden chairs, and glimmer of light filtering through the cob-
webs in the little window.

"Do you drink?" he said, bringing out the Guinness and putting it on the oilcloth. Later he asked sharply, "Is there tin there?" I thought it was unlikely, and that the most he could hope for under his circle was some fragments of bones and perhaps pottery shards. If that were all, he thought, he had no need to worry about it. I hope there isn't gold there.

He took me to a neighbour who could produce many more stones in his place. "He'll give you the running of them." We went over and found him, a thin little man in a battered hat and glasses who gazed at me quizzically as I heaved off my rucksack outside his house.

"This fellow is going to spend a month with you," my companion told him before going off. He could not have brought me to a better guide, one more knowledgeable about the whole area, whose farm, with its fine crop of standing stones, appeared to have been an important site for early man.

One stone was used as a pier for a gate, another lay in the field behind, where it had toppled into the bracken, and there were many more. Probably this was a megalithic graveyard. Many archaeologists feel that putting up a modern gravestone is similar to the erection of an ancient standing stone and serves the same purpose. But it is comparatively easy, if hefty, work to hoist huge stones in the air, and they had many other purposes; some were used as boundary marks, others as monuments to important events, and many were sacred and had their part in religious ceremonies. Since they were the least elaborate means by which men could impress their personalities on the landscape in a permanent way, they were used over a long period of time and are not easy to date. Essentially they are mysterious; monolith, menhir, in Irish *gállán, déllán,* or *liagán,* perhaps it is best merely to regard a standing stone with the same awe that struck Samuel Pepys gazing at the stones of Stonehenge: "God knows what their use was, they are hard to tell, but yet may be told."

Behind the farm my guide nimbly showed me four more stones, then a cromlech, and a stone circle. "I had it from a priest that it is the most important circle in County Cork." He talked generally as we walked over the mountain slopes. About the Irish language; his father spoke it, no one bothered any

more. The marts killed it, and everywhere now English was
spoken. Here on the slopes of Musheramore was another sparse
mountainy area difficult enough to make a living out of; in
most places the forestry had the land or it went back to heather.
In the old days his father had owned a lot of it; but it was taken
off him by the English for his refusal to pay rent. Not that he
blamed the English altogether . . . the present government
would have done the same.

Finally he directed me to a *gallán* which I could see about a
mile away, leaning over slightly from its great weight towards a
plantation of young trees. It was a long slender stone, far bigger
than the others, about fourteen feet high, set apart, attended by
a small stone circle; it seemed to command and dominate
Musheramore towering beside it.

"I can't go up a hill and see a cromlech," the sculptress
Barbara Hepworth has said, "and not want to pat it, or pick
some flowers and put them on it; it's very ancient, this feeling,
and very pagan."

I walked towards Millstreet, which from the circle seemed to
be at the end of a vapourish green valley surrounded by more
empty hills turning golden in the evening light. All the road
signs in the area had been mutilated; a few were chopped clean
off, others were twisted around or pointed upwards into the
sky. A farmer gave me a curious direction to "follow the horse"
and for a time I did follow a frisky animal which paused now
and again to seize a piece of grass before gambolling away in
front of me.

The light was going quietly, shadows deepening and falling
across the fields, covering a patch of fern, a slope of dead grass,
splinters of bramble, taking the shine out of red berries in the
hedge. Cattle waited to be milked and rooks began assembling
for their fussy evening doss down. There is a tradition, not in
the written accounts, that O'Sullivan had to fight off or
frighten off a small body of men from Kilmeady Castle, just a
mile or two outside Millstreet. Walking down to the town I
could make out the squat tower stiffening the shadows just
before the sun slid behind Mullaganish.

In Millstreet the West Cork Gaeltacht is left behind. Voices
seemed flatter, less musical and a good deal easier to understand.

At the hotel I luxuriated in a bath before going downstairs to the fry. In the dining-room a couple of farmers wearing gum-boots, hats pulled over their eyes, prepared to tackle their mounds of chips on which that trinity of the frying pan, sausage, egg and bacon, were geometrically arranged. Voices sank to a whisper, teacups clinked below a notice on the wall that adver-tised a holiday in Jerusalem and a special audience with the Pope thrown in on the way.

"How's tricks?" the waitress asked a morose man drinking tea in the corner.

"Good."

One painted arm pointed to the LADIES, another to the GENTS. I sat down among kitchen fumes and bottles of ketchup; a clock broke the hour with a ponderous chime and outside the black shape of a priest scurried past in the rain.

Just how long the tradition of "lazy cooking" has gone on in Ireland is hard to say. The earliest reference I can find is a note by Lithgow, a much travelled Scotchman who came to Ireland in 1619. The inns where he stayed offered him very familiar menus, "a regimen of bacon and eggs, varied perhaps by eggs and bacon, on rare occasions a chicken, or perhaps a joint, if such could be procured at the time".

Afterwards I went outside where the rain was pouring, so that the miracle of the fine evening I had seen an hour ago was a memory of better times. Down the long street pubs and shops, spaced like beads in a necklace, alternated with the occasional solicitor. It was a town of two banks, a large church dedicated to St Patrick and a cream-coloured convent with some plastic storks keeping sentry. Holding my umbrella over my head I inspected the shop windows and their displays of Calvita cheese, Kimberley biscuits, shoeboxes of chocolate bars, obsolete copies of the RTE guide, convex mirrors with wrought iron frames, holy pictures and statues, apples in cobalt tissue-paper, neat little holy-water stoups. Between the Queen of Heaven and the Infant of Prague a notice sellotaped on to the glass said "Found Rosary Beads". Some of the bars and shops had em-bossed gilt lettering, or golden names picked out against darkened glass, and inside I glimpsed old wooden counters, vast japanned tea caddies and a pair of scales on chains hanging down from the ceiling. This is not to suggest that Millstreet did not have the usual quota of supermarkets and shops where the TV sets, showing programmes duplicated like the facets of a fly's eye, had just been turned off. There was a cinema and a library, on the wall of which someone had scribbled, "sex is my bread".

I found a chiropodist, Miss Josephine Gubbins. "All foot ailments treated. Homes visited by request." Perhaps she was out visiting; the old lady who came to the door was too deaf to make out the nature of my malady, even when I took off my boots and showed her my blisters. So I retired to a pub. A recent study had suggested that much of the preference of Irishmen for small crowded bars can be blamed on early segregation at school, which also results in an old-fashioned attitude towards women.

"Will you hurry up there, Noreen?"

"Ah, leave the girl!"

Noreen, a teenager with hair screwed into multicoloured curlers, was a machine for filling glasses. No flirtation, no banter or exchange of jokes with her customers. Two high-coloured old men argued about beer and stout. "Beer will cut the kidneys in two," one said. "It's a poisonous English drink." He had strong prejudices. Later he leaned across and said to me: "Do you know how many pubs there are in Millstreet? Twenty-four. And there used to be more before the marts. And do you know why? The English allowed them to license as many as possible. It was in order to corrupt the children!"

For a time I talked with a whiskey drinker who claimed he knew all about O'Sullivan Beare. "He was kicked along the street like a dog." And he was right. This was the first person I had met who regarded walking with something like pleasure. "A good view is from a boat. A better view is from a car or train. Better still from a bicycle; but the best of all is to be had by walking. The cheap seat."

Another blue-suited figure entered the pub. "Hello, men." Cars have made a difference to drinking habits; farmers from remote areas can desert their television sets to drive into the town.

"Another one, Noreen."

An American had returned after forty-five years to live on his pension. He couldn't say a good word about the old sod. "The Irish are a race of topers," he mused sipping his whiskey. "I endorse that." He declaimed conventional views about hard-working Germans and Swedes. "If you ask an Irishman to come at eight, he'll be sure to come at eight fifteen." The town, he said, hadn't changed all that much since he was a boy. "It would take an atom bomb to make any difference."

The atmosphere grew cosier, solid; we were like mice under straw. Long after midnight the customers began to exert themselves, and one by one leave the warmth and intimacy of the snug. Even then groups of them hung around in the stinging drizzle, reluctant to make the weary final journey home, whether it was to empty houses or to sleeping or waiting wives, mothers and sisters. Noreen was left to the loaded ashtrays and the clusters of Guinness-stained glasses.

CHAPTER FIVE

Millstreet—Churchtown

> Covering twenty-four miles in that day he pitched his tents at nightfall at O'Keefe's country. Sentinels being posted, the soldiers abandoned their way-worn limbs to rest, but the natives annoyed them throughout the night rather by yelling than their hurting. Hunger had also weakened them, because they had no food the whole day, the provisions which they had taken with them for only one day, being consumed.
>
> Philip O'Sullivan

WITH ONE NIGHT'S stop at Eachros, O'Sullivan Beare reached the neighbourhood of Millstreet less than forty-eight hours after leaving Glengarriff. (Walking leisurely I had covered the same sixty miles at about half his pace.) When he "pitched his tents" it is well to remember that these would have been nothing like the orderly rows of a conventional army bivouac. Early illustrations of Irish camps show small humped structures, not unlike those put up by modern itinerants, or like those that were erected at Donnybrook Fair which Jonah Barrington observed were made with peeled wattles. These were stuck in the ground in two rows, the tops twisted "like a woodbine arbour in a lady's flower garden" and tied together with ropes of hay. Barrington said that a tent fifty feet in length could be erected in a few minutes. Instead of cloth or canvas or the old quilts that itinerants use today, O'Sullivan's men would have cut out very thin sods of earth about four or five feet in length, and these were arranged over the sticks. Some may have had skins to keep themselves warm; the mantle, which Spenser had called "a fit home for an outlaw, a meet bed for a rebel and an apt cloak for a thief", would have protected most of the others.

A number of men had been wounded during the days of skirmishes. There is no mention of any fatal casualties in these encounters, but a few may already have died of wounds and exposure. We know very little about the women who went on the march except that only one survived to reach Leitrim. Some of the professional soldiers may have had wives or followers like O'Sullivan Beare's old ally, Richard Tyrell, whose wife followed him on his Muskerry campaign, the lady who fled half-clothed after him, pursued by Sir Samuel Bagenal. Women like her would have been accustomed to the hardships of guerrilla warfare and forced marches, since Tyrell, like most mercenaries, had fought all over Ireland.

O'Sullivan Beare had left his wife, together with Philip O'Sullivan's mother, Johanna McSwiney, along with some companions in hiding above Glengarriff somewhere in the region of Nead-an-Fhiolair, the Eagle's Nest, what Philip O'Sullivan described as "the gorges and the tops of the mountains". Also hidden was Dermot, the second son of O'Sullivan, who was only two years old; he is said to have been looked after for two years by "some gentlemen of rank" before going to Spain. The idea was that these refugees should make their way to the ship which was moored off Dursey, ready for instant flight. Unfortunately this ship was captured when the unhappy island was again attacked by a Captain Fleming who arrived with a pinnace. "He took there certain boats and an English bark which O'Sulevan had got and kept for his transportation into Spain when he should be forced there. They took also certain cows and sheep, which were reserved there as a sure storehouse and put the churls to the sword who inhabited therein." The women did get away to Spain, under the care of another West Cork exile, Cornelius O'Driscoll, who arrived back on the south coast and took them off to safety about the same time that O'Sullivan Beare arrived in Leitrim. According to legend, while the lady O'Sullivan was in hiding, she had as a bodyguard a man named Gorrane, who was, like Philip O'Sullivan's mother, a member of the MacSwiney family which had come down from Antrim a century earlier to act as constables to MacCarthy Mor. Gorrane found it increasingly difficult to find food for her. He searched the seashore for carrageen and shellfish and climbed the mountain to the eagle's nest on the summit, where he caught and tethered the eaglet he found there. When the parent bird brought it game to eat, he stole a share to feed his mistress.

D

All night long the camp was harassed by the threatening yells of people who lived in the neighbourhood. They might have sounded like the cries of wolves. "It is the custom of these savages to live like wild beasts in the mountains," wrote the shipwrecked Don Cuellar who had such a bad time in Ireland. Various theories have been put forward to try to explain the malignant, persistent enmity that O'Sullivan's people experienced for so much of their journey. The reward for his capture, the need for self-preservation, the fact that the marchers—in spite of having money—had to resort to plunder in order to obtain food are among the reasons given. Once he was beyond his territory, he was a stranger without allies in a country that was dominated by the English. Only when he reached the remoteness of Connacht, which was land still outside the control of his enemies, did he find aid and friendship.

From now on daily battles and skirmishes would become routine. But the most pressing problem was food. Cuellar had observed that the Irish "eat only once a day, and that at night-fall, their usual food being oaten bread and butter". The custom of eating just one daily meal continued to the nineteenth century, both before and after the Famine. It was not necessarily a sign of extreme poverty; among rural people, fishermen or shepherds, for instance, it would have been a convenience.

The refugees had eaten one meal since their departure—at Eachros they consumed the rations they had brought with them. The speed and pressure of their flight had given them no time as yet to forage through the winter countryside. At this stage of the march, after the long day's fighting, they were not yet starving; merely sleepless and very hungry.

The dim morning light lit up the Probationer's Card on the door. "Heroic offering to the Sacred Heart—to be repeated night and morning." Then downstairs to a breakfast enlivened by a bowl of tinned fruit salad. The winter tourist in a small market town like Millstreet is something of a freak. While the rest of the world is going about its business, here you are gazing into old shopfronts, and darting down alleys with umbrella and notebook like Gogol's Inspector General. Some people were suspicious; one old lady bolted her door and climbed up to a top window to gaze down at me until I left. But others went out of their way to supply me with local history, the name of a river, traditions and so on, farmers and shopkeepers searching their minds to humour me. The bank clerk who showed me the photograph dated 1903 of the old mill—the town's name derives from its ancient milling industry—told me not to miss the particularly large rat poised on the wooden wheel. Sister Basil of the Holy Infant let me round Millstreet's most imposing building, Drishane Castle, which is run as a boarding school for girls. The MacCarthys who built it stayed out of trouble for a long time, and it was not until after the Williamite wars that Drishane passed out of the possession of the Earls of Clancarthy to an English company for making Hollow Sword Blades, which was seeking to recover money advanced to King William to conduct his war in Ireland. Six years later the castle was resold to a family named Wallis, who remained in possession until 1909, when it passed to the nuns. The house to which the castle is attached was remodelled in the nineteenth century, and the Victorian detail and scale of rooms blended with the scrubbed atmosphere and the creak of brogue shoes and rustle of habits on waxed floors. Sister Basil showed me over the main rooms, exuberantly filled with Buhl bought at a local auction, and a display of souvenirs brought back from the mission field. A miniature Chinese temple, and a good deal of ivory and sandalwood clutter—in another room was a wooden mantel-piece put in by the MacCarthys in 1663, which had survived three hundred years of upheaval. The old grey tower of the castle is restored and gleaming, given a new lease of life by the Board of Works. The Board only takes the more important of Irish ruins into its care, nailing the little black-and-white notice on old walls as a sort of Good Housekeeping Seal.

During the night there had been hoarfrost, and now the morning was breathlessly cold with pools of milky ice and frozen reeds sticking up in the fields like glass knitting needles. To get from Millstreet to Newmarket the river Blackwater has to be crossed. O'Sullivan Beare avoided Drishane, and one tradition states that he forded near the Boeing, the curiously named castle on the north side of the river, where some years later, Cardinal Rinuccini, the papal legate, stayed on his way to the Confederation of Kilkenny. A ford was marked on the map just beyond the station, and this I took to be the place, as I could see the Boeing beyond. I asked a woman if it were possible to use, and was told that well, perhaps I couldn't. What was wrong with the perfectly good bridge a mile or so further up?

What indeed? I did not analyse the motives that sent me down an icy black path to the water's edge. The width from bank to bank was about fifty yards. I took off boots, socks and trousers, rolled up the combinations above my knees, balanced my pack and stepped in. The shock of the cold water nearly threw me, even before I began feeling my way over the ford's flat slippery stones. But at its deepest the ford only came above my knees and I was able to reach the other bank without difficulty. The Boeing was a few minutes away. Dressed, I walked over the remains of a massive curtain wall with towers at each end, a gaunt structure humanized by the way that ordinary life was still carried on beneath its warlike keep. Here was a barn, cattle sheds and nearby a farmhouse. The farmer's wife had me in and gave me strong tea while children gaped across the kitchen table piled with egg-stained plates.

"No one pays the old building much attention. There's meant to be a passage linking it with Drishane. The nuns might know."

Drishane was visible from Boeing, rising out of the trees; behind I could make out the bare anvil head of Claragh mountain, and in the far distance the Paps, according to traditional folklore the breasts of the goddess Ana.

"These two mountains," a nineteenth-century traveller pointed out, "have derived their names from their round and equal form, resembling the human breast; two little protuberances in the centre of each (which I suspect to be cairns), make the resemblance still greater and their title more appropriate. . . ."

The temperature rose slightly as I walked north of the Blackwater and mist began to fill the valley. A ghost train rattled past. The lady at the Boeing had told me that Keale bridge was a long mile ahead—a very long mile that took me half an hour before I rested sitting on the parapet miserably chewing a tag end of dates and speculating whether it was likely that O'Sullivan had crossed the Blackwater near the O'Keefe castle of Dromagh a couple of miles from here.

In the post office I slid off my rucksack before the fire. "Are you taking a holiday?" the postmistress asked. "Even in summer we don't have many tourists." I had what she described as a "temporary drink" and a few cakes before going on my way. The frost was melting now, so that the hedges and telephone wires were beaded with drops and the asphalt rang with little tinkles of falling ice fragments. But the fog grew thicker, filling up the valley. I tried to put myself in the frame of mind of that intrepid walker, Dorothy Wordsworth, who had something good to say about most manifestations of nature. She had actually liked "the shape of the mist slowly moving along, exquisitely beautiful; passing over the sheep it seemed to have more life than those quiet creatures". I made out a few details of boggy fields and some houses without gardens. The colours of summer were hidden in the dried stalks of the melting hedges, overlaid by a sweet odour of silage. Pleasures of company were limited to the occasional glimpse of women collecting water in bright pails from lion-headed pumps, or a spectre draped in a ragged coat whistling in the cows.

Near Boherboy I stopped at a farmhouse to ask the owner about his fine thatched roof. In the early seventeenth century most houses in the country outside the walled towns were circular. "Built of sticks and reeds in homely wise and walled with sods around." They were thatched with whatever material was available—rushes, marram grass, flax, reeds, heather, oaten straw. Some huts were made entirely of straw. The roofs were kept down with masses of bog fir, sally or heather ropes pegged into the thatch to prevent the wind from lifting them off. Today thatching seems doomed to extinction unless the tourist people can keep it going. It is indelibly associated with poverty, inconvenient to maintain, and the men who had the skills for it are old and dying.

"There's only one man in Boherboy who can still do it." The owner of the house brought me into his kitchen and I drank tea under his rigid wedding photograph, himself heavily moustached standing above a stiff-seated bride, a picture paralleled by a large, tinted, rather formidable profile of Pope John. As I gratefully warmed myself beside the prickle of silent-burning turf, he told me that he was the man who had thatched the roof himself. Now the price of spars was thirty shillings a thousand, while the straw, which came from Limerick, was eleven to twelve pounds a ton. One of the troubles was that oats, from which the best straw came, was an unpopular crop which farmers no longer found it economic to plant.

This side of Newmarket I explored a huge cemetery, full of Celtic crosses and obelisks, some ivy covered, which loomed out of the mist in Gothic manner, looking in vain for the grave of Sarah Curran. I gave up the search as darkness fell, and made for Newmarket, past the site of the MacAuliffe castle which used to overlook a gorge of the Dalua river. In O'Sullivan Beare's time the MacAuliffes were lords of the area. Newmarket was a swirling ghostly town, where I found the "sort of hotel" which had been recommended to me. It had nicotine-covered walls and damp sweating through the paint; one part consisted of an old-fashioned bar-cum-shop with tins of biscuits, a wall of mahogany drawers, empty barrels and some mirrored advertisements for whiskey. On the other side was the dining-room with a good fire and a communal table laid for eight, and behind this was an old-fashioned kitchen. It all put me in mind of a nineteenth-century Russian inn, described by Turgenev, with a "dark parlour . . . divided in two by a partition . . . labelled bottles of various kinds stand in rows on the shelves directly opposite the opening. In the forward part . . . which is given to the patrons, there are two benches, one or two empty barrels and a corner table . . ."

Oddly enough, the proprietor invoked Russia as he wiped the head of froth off my stout. Did I know what a debt we owed to the Russians, who were the first to get rid of feudalism? But now we had bureaucrats in place of feudal lords, and much worse too. When I asked for accommodation, he twisted his face to a frown, reluctant to take on the burden of an extra guest. Since the new factory had been built, any help that he used to get had vanished. And how could he afford to pay a young girl fifteen or twenty pounds a week? While I drank he made up his mind at last to give me a bed if I didn't mind waiting for breakfast. We agreed on ten o'clock being a reasonable hour.

He showed me a room at the top of the house with a vast double bed beside ancient red velvet curtains. Under a buckled picture of the Virgin, held in her frame by matchsticks, was a basin and jug of water which I regarded with regret; walking in the mist, I had pictured the exact moment of pleasure when I could step into a hot bath. I went down a storey and explored, finding a fat family-sized bathtub which the claw feet beneath supported with some difficulty. I turned on the brass taps and stripped off my clothes. But Hot, after spitting out a kettle full of boiling water which immediately dissipated in steam, soon reduced to a dispiriting little lukewarm gush which chipped off some more of the enamel that covered the tub's fat girth. There was no bath for me in Newmarket that night.

I ate alone at the communal table, enjoying a great plate of delicious home-cured ham, the best of all traditionally Irish meals. "They were insatiably fond of swine's flesh," wrote Sir Charles Harrington in 1599, "and so abundant was it, that Canbruensis declares that he never saw the same in any country . . .". The best time to eat while travelling in Ireland was during the eighteenth century. In those days no self-respecting inn was without its wine or claret; a typical dinner consisted of roast goose and old ale, claret and brandy with tea and hot cakes afterwards.

At the easy chairs in front of the fire sat two old men, one enjoying a glass of whiskey, the other, a commercial traveller, doing his accounts on numerous pieces of graph paper. He had been in the business a good fifty years, years spent on the road. In the old days he used to arrive at Newmarket by train and hire a jaunting car. During the thirties he had a Ford V8, but when the Emergency came and there was no petrol, it was back to the horse and cart and even the bicycle. So many shops, so many musty country pubs still buying the same things, Oxo cubes, Jacob's biscuits, Cadbury's chocolate, bright coloured orangeade. He had supplied three generations of shopkeepers, and grandchildren were giving out almost identical orders to those made by grandparents forty years ago.

I woke to sunshine, doubly welcome after the mist; a slice of orange moon hung in the sky, and the only sound to break the morning came from a couple of barking dogs. After a breakfast almost up to eighteenth-century standards, I signed the visitor's book.

"Do you know who that is who signed just above your name? He's the world underground champion, who spends most of his life being buried alive in a coffin."

Later I found further association with burials in the church-yard belonging to the Church of Ireland. It seemed that the retreat for vampires that I had searched the day before had been the wrong cemetery, and that Sarah Curran was buried here in the Curran family vault. Robert Emmet's sweetheart was born in Newmarket, where her father, John Philpot Curran, had spent his youth. In those days Newmarket was an Irish-speaking area, and Curran was unusual among Anglo-Irishmen in being bi-lingual. He moved to Dublin, where he became a brilliant lawyer with a reputation for wit. (When he fought a duel with his friend Egan, with whom he had quar-relled, Egan complained that he was at a disadvantage because he was a large man and Curran small. Curran suggested that his size should be chalked out on Egan and only shots fired within the target area should count.)

My guidebook said rather spitefully that after Robert Emmet's execution in 1803, Sarah . . . "married an English officer, but Thomas Moore's

> She is far from the land
> Where her young hero sleeps

has assured her an unmerited reputation for fidelity to Emmet's memory".

She seems to have been more pathetic than unfaithful. In 1803 her widowed father, who had recently lost his favourite daughter, Sarah's sister, had grown embittered. For most of his life he had been a moderate Republican; earlier he had defended nearly every United Irishman who came to trial in Dublin—Napper Tandy, the tragic Sheares brothers and Wolfe Tone among others. But he would have no part in Emmet's bungled patriotism which resulted in his aborted attempt at rebellion. He considered that Sarah was disgraced by her association with the doomed young rebel and brutally threw her out of her parental home after he was hanged. "I never did tell you how much I idolized her—my love Sarah . . ." Emmet wrote to his brother the day before he died. A contemporary described her as "about the ordinary size, her hair and eyes black. Her complexion was fairer than is usual with black hair, and she was a little freckled. Her eyes were large, soft and brilliant, and capable of the greatest variety of expression. . . ."

After Emmet's death and her father's rejection she must have found some peace in marriage to Captain Sturgeon. She died five years later, it is said of a broken heart. The main number of the *Gentleman's Magazine* of 1810 carried her obituary. "At Hythe in Kent of a rapid decline, aged twenty-six, Sarah, wife of Captain Henry Sturgeon, youngest daughter of the right honourable J. P. Curran, Master of the Rolls in Ireland." Most broken hearts then were instigated by T.B. (Sturgeon was one of the most capable engineers in Wellington's army. During the Peninsula campaign, on Wellington's orders, he managed to construct a suspension bridge across the Tagus between the two arches of an ancient bridge built by Trajan.)

In the same churchyard is the grave of Mrs Aldworth. As Viscountess Doneraile she had become the only woman ever to be enrolled among the Freemasons, when she was discovered in Doneraile Court hiding in a clock to spy on their cranky secret rituals. Newmarket owed its foundations to the Aldworth family in the time of James I. During the second half of the eighteenth century the town was a centre for the wool trade; later the Munster RIC had their headquarters here, before transferring to Kanturk. "Kanturk came up and Newmarket went down." The great house belonging to the Aldworths, a large Georgian block with a fine sweeping staircase, was turned into a convent, like its equivalent in Millstreet. But vocations were not what they used to be, and the place was now up for sale. *Tout passe.*

I was on the road again in sunshine with Newmarket strung out behind me in a pool of green fields. Ahead the road sloped to Stanner's glen, a deep cleft in the hills with trees bordering a curling river. Until recently the ruins of Curran's old home

stood here, built originally in the cottage orné style, with a
thatched roof, round towers and an ornamental pigeon house.
But a patriot's memory could not save it, and now a few stately
old trees are all that is left to show where it stood.

I was approaching Spenser's Arcadia, "a most beautiful and
sweet country as any under heaven; seamed throughout with
many goodly rivers replenished with all sorts of fish, most
abundantly sprinkled with many sweet islands and goodly
lakes . . .". The next green valley led down to the Allow, which
with the Awbeg and Bragoge made up the Spenserian trinity
of rivers. Here by the Ford of Bellaghan O'Sullivan Beare had
to fight his way across. *Pacata Hibernia* says that he was attacked
by John Barry, the brother of Viscount Barry, with eight
horsemen and forty foot: they were supposed to have come from
Liscarroll Castle. Philip O'Sullivan mentions specifically a
Captain Cuffe as already holding the crossing with a superior
force of Englishmen. This is one of the few references to Englishmen as enemies. One has to remember that throughout
O'Sullivan Beare's fighting career most of his opponents were
Irish. It was true at Kinsale, before Dunboy, and throughout
the march. English troops did not care to volunteer for Ireland,
which had a reputation as a graveyard; they were particularly
susceptible to disease induced by the harsh conditions and the
damp chilled climate.

Most English regiments contained large numbers of im-
pressed countrymen and criminals, "poor old ploughmen and
rogues" who were often kept half starved and inadequately
clothed. "It grieveth us," wrote the Lord Justice to the Privy
Council in 1598, "to see the nakedness of the soldiers for want
of clothes and their poverty for lack of lending." There were
many complaints about the condition and battleworthiness of
these drafts. The Mayor of Chester noted one lot in which
"many were diseased and many mad". The Mayor of Liverpool
lamented that "the return of sick and poor soldiers from Ireland
has infected the town, that a number of honest householders are
dead and their houses dissolved". The conduct of such soldiers
on the battlefield was often less than sparkling. Mountjoy, well
aware that most of his victories were won by Irishmen, described on one occasion how "our new soldiers for the most part

could not tell how to handle their pieces so that the captain was driven to take away their bullets and powder and give them to the Irish".

At Bellaghan, however, Captain Cuffe's men are reported to have put up a good fight. "The ford was contested with red hot balls from both sides for about an hour until Cuffe was forced to abandon the place." His soldiers killed four on the Irish side and wounded many more. "The Irish, through hunger and weariness, could not pursue them." The dead were buried by the ford and improvised litters were made to carry the wounded, for whom there was little hope or comfort. If they had been left behind on the battlefield they would have been killed off. Their wounds were treated with remedies prescribed by folklore, which recommended groundsel juice or plantain as healing agents; blood was staunched with wads of moss.

This ford of Bellaghan is probably in the present townland of Ballebahellagh beside the Freemount–Kanturk road. I paused at John's Bridge, which may have replaced the old ford, a lonely place which I shared for a few moments with a heron picking its way through the trickling waters of the Allow. The encounter had taken place on 3rd January—then from here O'Sullivan by-passed Liscarroll and made his way to the Awbeg, travelling along its banks towards the relative safety of the Ballyhoura hills. This is a countryside of rolling fields and prosperous farmhouses.

I slept for a while in the sun, just strong enough to paint my limbs and face with a pale warmth. Then I walked on to where a town stood below me in a valley capped with feathery brown trees, whose great castle dominates it like a Potala. This was Liscarroll and its castle is at least as large as the town itself, which appears to be an overspill outside its vast rectangle. The formidable size of the fortress is illusory, since all the buildings within it have vanished, and the massive walls, which average twenty-five feet in height and are five or six feet thick, surround nothing but a field. Three or four corner towers survive. Charles Smith thought that "the ruins of its several turrets and other works afford the imagination a more pleasing idea than the most magnificent structure could do; as one looks at the wounds of a veteran with more veneration than the most exact proportions of a regular beauty". However, he seems to have credited it with more action than it deserved.

No one is sure about Liscarroll's origins. Like other Norman castles in Ireland it has been attributed to King John, but it was most probably built by the Anglo-Norman de Barrys late in the thirteenth century. During the Elizabethan wars these Barrys sided with the English, and hence were prepared for a foray against O'Sullivan Beare, who is said to have plundered their territory on a previous expedition. (Even if it were Captain Cuffe who mounted the ambush at Bellaghan, it is more than likely that he had Barry support.) Not until 1625 was the place foreclosed and confiscated, becoming the property of Sir Philip Percival. Seventeen years later this huge edifice, constructed for warfare, had its only real experience of fighting in seven centuries. On 20th August, 1642, it was attacked by Garret Barry, general of the Confederate Catholic army of Ireland. He forced the garrison to surrender on 2nd September, but could only hold the castle for a day; on 3rd September it was retaken by an English army led by Murrough O'Brien of the Burnings and Sir Charles Vavasour. After that no more history; merely some mild disintegration as the neglected property of the Earls of Egmont, descendants of Sir Philip Percival. But plenty of it still remains.

Shadows tugged at the last rays of sun as I trudged to Churchtown four miles on. Even in such a short distance there was a change of landscape; banks and hedges were replaced by grey demesne walls, fields by parkland. The sloping rays shone on the dark trunks of specimen oaks and the silver of beeches. Coming into Churchtown there was a whole avenue of beeches, topped by another restless noisy rookery settling for the night.

CHAPTER SIX

Churchtown—Ardpatrick

The Catholics, having buried their dead and in turns
carrying the wounded in military litters, accomplished a
march of 30 miles that day, and on a stormy night pitched
their camp in a desert place and vast solitude near the woods
of Aherlow, the guards being scarce able to keep awake
through hunger, weariness and fatigue.

Philip O'Sullivan

SMALL MANORIAL VILLAGES which owe their inspiration and
development to one landlord or family of landlords are not
uncommon in Ireland. Enniskerry in Wicklow and Adare in
Limerick are probably the best known, architecturally quite
different from the normal straggly development of Irish towns.
The alien prettiness of the neat rows of cottages bears the
imprint of the landlord, just as the walls of his mansion do.
Similarly Churchtown, with its attractive limestone houses,
school and handsome market building, is just a shade too neat,
and has the slightly operatic air of an ascendency creation.

The present village dates from the mid-nineteenth century,
after most of the older buildings were burnt down in 1832
during some fierce Whiteboy riots. The last public execution of
a woman in Ireland resulted from these riots. A small inscription on the old market house states that it was erected by Sir
Edward Tierney Bart., in AD 1846. Anyone reading it might
believe that Sir Edward, the builder of modern Churchtown,
was a typical landlord of the period. But this is not so.

The Tierney brothers, Matthew and Edward, were the sons
of a poor weaver from Rathkeale in County Limerick; both of
whom became millionaires by their own exertions. Matthew,
born in 1776, emigrated to London, where he became an
apothecary and a friend of Jenner, the pioneer of vaccination.
In 1800 he had the good fortune to revive the Prince of Wales,
who had fainted while walking round the streets of London.

"His Royal Highness was brought to the nearby shop of a poor Irish apothecary, Matthew Tierney . . . Tierney burnt some feathers under the royal nostrils, and the ammonia thus released revived the princely patient."

This course of treatment, perhaps inspired by Prinny's coat of arms, brought Matthew Tierney instant success. He became personal physician to Mrs FitzHerbert, and in 1818, as the result of royal patronage, was created a baronet. Meanwhile his brother, Edward Tierney, born in 1780, had an equally prosperous career as a solicitor. It is said that he became the owner of the Churchtown estates, which had belonged to the Earls of Egmont, by highly questionable means. He succeeded his brother to the baronetcy and built up the town; but after his death in 1864 the estate was rebought by the original owners.

The Earls of Egmont were of the same family which took over Liscarroll and the Barry lands. In the eighteenth century their Irish estates totalled ninety thousand acres, and Church-town and the surrounding lands formed part of their posses-sions. The original Burton was one of the few big houses in Ireland of the Caroline period. It had tall windows, ten feet high, and at one time was crowned with a lantern on which sat a large copper ball three feet in diameter. It was built by John Percival, together with a church. He also thought of establishing an inn, "but in ye meantime I think it will answere the Charge if I run up a stable of cabins in the towne with a sign to show Strangers there is room for their horses tho there is none for themselves". The "stately new house" in its "large noble park" observed by Sir Richard Cox in 1688, was destroyed when King James the Pretender's forces passed through on their way to burn down Charleville. The present Burton Hall, on the out-skirts of Churchtown, was not the main house of the Percivals, but the residence of their agents, the Purcells. It is Georgian in concept, although it did not escape a Victorian overlay which gave it, among other architectural features, an ornate baronial-style gateway. Its atmosphere is typical: "Large, intensely solid, practical, sensible, and of the special type of old Irish country house that is entirely remote from the character of the men that originated it," Edith Somerville wrote of a similar building, "and can only be explained as the expiring cry of the English blood. . . ."

In the hall stands a tattered flag of the Royal Cork Volunteers, dated 1745. Beside it The Knife hangs on the wall, an old carving knife which looks as if it did long duty on mammoth sides of beef and roast goose. It may well have, but it is also the same instrument with which Mr Purcell killed a number of intruders and earned himself a knighthood. *Tuckeys Remembrancer* gives details of the incident: "July 12th, AD 1811 . . . the Duke of Richmond knighted the venerable Mr Purcell, whose singular intrepidity in resisting the attack on his house by a gang of ruffians, five of whom he either killed or wounded, had been a subject of admiration and surprise." Probably the invaders were Whiteboys. After the attack, Mr Purcell, who was seventy years old, afraid that more would come to his house, hid himself in the back yard between two heaps of anthracite slack, emerging at daybreak covered with black dust and the blood of his victims.

I stayed at Burton Hall as guest of the Ryan-Purcells, descendants of the Knight of the Knife. It is getting rare to find a place in Ireland like this which is still in the possession of its original owners. In the struggle to survive the servantless post nineteen-forties, the family had resorted to the well-known expedient of Bringing up the Kitchen. I remember, in other houses, the last descent of the creaking old lift towards the damp underground basement with its burden of dirty cutlery and plates; the Aga and the new Formica-topped tables installed in converted library or study so that for the first time in two or three hundred years food appeared at the table reasonably hot. Here the old billiard room had become a combined dining-room and kitchen. Antlered heads still gazed down from the wall and green light shades gave their illumination to the kitchen table, where billiard balls once cannonaded and clicked.

Next morning I set off for the Ballyhoura hills. On his way to Ardpatrick it is probable that O'Sullivan Beare skirted the Ballyhouras and went by way of Ballyhaght. On this route the going would have been easier, and he would have had the safety of the forest-clad hills to fall back on if he were suddenly attacked. At the main junction of 'the Charleville–Buttevant road I decided to go off his route to Kilcolman, which derives its name from St Colman, one of the fifty-odd saints on the Irish calendar of that name. This one, a friend and disciple of St Finbarr, was a poet. But the place is more strongly associated with another poet.

From as far away as Buttevant there are signposts along the interminable dull road directing the traveller to Spenser's Castle. However, when you finally arrive they cease abruptly and not so much as a footpath guides you to the little tower camouflaged in ivy which stands among fields before a wild stretch of bogs and a small crescent-shaped lake quivering with birds. I heard the constant snap of duck taking off and landing on water, and watched two whooping swans flying overhead trumpeting asthmatically. You get teal here, widgeon, a few pintail and quantities of mallard. The Kilcolman Trust for Wild Life Preservation has obtained over seven hundred acres of the surrounding bog and lake for the recreation of these visiting birds. A local man told me that the Trust "made it saucy for the boys around". Trespassers are discouraged; there is an unresolved conflict between the conservationists and dedicated pilgrims who wish to cross the fields to view the poet's ruined home. No notices direct them to Kilcolman, nor do they have any right of way; their approach disturbs the birds on their nests.

When Spenser lived here the rectangular castle was flanked by a tower containing some small rooms reached by a turreted staircase. Part of the staircase survives, and what I took to be the poet's thunderbox. The view from the battlements once looked over five counties, sweeping from the Comeraghs in Waterford to the mountains of Kerry. It is a bleak enough place today, and in 1586 when Lord Grey's ex-secretary received the old Desmond Castle, together with 3,028 acres of forfeited lands, it must have seemed a wilderness. Kilcolman Castle, built in 1347 above a stretch of bog, was an austere home. But life here for Spenser would have been materially a lot more comfortable than for O'Sullivan at Dunboy.

Although the castles were roughly contemporary, it is likely that Kilcolman was the more substantial building. Dunboy was a typical coastal tower house, one of many scattered from Cork to Donegal. Like Kilcolman it had a large cellar, a hall, sleeping accommodation on the higher floors and chimneys and fireplaces—the last an unusual feature for small coastal castles. There is speculation that Dunboy was used mostly for ceremonial occasions, such as the entertainment of the paramount chief of the MacCarthys Mor, while the actual residence of O'Sullivan was at Ardea. The excavations at Dunboy have brought to light little more than some brownware pottery, and it seems likely that the furnishings there were simple and traditional. It would have contained a few solid pieces of furniture; rushes would have been strewn on the floor and illumination would have come from peeled candles or pilchard oil. Perhaps there were a few luxuries. Pewter and brass utensils had become fairly common household articles; they were made up in Ireland from imported metal and sent abroad. In 1585 about 2,300 loads of old brass and pewter were exported to Chester. An inventory of the forfeited goods of the Earl of Tyrone gives a useful index of the sort of things which could have been found in Dunboy. Two long tables, value ten shillings . . . an old bedstead . . . a powder tub . . . six pewter dishes . . . a brass kettle . . . an old Irish harp.

There are a few contemporary somewhat bizarre descriptions by visitors of life in these remote Irish castles. A Bohemian nobleman, the Baron of Dohna, who visited the castle house of O'Cahan in 1601 was met at the door by "sixteen women all naked except for their loose mantles". He was invited by the Chief to take off his clothes by the fire, where the ladies sat "crosslegged like tailors". But the Baron, when he came to himself after some astonishment at this strange sight, professed that he was "so enflamed therewith as for shame he durst not put off his apparel". (One should add that this story comes from Fynes Moryson.) In 1620 Luke Gernon, enjoying traditional Irish hospitality, was offered a meal of deer and mutton, with beer, sack, whole ale and acqua vitae, which was a form of whiskey. "Towards the middle of supper the harper begins to tune and singeth Irish rhymes of ancient making. If he be a good rhymer he will make one song to the present occasion. Supper being ended it is your liberty to sit up or depart to your

lodging . . . when you come to your chamber do not expect
canopy or curtains. It is very well if your bed content. . . ." In a
castle like Dunboy beds would have been something of a rarity;
Don Cuellar remembered that "they sleep upon rushes, newly
cut and full of ice and water . . .".

Spenser may well have brought over a shipload of Elizabethan comforts. Pewter, tin and silver had become general
among the leisured classes in England where they had largely
taken the place of earthenware dishes and wooden spoons. He
would have had beds with feather-and-down mattresses,
furnished with sheets and soft pillows, which had formerly been
considered only suitable for women in childbirth. Tapestry,
Turkey work, fine linen, a silver salt cellar, silver spoons would
have lessened the discomforts and helped to give an assurance
and a sense of superiority.

Ostracized by his neighbours, Spenser not only stuck Kilcolman, but derived his disciplined Arcadian inspiration from
its surroundings—the gentle Molla, which is identified with the
Awbeg, Old Father Mole up on the Ballyhouras, and other
landmarks that formed the background to the "rude rhymes,
the which a rustic muse did weave on a savage soil far from
Parnasso Mount". Among his loveliest poems is the Epithala-
mion, written when he married Elizabeth Boyle. Here, too, the
Awbeg is invoked, or rather, the "nymphs of Mulla", tending
the river fish ("those trout and pike all others do excel"), who
are told to look their best while attending the bride. Germaine
Greer has pointed out that this exaltation of his wedding is
probably the first public-relations work for marriage. Possibly
Spenser was making the best of things; isolated at Kilcolman he
could have had little opportunity for any alternative adventure
into courtly love.

With his work as a provincial official and poet, his life could
not have been all that disagreeable, but it must have been
lonely. His refusal to remain anything but detached from the
society of Irishmen which he regarded as steeped in brutish
barbarism was common enough at the time; yet it is always
disturbing that so sensitive a poet should set out the attitudes of
the Elizabethan planter with such eloquence.

His opinions are unpleasant, allowing for the effects of

loneliness and litigation with Lord Roche, and his reputation must be blighted by *A View of the Present State of Ireland*. He did not originate, but set out very clearly, the policy which was continued during the seventeenth century of breaking down the powers of chieftains and destroying the customs and laws on which depended the unwieldy structure of Gaelic society. He advocated plantation. He is believed to have given Mountjoy many ideas, among them the scheme of reducing the Irish by deliberately induced famine. He set out the advantages to be gained from fighting in winter, and conveys something of what it must have been like for O'Sullivan Beare and his companions that January. "It is not with Ireland as it is with other countries . . . but in Ireland the winter yieldeth the best services, for then the trees are bare and naked which use both to clothe and house the kern. The ground is cold and wet which useth to be his bedding; the air is sharp and bitter and the cattle without milk which useth to be his only food; neither if he kill them will they yield him flesh, nor if he keep them will they give him food."

He was at Kilcolman for twelve years, apart from a brief visit to London in 1590 to present a copy of the *Faerie Queene* to his sovereign. Raleigh came to stay, he took a second wife, Elizabeth Boyle, and then his life was destroyed. Those who burnt his castle in October, 1598, in which his infant son is said to have perished, set up his own death; the experience of becoming a dispossessed refugee led to his dying a pauper a year later in London at the age of forty-seven.

His descendants returned to Ireland and continued until the late eighteenth century. One of the last, John Spenser, is supposed to have loved his housekeeper. "She was shaving him on the morning of his marriage to another lady, and she cut his throat."

It is tempting to imagine that four years after the Munster rising, O'Sullivan Beare, also a refugee, may have passed the blackened stump of Kilcolman and viewed it, perhaps even with the knowledge that Mr. Spenser had fled and was dead in England—but the castle is too far off his route.

From Kilcolman the Ballyhouras, a fat roll of green topped with firs, rose ahead. Passing Castle Pook, another crumbling tower, I thought I could walk through the extensive forestry plantation and come out above Ardpatrick, where O'Sullivan made his third camp. A forester gave me complicated directions which simplified themselves into one piece of advice—go north. Unfortunately I did not have a compass, and weaving among the forestry paths, hemmed in by trees on either side, was like trying to find a way through a giant maze. I floundered up the Z-shaped route, upwards and horizontally from path to path in a direction that I assumed to be northwards, until at last the conifers expired and I found myself on a windswept plateau covered with white bog grass. The hump of the mountain ahead I thought must be Carron (1,469 ft), and the land dropping away to the right must be the edge of the Limerick plain. At that moment it began to rain, and visibility immediately closed to a few yards. I started walking blindly downwards. Hours later, tired, wet and peevish I reached a small tarred road which led through yet more forestry plantations with a glimpse of a green plain at the end of them. I had been on the move for the best part of the day, and filled with thoughts of food and rest, I did not notice at first the old tower that stuck out of the trees and the vaguely familiar pattern of the countryside. I told myself there were other towers—other castles—I could not have been so foolish. At the first inhabited cottage I asked the way to Ardpatrick.

"Ardpatrick? It's a good thirteen miles away on the other side of the mountain. That? That's Castle Pook." I had made a great circle and come back to within a few hundred yards from where I started.

"Where's the nearest town?"

"Doneraile. About four miles from here." I knew the place, built on Spenser's land, with its wide main street and sad empty court abandoned by the Doneraile family.

"Would I find accommodation there, do you think?"

"No. I don't think there would be anything like that." In a mood of weariness I set off to examine the possibility of camping. I found that Castle Pook, the Castle of the spirit of Pooka, or the Spook, was drowned in mud and totally uninhabitable. Then I thought of the caves nearby, which I knew were substantial enough to contain the bones of prehistoric animals. They had been explored at the turn of the century by Mr

Ussher and his butler, who discovered a vast system of galleries. "We lost our way; while seeking to find my attendant, John Power, came upon the scapula of an adult mammoth, deeply gnawed, as it proved, by the teeth of a hyena." They found rhinoceros, bison, musk ox, lion, Irish elk and Arctic lemming. Plenty of room for me to lay down my sleeping bag, if all the caves and galleries had not been blocked up with rubble by local farmers fearful for the fate of wandering cattle.

I had no tent with me and it was damp for sleeping out. Since I felt that it was too late now to try to retrace my route across the Ballyhouras, I decided to go the longer way round by road. The road, too, was tricky to find, and I set off hesitantly, only to be stopped a few miles further on by a car. It was driven by the man who had given me my location: "We didn't like to think of you getting lost on the mountains again." His job as a forester made him aware of the discomforts, not to say dangers of being caught out at night. I felt I should be prepared to camp in the ditch; but I climbed gratefully into the back.

As darkness fell I stood outside Clonodfey House, a Victorian mansion of gigantic dimensions looking like the Palace of Westminster transposed to the edge of the Limerick Plain. It was built in old red sandstone on the site of the earlier house named Castle Oliver, some time after the famine, by the Misses Isabella and Elizabeth Gascoigne Oliver. The architect, Fowler Jones, preferring the "old Scotch castle or manor house style of Scotland", incorporated in his design forty bedrooms and a front hall the size of a swimming pool with stained glass windows showing scenes from the life of St Patrick designed by the Misses Gascoigne.

Mrs Trench takes guests. The kitchen has been brought up, ceilings lowered and Calor gas stoves are scattered about, giving off as much heat as candles in a cathedral. In the main room, nicknamed Siberia, we huddled over a big fire and talked about keeping warm. Strenuous efforts have to be made during those weeks in midwinter when parties of Americans arrive to stay and hunt with the Scarteens. Mrs Trench told me she once asked a central-heating specialist to give her an estimate, but he took one look at the house and refused to climb out of his car.

The three hundred acres that she farms today are a fragment

of the original estate acquired by her husband's ancestors. A letter exists in the family from Captain Robert Oliver to Sir Richard Aldworth of Newmarket, dated 22nd February, 1676, describing a violent thunderstorm which partially wrecked the original house. There were sixty-odd guests staying at the time, among them Lord and Lady Baltimore. The storm "broke down the hangings, threw my lord from his chair, his lady on the bede, his head was under the bede".

When Arthur Young came here, the house was newly spruced up. "Castle Oliver is a place almost entirely of Mr Oliver's creation, from a house surrounded with cabins and rubbish he has fixed up a fine lawn surrounded by good wood." Young enjoyed the hospitality, but on a later visit rather regretted the meals he had eaten when he passed into the squalor of the kitchen. "Etna or Vesuvius might as soon be found in England as such a kitchen."

Mr Silver Oliver's successor, Captain Oliver, was a landlord of unusual imperiousness. His neighbour, the scholar P. W. Joyce, described him as a Lord of the Soil. Around this area a lazy man, driven to work by unavoidable circumstances, was said to have got Oliver's Summons. When Captain Oliver needed workers at a certain season, he used to send around to the houses of those he wanted two men with a horse and cart who were authorized to impound goods and chattels. Next day he was sure to have half a dozen people prepared to work for him, and after they had finished their tasks, their property was returned.

In 1818 Lola Montez was born at Castle Oliver, where her mother, a member of the Oliver family with Spanish blood in her veins, christened her Marie Dolores Eliza Rosanna. Her father, Edward Gilbert, was gazetted an ensign in the 44th foot, and moved the family to India for a few years, from where, in 1826, Marie was sent to Scotland to be educated. Ten years later, in order to avoid marriage with the aged Sir Abraham Lumley, she eloped to Ireland with Captain Thomas James, whom she married in Meath, using the name of Rosanna Gilbert, spinster. He was the first of three husbands and a long succession of lovers who included the Viceroy of Poland, Liszt, and the son of Robert Peel. After her divorce from Captain

James, she took lessons in Spanish dancing and changed her name to Lola Montez. When she first appeared in London, her energetic tigerish performance was well received until the moment that she was denounced amid uproar from the box of her ex-lover, Lord Ranelagh, and a hissing party of his cronies. "That woman isn't Lola Montez. She's an Irish girl, Betsey James!" The audience called for their money back and told her to get back to the bogs. She swore, stamped on the bouquet she was holding and kicked it at them. Then she went to Europe, where she became notorious. Her activities included throwing her garters and drawers at a Parisian audience, horse-whipping a Berlin policeman, causing a riot in Poland and dancing on the tables during a civic banquet in Bonn at a time when Queen Victoria was paying a state visit. But her triumph was in Munich. When King Ludwig, enraptured by her dark beauty, doubted the promise of her seemingly ample bosom, she is said to have pulled down her dress to convince him. "Gentlemen," he told his courtiers later, "I present you my best friend." Lola stayed with him for a year and virtually ruled Bavaria, rather better than most of the Wittelsbach. But the citizens of Munich could not accept her; their dislike echoed strongly again twenty years later when they remembered her in their detestation of Wagner who infatuated another Ludwig. In 1848, the year of revolutions, both mistress and monarch were forced into exile. According to a contemporary, Lola "found consolation in the arms of a 21-year-old ex-Etonian, a virile young guardsman named Heald, whom she subsequently though bigamously married". After wandering to Australia and all over the world, she died in America. Her grave in Greenwood cemetery, New York, says simply, "Miss Eliza Gilbert: Born 1818. Died 1861."

Setting off across the fields I looked back at Clonodfey House, which like many mock baronial buildings became more attractive the further away it was viewed. From a distance the towers and battlements glowed red in the sunlight against a background that was lush and verdant, even in winter; a luminous fairy castle set in a fairy landscape. I was reminded again of its odd link with Bavaria and its kings, and the even more dreamlike creations of mad Ludwig, grandson of Lola's lover. What were the motives of the two Miss Gascoignes in spending a fortune to erect an Arthurian fantasy on the Limerick plain? I wondered if they had also built the folly known locally as Castle H, two small towers and a couple of castellated arcades prominent on a hillock in the grounds of Castle Oliver. Local history can become distorted, and a man told me that Cromwell hanged rebels from it. Possibly this myth arose from confusion of the name Oliver; in fact it is a folly, erected to give employment during the Famine. The demesne used to have blocks of trees planted to represent the formation of Napoleon's soldiers at Waterloo.

During the eighteenth century the surrounding area was settled with Palatines, the German Protestants from the Palatinate of the Rhine who were driven out during Louis XIV's French wars. In 1709 Queen Anne sent a fleet to Rotterdam which brought over about seven thousand of these refugees to England. (Two thousand others, who were found to be Catholic, were hastily shipped back to the Continent.) Some stayed in England, others went to America, and a group was encouraged to come to Ireland, not for any humanitarian consideration, but because it was thought that such industrious people would improve the agriculture and strengthen the Protestant interest. Most of them settled in Limerick around Rathkeale, where about twelve hundred people were brought over in a colony organized by Sir Thomas Southwell. Although they got on well with their Catholic neighbours, they remained a closed foreign community up until the end of the eighteenth century. German was taught in their schools, they wore their distinctive mid-European dress and had a burgomaster to deal with their disputes. They lived in poverty that horrified John Wesley when he visited Limerick in 1756. "I stand amazed," he wrote, "have the landlords no common sense (whether they have humanity or not) that they will suffer such tenants as these to be starved away from them?" He noted that they had no minister, and as a result they drank, swore and neglected their religion.

> If you see my home and folk,
> They'll give you wine and brandy,

sang the Palatine lass to the boy at the fair. But after a spell of Wesley's influence their ways changed. "They are washed since they heard and received the truth." Two Methodists of Palatine descent emigrated to America and helped greatly to establish the religion there. Philip Embry, the carpenter and preacher, and Barbara Heck, the "Mother of American Methodism", both came from near Rathkeale, and American Methodists still make a pilgrimage to the little church of Ballingrane where they are commemorated.

From the parent colony of Rathkeale thirty-five Palatine families were brought over to Kilfinnane and the land around Castle Oliver in 1776 by Mr Silver Oliver. I went in search of Mr Steepe, who is of Palatine descent, and lives in the little hamlet of Glenosheen on the lower slopes of Seefin—just a few houses, an old schoolhouse, now a shop, and above the fields and dark woodlands the tawny cap of the mountain. Mr Steepe told me that his house had been lived in by at least five generations of his family, which was awarded eight acres of land when they had first moved over to Rathkeale. After all this time he possessed the same eight acres; no one could accuse his people of aggrandisement. There are about 450 descendants of Palatines still living in County Limerick, most of whom are absorbed into the Catholic population. But Mr Steepe said that the families who survived around Kilfinnane—Alton, Steepe, Switzer—remained largely Protestant.

In the same small village, facing the grandiose pile of Clonodfey House, is the small cottage which was the birthplace of the Joyce brothers, P. W., the historian, and R. D., the song collector. Sons of a cobbler, they strove to educate themselves, starting as historians immersed in local tradition, rather like the brothers Grimm. Their scholarship became national, resulting in *Irish Place Names, Ballads of Irish Chivalry, Irish Folk Music and Songs* and other fundamental textbooks of social history. P. W.'s son Weston St John Joyce, continued the tradition of family scholarship, writing about Dublin and its neighbourhood.

The bright green dome of Ardpatrick, a conspicuous landmark for miles around, stands out only a few miles from Glenosheen. St Patrick founded a church on the top of the hill, whose monastic successor is represented by the stump of a round tower and church. The monastery, once extremely powerful, and linked closely to Armagh, was burned by the Danes in 1114; later, when it was suppressed in Tudor times, its bells were concealed and there is a tradition that at Christmas and Easter five bells ring out magically over the countryside. On the fields leading up to the summit scratch marks made by ploughs show the medieval field systems used by the monks. An ancient entrenched pathway called *Rian Bó Phádraig*, the slug of St Patrick's Cow Horn, winds up the hill. St Patrick's little cow kept him regularly supplied with milk, and she used to be suitably remembered in this dairy county by being pictured on signboards. On the domed summit the scattered ruins are composed like a Victorian illustration of Celtic Ireland. The squat cylinder of the round tower, nine feet in diameter, stands outside a graveyard bounded by the old monastery walls. Inside, among graves old and new, I found a heap of yellowed skulls and thighbones brushed up under a tree. (Like a bloody battlefield, a man I met on the road called it.) Here is the famous well of ill omen, now blocked up by stones. If you did not see your shadow in the water, the outlook was extremely grim.

Ardpatrick is locally regarded as the highest green hill in Ireland, and the fields lap its base all round. The Limerick plain to the west and north is the richest pastureland in Ireland, the centre of the dairy industry. The landscape is dominated by Queen Cow; where the fields are not brilliant green with lush grass, there is scarcely a clod of earth that isn't dented with a cloven foot or enriched with manure. From the summit of the hill the view is of a country drawn with a Dutch perspective, full of rolling shadows, patterns of fields with distant towers and church spires shining in the sun—and dotted all around, the browsing flicktailed herds of cows that Cuyp would have posed and painted.

Here, at a time when this pasture was forest, O'Sullivan Beare spent the third night of his march. There can be little doubt that the "desert place and vast solitude near the woods of Aherlow" which Philip O'Sullivan writes about was Ardpatrick. He stopped here deliberately, just as he had paused at

Gougane Barra, Eachros and Ballyvourney. Throughout the march he favoured stopping places which were also centres of pilgrimage and worship, and although they were under constant pressure of flight, his people made time to pray. O'Sullivan himself was extremely devout; in exile, where perhaps he had time to fill up, he went to mass two or three times a day. During his flight it was natural to combine what might be termed a rest period with prayers for deliverance; also the old medieval idea may have lingered in his mind that a shrine was a place of sanctuary. Special visits to shrines were often part of a battle campaign; Hugh O'Donnell had gone out of his way on his march to Kinsale to visit Holycross and ask God's help—which was not forthcoming.

The shrines where O'Sullivan stopped were on pilgrim routes. From ancient times there was a system of roadways around Ireland, later used by Normans and Elizabethans, and places like Ardpatrick or Gougane Barra would have been landmarks along them. They were not very good roads; the Scottish traveller, Lithgow, described the discomfort of winter journeys when every day his horse constantly sank to its girths in the boggy road, and his saddle bags were destroyed. He often had to cross streams by swimming his horses; during a period of five months six of them drowned. In the end he felt as worn out as any of his steeds.

O'Sullivan would have kept in touch with these routes as much as possible; in spite of his enemies he had to use recognized mountain passes and forest paths, to cross bogs by the usual *toghers* or causeways if he were to move at any speed at all. At this stage he obviously stayed near them as much as he could, avoiding guarded villages and the posses, who, notified of his swift approach, constantly came to attack him. Later, west of the Shannon, where roads were wilder and more uncertain and he was in utterly strange country, he got lost.

Until he reached Ardpatrick he had avoided any serious battle with his enemies, since he moved through mountainous areas. Now he had to dash across the Limerick plain, a perilously populated area, to the relative refuge of the next range of mountains, the Slieve Felim. He could see the towns from the summit of the hill, the lights of Kilmallock where the Sugan

Earl of Desmond had made his submission to the crown three years before, and in whose Franciscan Abbey O'Sullivan's enemy, the White Knight, would eventually be buried. Perhaps there was a glimmer from the neighbouring town of Hospital and even a distant glow from Limerick. Ahead on the great dark plain and beyond was danger and suffering; the three days he had marched had been easy enough by comparison to what he would meet. The ruined church and tower blessed by St Patrick would have called him to prayer on that cold hungry January night.

CHAPTER SEVEN

Ardpatrick—Lough Gur

On the following day they refreshed themselves with cresses and water and hastened along in a direct route before sunrise. The inhabitants in their usual way pursued.

Philip O'Sullivan

MEN IN IRELAND had long been used to eating raw materials provided by nature. When John Derricke wrote "my soul doth detest their wild shamrock manners", the word shamrock summed up a whole way of life which he considered wild and strange. In good times a favourite dish among the Irish was beef flavoured with roots, shamrocks and other herbs. Shamrock was often confused with wood sorrel, whose refreshing acid-tasting leaves made a garnish in season. Nettles were a popular remedy against sickness and fever; St Kevin lived on them for years. Other ascetics had enjoyed a diet like mad Swiney's of fruit plucked from the countryside.

> Watercress . . .
> Apples, berries, beautiful hazel nuts,
> Blackberries, acorns from the oak tree;
> Haws of the pricking sharp hawthorn,
> Wood sorrels, good wild garlic,
> Clean topped cress, mountain acorns,
> Together they drive hunger from me.

As late as the nineteenth century it was a fairly common practice for countrymen to eat nettles and charlock during the months of May and June before the potato harvest.

The belief that Irish rebels lived on grass alone was probably encouraged by the general use of herbs and nettles. But at the end of the sixteenth century this could largely be said to be true, and a terrible diet it was. Elizabethan officials had long considered "that a barbarous country must be broken by war before it will be capable of good government". The scorched earth policy had made most communities sensitive to famine; the practice of burning crops meant that meagre supplies of meal and grain were hoarded. The devastation after Kinsale shocked Mountjoy, even though he was responsible for it, and he wrote to the Privy Council of his progress in the north where "we found everywhere men dead of famine, in so much that O'Hagan protested unto us that between Tullogh Oge and Toome there lay unburied a thousand dead". Famine following war was nothing new; Spenser's famous description of the starving refers to the terrible Desmond wars: ". . . they looked anatomies of death, they spoke like ghosts crying out of their graves, they did eat of the dead carrions . . ." The people whom O'Sullivan Beare encountered twenty years later would also be close to starvation, since the settled countryside, according to Philip O'Sullivan, was almost entirely laid waste and destroyed. Fynes Moryson wrote that no spectacle was more frequent in towns and especially in wasted counties than to see "multitudes of these poor people dead, with their mouths all coloured green by eating nettles, docks and other things they could rend above the ground". Sir William Petty, with characteristic preciseness, estimated that 616,000 people perished during the Elizabethan wars. Any estimate that claimed a rough accuracy would come to about a quarter of the population.

The watercress eaten by the fasting O'Sullivans on 4th January would have been *nasturtium officinale*, called *biolar* in Irish. It would have tasted crisp and good, but would not have been very abundant, torn out of its icy winter stream. Spenser wrote of such a scene: "If they found a plot of watercresses or shamrocks, where they flocked as to a feast of the time, yet not able long to continue there withall, that in a short space there was no more almost left." A fierce pamphleteer whose verses appeared in London a short time after Kinsale had been won echoed his description:

> The Irish rebels now do keep their caves
> Amid the woods like wolves or ravening beasts;

Where all the outlaws or uncivil slaves
On grass and shamrocks now they take their feasts.
O England, never better news can be
Than this to hear, how God doth fight for thee.

Near Ardpatrick was the thickly wooded Glen of Aherlow, which had been the hideaway of the Geraldines for centuries, and which Spenser described typically as being full of wolves and thieves. When the Geraldines destroyed Kilmallock in 1571, "they were engaged for three days and nights in carrying away every kind of treasure and precious goods including cups and ornamental goblets, up on their horses and beasts of burden to the woods and forests of Aherlow". After the wars this forest was soon chopped, and by 1670 it had shrunk to a thousand acres. "The first step to civilize a country is to cut down the woods," considered the French traveller, Latocnaye, and so it happened.

In order to cross Aherlow O'Sullivan Beare might have been tempted to skirt the mountains of Galbally, which led to the vale of Aherlow, and then strike out boldly for the Slieve Felim twenty miles away. It is more likely that he moved straight across the Golden Vale by Hospital and Emly. His route is conjectural, and having a choice, I mapped out a way for myself towards the Slieve Felim which included these towns. Up until now I had walked mainly in mountain areas, and now I was very conscious of the descent from hill to plain, where for the next few days there would be no easy escape from the long stretch of roadway. In winter very often there were days when the whole plain was covered with mist. I remembered a remark of a friend who lived near Kilmallock. "All Limerick villages are ghastly. It's something to do with the dairy industry."

I came down the side of Ardpatrick towards Kilfinnane, only a few miles away. Just below the hill I found a remarkable pub owned by the O'Brien brothers, venerable local scholars continuing a tradition started by the Joyces who had lived down the road. Shop and pub combined were spread around spacious floors and ample wooden counters decorated with a couple of faded old Players advertisements dating back thirty years. "We

are all equipped for the tourist," one of the brothers commented
when I asked him about Ardpatrick, and he pulled out a heap
of learned books from behind the bar. Among the regular
drinkers we started a discussion about the round tower and the
monastery, or rather the O'Briens talked in between filling up
glasses and I listened—I was out of my depth. Before long one
of them handed me a note on which he had scribbled in pencil:
"We can talk better in the next room." I followed him away
from the line of men sipping stout into his study, where he
locked the door to make quite sure of no disturbance. Here for
an hour or more he entertained me with a formidable stream of
information which took in everything about Castle Oliver,
Ardpatrick, Lough Gur, Kilmallock, O'Sullivan Beare, the
White Knight. Occasionally there would be a hammering at
the door, which he would ignore. Twice he got up, undid the
lock and went out to fetch more books.

I was reeling with knowledge when I finally left him and set
out walking to Kilfinnane. About a mile from Ardpatrick I had
my lunch sitting on a bank opposite a farmhouse with a new
porch built over the Georgian doorway and every window
striped with Venetian blinds. A line of ivy-hooded trees was
echoed by a line of washing, two white shirts, a couple of little
girl's dresses and a pink towel. In the farmyard a half-eaten
haystack leaned over pools of muddy water and patches of
manure. I thought about the O'Briens and all the other local
historians. Nearly every part of Ireland has people who mark
out and claim their territory with the imperative instinct of
wild birds; then they spend their lifetime discovering every
available scrap of information about it. There is not a townland
or an archaeological site or a hero which they cannot discuss
and theorize about. Such scholarship has a long tradition, but
unfortunately it is largely an oral one, and too seldom does such
accumulated knowledge get sorted out and written down.

Natural history is seldom studied with anything like the same
enthusiasm. Medieval poets, scholars and saints wrote endlessly
of nature, and poetry is full of references to stags, eagles, black-
birds, oaks, foxes, and so on. Perhaps it was the destruction of
the forests that made Irishmen lose interest in the details of
their surroundings. During the eighteenth and nineteenth

Palatine Wood, Kilfinnane

Old farmhouse, Elton

Remains of the
old cathedral,
Emly

Fort at Donohill

centuries when Linnaeus, Buffon and Cuvier inspired observers and naturalists throughout Europe to identify and classify natural species, hardly any of this work was done in Ireland. In England and Scotland the clergy, in particular, used their possibly abundant spare time to speculate on such phenomena as the mysteries of hibernation; there was a strong strain of amateur naturalists among English parsons. We had no parallel movement here, no Gilbert Whites in country parishes, and we know comparatively little about Irish natural history during this period. Neither parish priests nor Protestant clergymen had the tranquillity, nor amateur scholars the interest, to observe animals and birds to write about them. This lack of interest largely survives today. For example, Philip O'Sullivan compiled a natural history of Ireland in the early seventeenth century, from information which he must have collected by hearsay, since he left the country as a child. It is written in Latin, and no one has ever bothered to translate it.

Kilfinnane was a market town perched on a small round hill above the Limerick plain, its line of shops and pubs and the Munster and Leinster bank all solid and old fashioned. There was an O'Shaughnessy Boots and Hardware, founded in 1853, a substantial hotel called Doherty's painted in pink and blue, a shrine, and the walls of an old castle no one seemed to know anything about. The interior of the church was brightened up with lines of red marble pillars. Facing the wide shiny main street with its rows of battered country cars was the market house, a delightful little eighteenth-century building which should have been a feature of the place, but had been allowed to decay, with the arches on its ground floor bricked up. Just outside the town opposite a permanently grounded caravan marked CHIPS was a great trivallate mound surrounded by three concentric banks and fosses, a platform type of ring-fort probably pre-Norman in construction.

From this mound I set off for the Cush crossroads and Slieve Reagh, a narrow line of mountains that come down almost at right angles to the plain. Earlier writers have described them as a "sleeping lion" and noted that they can be seen from as far away as Clare or the belfry of Limerick Cathedral. The road led down Kilfinnane hill past a cluster of tourist cottages with

E

their roofs of orange straw, sugar-white walls and central heat-
ing, to where a track branched off past the Palatine wood. This
was a hill covered with tall Scotch firs where the Palatines used
to meet and discuss their affairs. The men in their stiff German
clothes, the women in wide-brimmed straw Palatine hats and
traditional short skirts and aprons would have looked down on a
landscape which has not changed much—on one side the
Limerick plain, and behind and around them the hills wrapped
in a threatening black sky.

On the slopes above Cush, among sedge and dead grass the
colour of old bones, is an important burial site which was
excavated in the thirties. I met a farmer who told me how it
used to be called White City from the amount of remains, and
remembered how a neighbour of his unearthed two large urns
while digging his garden. Neolithic sites are often hard to find,
but at Cush there was no problem in picking out the line of
little ring-forts, which are scattered like doughnuts on both
sides of the Slieve Reagh hills. They were lived in from the late
Bronze Age up to the first century BC. A whole colony of early
man settled around here and made a community which lasted
for centuries. One of the forts was turned into a Bronze Age
cemetery after it stopped being inhabited. The farmer said that
up above was a heap of stones like a wain of hay, under which
some old king was buried. But there was a fir plantation up
there, and after walking around for a bit I abandoned the
search and left him to his slumbers.

Returning to Kilfinnane I spent the night in Doherty's
hotel. The woman who received me gazed curiously at my
rucksack and umbrella. "You're a stranger . . . it's bad weather
for walking . . ."

I asked if she thought it would hold.

"If the wind comes from the market house it's going to rain.
But since the astronauts have been going up, there is no safe
prediction."

I don't know how the wind blew, but next morning I woke
to the beat of rain against the window and the sound of slam-
ming doors. All the indications pointed to a very wet day. I lay
for some minutes under blankets with the feeling that the sun
had soared off into space. I dressed and came down reluctantly

past the picture on the landing showing an outsize angel watching a child pushing a pram, and the rows of humorous sporting prints, to the dining-room, where a fire was already lit.

"We have to expect it now," the cook said with fatalism as she brought in the fry. I toyed with the idea of postponing my walk for a day. But it might rain for weeks, and then I would not get to Leitrim until around June. Today I had planned to make another detour off O'Sullivan's probable route; instead of going directly to Hospital and Emly I wanted to go round by Lough Gur and add an extra twenty miles to my journey. I thought I had better get on with it; a day spent rainbound here would be very long. I put on my wet-weather gear, two pairs of plastic trousers, an anorak, and my Japanese hat, and prepared to open my umbrella as the maid unlatched the front door.

"There's a bus to Kilmallock," she whispered temptingly.

I stepped out into a beleaguered main street where some brown water swept over its surface into the drains, while cascades of rain dripped on to rooftops from scudding black clouds emptying their burden as urgently as if they were putting out a fire. Householders had shut themselves up against it, closed their doors and withdrawn inside from the deserted streets. Outside the town was mile after mile of soused fields, full of sloppy cowpats, over the same flat landscape stretching to the grey horizons. After a while I began to experience a sense of irritable loneliness that I was the only person out in that weather; that the rest were indoors, while I walked in the lee of the hedge, my umbrella making a very small fragile shelter for me in these heavy gusts of wind.

"The rain here is absolute, magnificent and frightening," wrote Henrich Böll when he visited Ireland. "To call this rain bad weather is as inappropriate as to call scorching sunshine fine weather."

If it were any consolation to me, weather conditions during O'Sullivan Beare's lifetime were infinitely worse. There was a cycle of bad winters at the beginning of the seventeenth century, and contemporary accounts make much of the cold. O'Donnell's famous November march was in severe frost and snow; the Battle of Kinsale took place during weather which a historian has described as "appalling and unparalleled in modern times". Fynes Moryson wrote after a night watch before the Battle of Kinsale: "It groweth now about four o'clock in the morning as cold as stone and as dark as pitche, and I pray, sir, whether this is a life that I much delight in." During the campaign Mountjoy caught pneumonia and died from its effects four years later. In March, 1602, Stafford at Bantry wrote of the wind coming off the snow-covered mountains of Beare which "tested the strong bodies, whereby many turned sick, and some, unable to endure the extremity, died standing sentinel". After crossing the Shannon O'Sullivan was to endure extreme weather conditions.

On the fifth day of the retreat, back in Glengarriff, Wilmot, in the usual manner of the time, was teaching any followers of O'Sullivan Beare a lesson. "Sir Charles coming [on the morning of 4th January] to seek the enemy in their camp, he entered their quarters without resistance, where he found nothing but hurt or sick men whose pains and lives by the soldiers both were determined." These were soldiers who had been wounded when they were defending the *creaght* and trying to prevent its capture. After slaughtering them, Wilmot moved on and "caused all the country of Kerry Desmond, Beare, Bantry and Carbery, to be left absolutely wasted, constraining all the inhabitants thereof to withdraw their cattle into the east and northern parts of the County of Cork". At the same time he sent off a troop commanded by Lord Barry in pursuit of O'Sullivan's people, not realizing how far they were beyond Glengarriff by this time. "They flew so swift with the wings of fear," wrote Stafford, "that passing by many preys directly in their way, they never made so much stay as to molest either their cattle or their keepers." Stafford seems to have been misinformed, since from Philip O'Sullivan's account the first opportunity the refugees had of forcibly obtaining food was when they plundered the fort at Donohill.

Wilmot's activities, which were meant to discourage O'Sullivan from returning, must have brought death by starvation to a good many people during the course of the winter. O'Sullivan knew that his wounded soldiers and the people of Beare could expect no mercy from Wilmot's army. The compulsion that made him decide to try to ally himself with O'Neill and continue the war in the north must have been very strong. The loss of his cattle to Wilmot left him without supplies; it was also a bitter blow to morale. But there were factors that should have kept him in Beare. He still had a small paid-up army and money with which to recruit supporters and perhaps morally he should have stayed, even against the odds, to rally his diminished forces and protect the people who lived in his patrimony. There were still groups of soldiers in Munster who opposed the avenging English armies, like the MacCarthys with whom Owen MacEgan allied himself. But O'Sullivan finally decided that it was useless to carry on the struggle in the south; his clansmen were disposable, and he was prepared to sacrifice the unfortunate inhabitants of Beare in order to fight the heretics elsewhere. I have heard the theory put forward that the bravery and enterprise he showed on the march was an exorcism of his previous failures of character and judgement.

At the turn-off for Elton I passed a small river which rejoiced in the name of the Morning Star. Near here I joined forces with the local postman wheeling his bike, dressed in yellow cape and gaiters with a sort of bonnet over his cap. We trudged on together past a fortified house of the O'Hurleys full of rooks complaining about the weather. Suddenly the Scarteens burst towards us, a torrent of steaming horses and hounds filling up the road. Behind the famous black-and-tan hounds, panting and flecked with mud, came the riders, their elegance just beginning to be crushed by the rain. We thought we saw one or two drenched Americans. Behind them the followers were all dry in their cars, and behind them again a few laggards trotted briskly in an effort to keep up.

"All done for pleasure," said the postman.

Elton was packed with horse-boxes, and some grooms and girls and depressed horses standing in the rain. Other huntsmen were crowded in O'Sullivan's bar downing shorts of whiskey and vodka. I stayed among them until the downpour blew itself out and the day had recovered some of its presence. The Scarteens were still far away from base as I left the tiny village which is dominated by a long hiproofed farmhouse with a Georgian doorway and what must be one of the best examples of thatch remaining in Ireland. Later I saw it illustrated in a book of folklore. But while the phoney thatch goes up for tourists the real thatch comes down. This house was empty with some broken windows; the hearth was extinguished, damp was setting in and before long it would begin to crumble.

"The owner built himself a new bungalow."

Just below Knockainy were the remains of an O'Grady castle in a dark green jacket of ivy which flourished with jungle luxuriance. I climbed the hill, another low green saddle looking out over the flat landscape, a magical place associated with the sun goddess Áine. The storm had cleared and a hard light replaced the numbing greyness that had diffused the plain; the fields curved away to the mountains and a silver-tipped sky. Áine was usually a benign being who only demonstrated her malevolent power when she was invoked. Her influence, together with that of another notable hag named Bheartha or Vera, was widespread throughout the country. Up until the late nineteenth century, men used to bring torches of hay and straw up to the summit of Knockainy and make a circuit of three small barrows before visiting the surrounding farmlands to bring them prosperity for the coming season. The barrows are sunk to small depressions in the grass; there is a motte at the bottom of the hill and on the summit a cairn called after Áine, who seems to be well looked after.

CHAPTER EIGHT

Lough Gur—Emly

Attacked by the Gibbons, mercenaries of the White Knight,
natives of Limerick City, both sides fought with guns. Such
heavy showers of bullets rained on all sides that O'Sullivan
could not as usual bury his dead. . . . Such a cloud of smoke
from gunpowder darkened the air, that one party was often
unable to see the other.

Philip O'Sullivan

FAT CLOUDS FLOCKED across the sky like herds of contented
cows, and a cock pheasant, fluttering its feathers, ran indignantly up the road ahead of me. Beyond Knockainy there was a
peculiar change of landscape, as curious little outcrops of rock
appeared in the fields on all sides. These are volcanic in origin,
making this region a delight to the geologist, since for its size it
is one of the most varied and complete carboniferous volcanic
regions in the British Isles. Ahead was the lump of Knockdere
with a bite out of one side where a company had been taking
away the limestone. Sheltering behind it was Lough Gur and
the pub at Holycross which heralds one of the most abundant
megalithic sites in Europe.

Other countries might announce such richness with signs and
gravel paths. Here, if you are persistent and lucky enough to
see a group of these ancient monuments, it comes as a complete
surprise.

"Only one problem marred an otherwise superlative experience," an American visitor complained in a letter to the *Irish
Times*, "when I say 'searching' for monuments, I mean it literally. The point I want to make is that it seems altogether too
difficult to find many of the more interesting ruins and sites. At
Lough Gur, for instance, are half a dozen outstanding important things, but try and find them as we did, in the rain! Signs,
pointers, explanatory markers, just don't seem to exist."

Lough Gur is only one among many sites throughout the
country to be concealed in this way. Any site of importance is

protected as an ancient monument. But the fields around it belong to the farmers. If a sign were to be erected showing the way to a castle or ring-fort across a stretch of fields, it would condone a trespass, and in most cases the Board of Works or Bord Failte just has not got the money to buy rights of way. Until recently most farmers were only too delighted to see someone exploring the ruins on their lands. Tourism is beginning to change their attitudes. The odd sightseer is quite acceptable, but not the bus load. Sometimes farmers cash in on the situation and make a small charge for "the trespass"; who could blame them? "Every poor country accepts tourism as an unavoidable degradation," wrote V. S. Naipaul.

Most accounts of Lough Gur concentrate on the monuments scattered round the shores, and one is unprepared for the beauty of the lake itself. Golden reeds edged the horseshoe of water which was covered with a concourse of ducks and swans. "It was a personality loved, but also feared," wrote Mary Carbury in *The Farm on Lough Gur*. According to legend every seven years someone should be sacrificed to appease the waters. Also at intervals of seven years, the ghost of the strange poet, the fourth Earl of Desmond, identified in folklore as a fairy king after his disappearance in 1398, rises with his knights from the depths of the lake to perform military evolutions and gallop about the surface; he must continue to do so until the silver shoes of his horse wear out. Near here was found a magnificent bronze shield, now in the National Museum, engraved with six concentric circles, belonging to a vanished warrior who lived many centuries before the Fairy Earl.

Man has inhabited the lake shore from earliest times to the present day, a perspective that begins somewhere about the period when the great *lios*, the largest stone circle in Ireland, was erected here, and ends up at Riordan's pub at Holycross. Why was this particular area always so attractive? It may have been a combination of the natural defensive position afforded by the lake and the fertility of the light limestone soil. The land was probably unwooded, and no great efforts had to be made to cut down trees; it was therefore very suitable for rearing cattle. Grass on limestone is lush. "You can see them putting on weight while you watch," I heard a farmer say of his cattle.

The lake itself was a retreat in time of trouble, where crannógs could be built, and four of these artificial islands survive. In the late seventeenth century Thomas Dinely noted that it was full of perch, eels and roach, and these must have afforded an alternative food supply.

Because so much of Ireland has always been under pasture, nowhere else in Western Europe are the traces of ancient man's pastoral activities so clearly visible over large areas. The land around Lough Gur is still undisturbed by the plough, and a complexity of prehistoric field systems can be seen around the extraordinary variety of remains. Bronze Age sites, ring-forts, pillar stones, cultivation terraces, two fifteenth-century castles, a medieval nunnery, not to mention a penal altar—they are all here. Many of them can be found on Knockadoon, the carbuncle of bleached limestone around which the lake curves. At one time Knockadoon was an island with its approaches closed by two castles, the chief seats of the Earls of Desmond. Lough Gur Castle on the north-east side of Knockadoon is in almost mint condition with its tower surviving intact. Its alternative name is Bouchier's Castle, after Sir George Bouchier who settled here in the seventeenth century.

By contrast Killough Castle, also called Black Castle, on the southern end of Knockadoon is in ruins; a tree grows out of a broken wall and ivy threatens to topple more of its sparse remains. When Knockadoon was an island this castle had a motte and drawbridge connecting it to the mainland. Brian Boru is said to have fortified it and earlier still the site contained a secluded protection for Bronze Age man. In the Middle Ages it was one of the most formidable of the Geraldine strongholds. The culminating event of its active history was its surrender during the Munster rebellion to that expert besieger of castles, Sir George Carew. Killough, held for the Sugan Earl, was important since it commanded a strategic position beside the Limerick–Kilmallock road. It contained a garrison of at least two hundred men under John FitzThomas. Carew described it "as of exceeding strength by reason that it was an island encompassed with a deep lough, the breadth thereof in the narrowest place a caliver's shot over". He planned to frighten it into submission with the aid of an old cannon he brought up from

Limerick. "The surrender of a fort on the mere hint of a cannonade", Cyril Falls says, "is typical of the Irish wars. Dunboy, which fell three years after Killough, was an exception to this rule. By contrast Killough capitulated without a shot being fired, betrayed by one of its defenders, Owen Groome, for sixty pounds and a pardon.

I spent the next morning around the lake looking for places which would require a lifetime to study. It was a hectic experience. Before ascending Knockadoon I asked permission from the farmer who owned its approaches.

"You've got a couple of hours," he said, "while the bull is at the silage."

Less than forty minutes later, while I was making my way towards a group of ancient house and hut sites, I heard a snort behind me, and what had seemed at first just another red cow came bolting up the field. I had to jump over a hedge, while he stood on the other side pawing the ground and bellowing angrily. After a time he resumed his patrol of the hill where all the most interesting monuments were situated. I made a few half-hearted attempts to circumnavigate him, but he was too efficient a guard, and later I had to make my escape by the edge of the lake.

I went back to Holycross, where, a little beyond the pub, I found the great *lios* right beside the road. It is a colossal structure, like a huge mouth, consisting of an earthen bank thirty feet wide surrounded by uprights like a ring of decayed teeth. The excavation of this circle produced numerous finds, stone axes, bone points, bronze and pottery of the beaker type. It was deduced from these that the *lios* dates right back to the early Bronze Age, about the eighteenth century BC. There was no indication that it had been used for habitation, or burials, and it seems clear that so many dozens of stones were clustered together entirely for ritual purposes. The longer I sat among them the more they seemed to resemble teeth, and also to recall to my mind those stones in Brittany that are said to move from their base to crush unwary travellers.

Dusk was falling beneath a red sky as I returned to the road and walked along to another smaller circle and a drunken pillar stone in the centre of a field. Nearby were some Herefords and a man in tweeds smoking a cigar, inspecting them with a contented air of ownership. Since it was not a moment to have qualms about trespassing, I went over to apologize for tramping over his land. Colonel Galloway, who farms around much of the lake, was not put out by the tramp-like figure walking through his aristocratic cattle, even if, like other farmers, he does not actively encourage the inspection of megalithic remains on his property. Later at his home I enjoyed his hospitality with tea and a pile of potato cakes, watched by a mournful Pyrenean mountain dog the size of a heifer.

Next day I was walking again in rain, feeling my waterproof clothing yield little by little to the downpour as the rain seeped in. Through dripping trees I could make out the ruins of Grange House, a barracks of a place which had been partially pulled down by a builder scavenging for materials. In the same area I passed two more Georgian houses that had been knocked. The last occupant of Grange House was a Protestant named Croker. When he lay dying his clergyman came to visit him and give him comfort. "You're going to a better place, Croker." "I doubt it," he replied, and ever afterwards was remembered as I Doubt It Croker. I heard the story of I Doubt It Croker in three different pubs in that countryside, and in every one it was considered as uproariously funny.

From Sixmilebridge I followed the Camoge river towards Herbertstown. There was no trace of wind today, merely the steady sluice of water coming down vertically out of a uniformly grey sky. The Camoge was hardly distinguishable from the surrounding fields. Passing drivers glared through their windscreens, giving me a gloating look of self-satisfaction, repeated a moment later after a brief flick from the wiper, before they swished by drenching me with mud. I struggled on towards the wet rooftops of Herbertstown gleaming on a hill, where an old lady in a pub told me that the Irish name for the place meant the Town of the Lark. No larks were singing today; the only voices were those of housewives in the Cooperative near the crossroads, which sold everything from slabs of salty bacon to my daily packet of Iraqui dates.

After Herbertstown the rain stopped. I took the Kiltegan road with the small village of the name crouched under a bulbous-nosed hill. On the other side, separated by a slice of fields, was Cromwell's Hill, pronounced Cromell, and having no connection with the Lord Protector. Like Knockainy it is a rich centre of folklore and contains many ancient monuments; I duly found a stone ring-fort, an enfossed mound, a tumulus and a broken gallery grave with a thornbush growing out of it.

From Cromwell, I looked down on the usual view of pasture to a horizon bounded by the sharp line of the Galtees, their edges clear as cardboard, painted in a rich tangerine light. A bump in the surface of the flat landscape was the town of Hospital, and I went on to reach it during another swollen outburst. This is the town that takes its name from a hospice of the Knights Hospitallers, founded in 1215 by the English Justiciar, Geoffrey de Marisco. In the ruined church are the tombs of three de Marisco knights whose rather broken-down effigies, built into the walls, gaze across at each other with a stern-faced preoccupation. After the dissolution of the monasteries the Hospice became the property of the Browne family, and by a coincidence, O'Sullivan Beare was fairly closely related to these Elizabethan settlers. Nicholas, the son of Valentine Browne, who had become Surveyor General and Privy Councillor, married Julian, the daughter of an O'Sullivan Beare—probably a near kinswoman of Sir Owen O'Sullivan. In the year of the retreat, when he was passing through this area as a fugitive, one of the sons of the marriage, a Thomas Browne, married Mary Apsley, an heiress of Hospital. By a grant dated 16th May, 1604, he inherited "the entire manor, Lordship and Preceptory of Hospital of Anye, with all the appurtenances and all its castles, forts, lands and hereditaments . . . being the said temporal estate of the said Hospital, the church rectory and chapel of the said Hospital . . .".

The Brownes continued to do amazingly well for themselves, by means of the family policy of aggrandizement through marriage. The only daughter of this Sir Nicholas Browne married a distant relation, Sir Nicholas Browne, owner of vast estates near Killarney, and two great properties were united. Other Brownes married into the most important Irish families, the Fitzgeralds, MacCarthys and O'Sullivan Mor. Although they were Protestant when they arrived, they became Catholic, perhaps because of these alliances, and this fact, too, stood them in good stead when the family were ennobled by James II—one of the eight creations he made after he was deprived of his throne. The Brownes took the title of Viscounts Kenmare from the neighbouring castle at Hospital. By the nineteenth century, in spite of the Penal Laws, the Kenmare estate had become one of the largest in the country, and consisted of 130,000 acres with a rent roll of £30,000 a year. It was a respectability that did not prevent a Valentine Browne from being ridiculed by Egan O'Reilly because he was a foreign upstart who had taken the place of Gaelic princes as patron of poets, and had an absurd name for a man who considered himself a gentleman.

That my old bitter heart was pierced in this dark gloom,
that foreign devils have made a land a tomb,
that the sun that was Munster's glory has gone down,
Has made me a beggar before you, Valentine Browne.

In a house on the outskirts of Hospital there are some remaining bits of Kenmare Castle, a piece of stone wall that may have come from an old building, a heavy stone lintel made into a seat, and an intriguing system of medieval plumbing which incorporated a handy stream to flush out refuse.

Somewhere in this area O'Sullivan Beare and his followers fought the most ferocious battle of the march so far, against the allies of the White Knight. Only twenty years before the Geraldines had done much to fragment English rule in Munster. But in November, 1583, the last effectual Earl of Desmond was killed while a fugitive by a Moriarty in the woods of Glenagenty above Tralee, and after that the majority of his kinsmen went over little by little to the English.

"The most wyse subtil and valliant man in Munster, and of great following," Carew said of the White Knight after his submission on 22nd May, 1600.

Coming from the Lord President this was true praise. The White Knight had betrayed his cousin, the Sugan Earl, who had been captured in a cave near Mitchelstown. Now he was campaigning with a force headed by Captain Taaffe in the neighbourhood of Bandon. But his followers in Limerick realized that now the passage of O'Sullivan Beare through his territory should be halted if possible. His mercenaries, the Gibbons, were joined in the battle against O'Sullivan by some Englishry and some levies who are simply described as natives of Limerick.

Hospital, the White Knight's headquarters, had been made into a well armed aggressive garrison, recruiting local men as well as professional soldiers. From here they went out to attack the straggling column of people weakened by hunger. All across the Limerick plain the refugees had been vulnerable; now with the Ballyhouras well behind them and separated from the shelter of the Slieve Felim range by twenty miles of dangerous flat land, they had to endure a running fight which lasted for eight hours.

The weather must have been fine that day, to allow of such thick clouds of smoke from gunpowder. Descriptions of musket fire usually refer to "red hot" shot. Firing could cause such accidents as that reported of an English soldier who refilled his powder pouch from a barrel which blew up in his face. But if the weather had been anything like what I was experiencing, no muskets could have been fired at all. One dampened battle took place in 1595 between Hugh O'Donnell and the Lord Justice on the Erne river. "At this time there fell a shower of rain in such torrents, that the forces on either side could not use their arms, so drenched with wet were their powder pouches and the apparatus of their fine guns." When Cromwell told his soldiers to trust in God and keep their powder dry, he was not being rhetorical, but giving two important commands.

In eight hours of receiving constant gunfire from well trained soldiers, the O'Sullivans must have suffered a number of casualties. Even those who were slightly wounded must have had to fall out from the column making its swift contested retreat, and these would certainly have been killed off by the White Knight's men. There was no opportunity to make up litters for those who fell under the stream of bullets; only time to escape in the comforting darkness.

Limerick is oppressively peaceful now, I considered sourly as I splashed through deep pools and quagmires of mud, listening to gurgles of rushing water. A country of tractors, horses and donkey carts painted a liverish orange carrying churns to the creamery; old men in mackintoshes or with a sack around their shoulders, sitting sideways on the shafts, their legs dangling in the air, all in heavy country boots, old coats and crushed hats, looking out across the fields dotted with their cattle.

From a quick impression of Emly you could not tell that at one time there was an important town here and a religious see that predated the rise of Cashel. Long before Christianity the town was associated with religious worship, and there is a whiff of pagan mystery about its actual name, which derives from *imblech-ibair*, meaning the umbilicus of the yew tree.

The name is also said to derive from Ailbhe, the first bishop of Emly. Ailbhe means Rockliving—and he was called this because he was brought up in a wolf's lair. He was the son of a woman who belonged to a local king, but who deceived him with a lover. When the king commanded that the child should be killed, this order was not carried out, and instead the child was abandoned. A she-wolf came across him, and took him to her lair, where she suckled him and reared him with her own cubs, until he was discovered by a peasant and brought home to live among human beings once more.

Ireland was largely pagan at this time, but Ailbhe was baptized by a missionary. Later he is said to have met St Patrick; he became a missionary himself and was responsible for converting the area around Emly to Christianity. Once the people decided to have a wolf hunt. The quarry, a very toothless old she-wolf, ran straight up to the saint seeking his protection. He acknowledged that she had fed him when he was a baby, and from that day until her death he fed her himself every day. For a while he went to study in Rome, returning to Ireland as Bishop of Emly, which was to be the principal ecclesiastical see of Munster until Cashel took it over. The *Annals of Innishfallen*, which were compiled at Emly, say that he died in 528. Emly survived as a religious diocese until the Reformation, when the old cathedral was taken over by the Anglicans. In 1587 they united it to the see of Cashel. Catholics and Protestant bishops of this see still take their title from both Cashel and Emly.

In 1570 it was described as a "good town" with its cathedral and two castles. This was the time when James Fitzmaurice, a leader of the Desmonds, challenged Sir John Perrot, the Lord President of Munster, to meet him in single combat at Emly. Both combatants were to be dressed in scarlet "Irish trousers". On the appointed day only Perrot turned up. Fitzmaurice had second thoughts, after considering that the Desmond family was in a bad way since two of its members, the Earl and his brother, were detained as prisoners in London. He probably suspected treachery. "If I shall kill Sir John," he said, "the Queen of England can send another President into the Province, but if he do kyll me, there is no one to succeed me or to command as I doe, therefore I will not willingly fight with hym, and so tell hym from me . . ."

The old cathedral, part of which dated back to the thirteenth century, was a casualty of the wars, and in 1607 was said to have been totally ruined. But by the end of the century it was rebuilt, and Thomas Dinely was able to make a neat sketch of it. A hundred years later it was described in its visitors' book as having large windows, "lately put up in hewn stone, except the East one. The communion table, rails, pulpit and reading desk are in good order. The surplice is good, there are a bible and two prayer books, almost new, a chalice and paten and a copper poorbox." Even as these words were being written the whole fabric of the building was again falling into disrepair. In the high noon of classicism, no one was interested in maintaining a restored medieval cathedral, since the Romantic vogue, heralded by Walter Scott, would not come in for another half-century. Like Cashel, which was having its roof taken off around this time, the destruction of the cathedral at Emly was largely due to prevailing taste.

In 1827 a new cathedral was built, "a handsome structure of hewn stone in the later English style with a lofty spire". It had a very short career indeed. Within forty years it had been pulled down, partly because of the amalgamation of parishes, partly because of the disestablishment of the Church of Ireland. An offer by a parish priest of Emly to buy it was refused, and after it was broken up the stonework was sold for ten pounds. The new Church of Ireland at Monard was built with some of this material. But today even the church at Monard has gone, and I was told that a local contractor had brought the stones back to Emly.

In such circumstances it is hardly surprising that only a few fragments from the ecclesiastical past remain, some stone heads built into a wall, an O'Hurley crest, an inscription in Roman letters that reads, "Robert Jones became Precentor of Emly in 1628": that is all that has survived after centuries of Christian prayer. Except for St Ailbhe, who was lucky enough not to vanish with the rest. Among the crowded stones in the grave-yard is a crude cross which is said to mark his burial place. Here, too, is St Ailbhe's cell, which is visited on the saint's name day, 12th September.

From the graveyard there is a sweeping view towards the main range of the Galtees. "Those who are fond of scenery in which nature reigns in all her wild magnificence", wrote Arthur Young, "should visit this stupendous chain. It consists of many vast mountains, thrown together in an assemblage of the most interesting features, from boulders and height of the declivities, freedom of outline, and variety of parts." This view, like the ecclesiastical architecture, has undergone a drastic change; in the early eighteenth century it was bounded by a large lake which filled in the low-lying lands in the direction of Knocklong. The lake, like the cathedral, has vanished. In 1717 an industrious landlord, Robert Ryve, had the idea of draining it and turning it back to arable land. The experiment was not altogether successful, since much of the land is still bog, and a woman who lived nearby told me that it filled up with water a little more every winter.

CHAPTER NINE

Emly—Hollyford

At Donohill fort, which the soldiers stormed for the sake of getting food, whatever prepared food was there, the first who entered devoured right off. The rest set themselves to feed on meal, beans and barley grains like cattle.

Philip O'Sullivan

THE NEXT DAY once again the grey sky threatened rain, and soon it was falling like Moorish spears. If Lord Emly gazed out on the soaked street in 1874, he could not have got much joy from having called himself after this sad little town, following years of faithful service to the Crown.

But as I walked out of Emly the weather suddenly looked up. Birds sang in the hedges, the sky became brighter and the Galtees emerged from their cap of mist to display snow-covered peaks. The rain had released smells of damp earth, manure, slow-burning turf and frying bacon coming out of an open door.

About three miles away I came to Ballymeety and a small church dedicated to St Brigid. This was the place immortalized in Irish history by Sarsfield's daring raid against the Williamite siege train, which broke the back of the siege of Limerick. The surprise attack at 1 a.m. on 13th August, 1690, destroyed two of the eight siege guns—the other six were salvaged—and enough ammunition to flatten the town: forty wagons, with twelve thousand pounds of powder, three thousand cannon balls and a large quantity of match, grenades and carcass. The explosion made "a great light in the air and a strange rumbling noise", which was heard at a distance by John Lanier and eight hundred supporters of King William, as they approached too late to escort the train back to Limerick.

Behind the church is Sarsfield's rock, a curiously shaped gallery of granite bulging out of the grass with a hollow beneath it. The little hillock which it tops is a landmark for miles around. A farmer told me that for a time the rock was quarried, and human bones were found which he thought must have been bones of men who had died when the wagon train was blown skyhigh. He said that quarrying was stopped on the express orders of de Valera himself, and it was a good thing too. Now the rock was preserved for all time.

As you look across the wooded countryside from Ballymeety, the two main ranges of the Galtees and Slieve Felim begin to fill up the sky. The forests here were spared until after King William's victory in 1691; then they were the first to be destroyed in the clearances that followed, because they were thought to shelter the dispossessed landless men of Sarsfield's army.

> But now the woods are falling
> We must go over the water—
> Shaun O'Dwyer of the valley
> Your place is no more.

O'Sullivan Beare's route at this point would have been more or less the same as that of Sarsfield's cavalry, which a century later crossed the Shannon at Killaloe, and came down in the opposite direction to waylay the siege train. Sarsfield returned to Limerick by crossing the Shannon at Banagher, having evaded all attempts to intercept him. Walking along Sarsfield's Ride, which more than likely was O'Sullivan's ride as well, I looked across the easy prosperity of these rich farmlands to the low ranges of the Slieve Felim, whose domed heads, approached by cultivated slopes, had a gentle domesticated appearance compared with the mountains of Cork and Kerry. But this closely knit tangle of hills and narrow valleys was one of the original "fastnesses", from earliest days a place of refuge for rebels and rapparees.

They were still some distance away, and I was not quite off the Limerick plain yet. First I came to Cullen, another little cross snicked out of the landscape, edged with a few houses and shops and the inevitable bar, where a drunken old man sat pouring down glasses of whiskey. I sat nearby with an empty stomach, watching the light flicker on a formidable array of Mission boxes spread down the counter. Daughters of Our

Lady of the Sacred Heart, Irish Palatine Fathers, Salesian Sisters' Mission . . . Help Us to Help Them . . . Help us to Bring to Christ Other Little Mites Like Me . . . God Bless You.

Snatches of conversation: "Well, when are you going up to the North?"

Pause. "I'm too old. No one wants to die."

"You're drinking whiskey like lemonade. If you don't know the difference, you should by the price . . ."

When I came out I blinked in the sunshine that lit up stagnant pools and bare branches of trees, and gossamer was reflected in the tall hedgerows. I went up the hill to a lonely farm with milk churns standing outside the door, a storage tank for oil and a barn piled with rusty machinery. An old-fashioned reaper and binder was like the one I watched as a child performing miracles with its mechanical flail and ball of twine, creating little golden stooks of corn that kept falling apart before the rabbits scampered out with the last cut. A broken trap beside it also held a dusty memory for me.

I was looking for the golden bog of Cullen. I called out to the farmer who was carrying something for pigs in a battered galvanized pail.

"The Bog of Cullen? Never heard of it. There's no sort of bog around here. You mean the Bog of Allen."

I didn't. In fact the Bog of Cullen was about four hundred yards away in a small natural depression which remains undrained. A place which is filled with bright iris in summer, and which yielded up a marvellous treasure during a thirty-three-year period between 1731 and 1774. Not one of the pieces of gold that was found has survived.

Before 1861 the law of treasure trove meant that anything valuable discovered by chance belonged automatically to the Crown, without any compensation to the finder. Because of this law, when gold objects were found they were very often melted down before questions could be asked. In addition, the rings and collars of Celtic chieftains were frequently mistaken for bronze or brass. One hears of a gold ring made into a nose ring for a pig; another torc was used for years to fasten a gate. At Cullen things that came out of the bog vanished quickly, and all we have are the dismal records of the trickle of ornaments

that were sold off, melted and otherwise disposed of. In 1732 ...
"a poor woman, taking up black slimy stuff which lies very
deep to dye wool, found three pieces of bright metal of equal
size and weight in the form of hectes used in smoothing,
which weighed seven pounds and a half. She sold them as brass."
In 1742, "a child found a circular plate of beaten gold, about
eight inches in diameter—his mother gave it to a merchant to
make brass weights". In 1744 "Mr Joseph Kinsalloe, a
jeweller of Limerick, bought of John Clery, a shopkeeper still
living in Cullen in the County Tipperary, a small golden crown
weighing six ounces, this he melted, and he affirmed it had the
least alloy of any gold he had ever met." In the same year
"a poor woman found a small gold cup". And so on, more of it.
I came away wondering how much gold from bogs had been
disposed of in the past, and also whether more treasure might
be hidden beneath that tiny intensely green depression. It is
strange with all the mechanization of turf-cutting that so little
is recovered—the odd crock of bog butter and little else. Do the
great machines that have been moving over the bogs for decades
destroy what they find without anyone realizing it?

Monard is eviscerated by the Limerick–Tipperary road;
you can hardly call it a town, just a few houses and a national
school and garage forming an avenue for the traffic sweeping
through. The graveyard, where a few old headstones pricked
grey ears to the roar of lorries, surrounded the site of the demolished Church of Ireland, built out of the rubble of Emly
Cathedral. Further on was the oddly named Limerick Junction,
a railway station situated in Tipperary, at least fifteen miles
from Limerick city. Here, at this prairie station set in the middle
of fields, where the main line divides for Limerick and Cork,
generations of travellers have wasted hours waiting for trains,
sampling old sandwiches from under glass bells, rattling the
red chocolate dispenser and the name-tab machine whose brass
handle used to swivel to produce your name on a piece
of foil.

Another road led off to Soloheadbeg with its cavernous
church and steeple, a prominent landmark for miles around.
Soloheadbeg (from *sulchoid*, the sallow wood), is known for
being the site of two important military engagements. In 967

King Mahon of Thomond and his brother beat the Norse; on 21st January, 1919, Sean Treacy and Dan Breen staged the successful ambush that marked the sombre beginning to the War of Independence.

I was told that the earlier battle took place just beside the football pitch, which could be true. Only more recent heroes are remembered, on the wall just opposite the church, their names flanking the little flame of life on its red marble plinth. There are people who do not like the monument, because they consider that it commemorates an unhappy incident with which to initiate a fight for freedom . . . the sort of episode that has become familiar all over again fifty years later.

Carlton Younger described the ambush as "one that still brings a blush to the cheeks of some Irishmen . . . not much more than a piece of brigandage". A cart containing gelignite was being taken to the Soloheadbeg quarries under the guard of two constables—both local men—who were ambushed and shot dead. The ambush coincided with the first meeting of the Dail, but did not have its sanction. "Soloheadbeg was calculated by Treacy and myself," Dan Breen said in an interview late in his life, "the gelignite was only incidental. We were surprised that there were only two of them—we'd hoped we could take on ten. We knew that we'd get it in the neck from everyone." Irishmen too often kill each other for the wrong reasons, as O'Sullivan Beare knew well.

He camped in the region of Soloheadbeg. In a townland called *Rath ui Bheara*—which means the fort of Beara—stands a ring-fort, and there is a very strong local tradition that this was where the refugees spent the night. There can be no proof that it was their camping ground, but it seems very likely. The large square enclosure on its isolated marshy bit of ground was big enough to hold them. The enclosing walls of the rath would have provided some shelter from wind and wild animals, and would have concealed the light of their fires from the enemies who, they knew, were still in pursuit. Exhausted after enduring a day of battles and flight, frantic for food, they groped about in the surrounding darkness for plants and leaves, and dug at the frozen ground for edible roots. At the same time they had to scavenge for fuel to keep up the little bivouac fires around which they huddled. Under the frosty star-filled sky some of the weak and wounded must have died.

The farmer who brought me to the rath said that he and his people never cut any of the trees. It would have been unlucky. Only a year back he nearly had an accident with his tractor, and now they left the place alone.

I spent the night in one of the many farmhouses that during the summer take in tourists and combine it with normal farming activities. After dinner I sat with my host and hostess learning such things as preparing bulls for showing, the price of land in Tipperary—you would think there was oil under it— and grass-roots opinions about politics, while the television flickered and smouldered with the latest bulletins from Belfast and Derry.

Next day I began walking towards the gentle approaches of the Slieve Felim. I did the first few miles along the railway track, stepping from one sleeper to another, an irritating distance just short of a stride, until the sudden appearance of a train threw me into the safety of a ditch. Cursing, I remembered the long blank hours I have spent in my lifetime waiting around Limerick Junction; the last thing I expected to come bursting from that direction was a train.

I turned off the track towards the spread of obscene mole-hills created by the new Gortdrum mine, joyfully turning acre after acre of the best pasture to grey dust in the pursuit of copper and mercury. I was well into Tipperary now, one of the largest and richest counties of Ireland. In O'Sullivan Beare's time it was part of the patrimony of the Butlers, Earls of Ormonde, and enjoyed a partial independence much resented by many Elizabethan adventurers. It had not been colonized to any extent, and for a long time the English knew very little about it. In Speed's mid-seventeenth-century maps of Ireland it appears almost as a blank, and even by Charles II's time it was still largely unknown. "Of this country the most are in rebellion," a weary Elizabethan official reported, "especially the younger brethren [of the chiefs] and all the dependents, although the elders keep a show of obedience." In 1601 Carew wrote to Mountjoy that "the poison of rebellion rests nowhere in Munster but in my lord of Ormonde's country. As long as he liveth I look for no good establishment in these borders . . ."

At Donohill there stands one of the most prominent surviving relics of O'Sullivan Beare's march, a high artificial motte rising behind the village of that name. Donohill (whose name is derived from *Dún Eochaille*, meaning the fort of the yew wood) is on the ill-defined trail leading to the foot of the Slieve Felim which stretched from Munster across the mountains to the Shannon and Connacht. Sarsfield, O'Sullivan Beare, O'Donnell, all used this route. The place where O'Donnell camped on his march down to Kinsale is only a few miles from Rathyvira where O'Sullivan pitched his camp.

Donohill is the usual defensive "donjon" of a motte-and-bailey fortress; there was still a tower on it when O'Sullivan Beare attacked it, although by that time it was being used for storage. However, it was well guarded, because of the prevailing famine conditions. For centuries Donohill had been a centre for milling, with an ancient fair, and the meal stock of the country around was stored in the tower. Besides the beans and barley grains mentioned by Philip O'Sullivan there would undoubtedly have been oats, which were widely eaten. Unleavened griddle oaten bread, made with oatmeal and water, did not go stale, and was a favourite food of travellers. As late as the nineteenth century emigrants took bags of oaten cakes to sustain them on the long voyage in sailing ships. Very likely the supplies O'Sullivan's people carried from Glengarriff were in the form of oaten cakes. While the potato had been introduced into Ireland about 1565, it had not yet come into general use. Wheat was regarded as a luxury, and much of the crop was exported. (Fynes Moryson has a mischievous description of rural methods of milling. In Cork he saw "with these very eyes young maids grinding corn with certain stones, to make cakes thereof, and striking off into the tub of meal such reliques thereof as stuck upon their body, thighs and more unseemly parts . . .".)

The precious grain was guarded by the O'Dwyers on whose land stood the motte of Donohill. Although O'Sullivan had money, he made no attempt to bargain for a supply; it was worth more than gold. Instead, his soldiers stormed the steep side of the motte, which stands thirty feet above the level fields, and broke open the main gate. It was a difficult manœuvre, but probably they had the advantage of surprise, and were able to capture the store in spite of the fire directed at them from the top of the high walls. There may have been casualties; in a quarry at nearby Tulla hill some human bones were found that have been linked with this battle. Like the remains found at Sarsfield's rock, they were conveniently near, but there must have been many other fights and skirmishes in both areas that produced bones. However many men died when the O'Sullivans stormed Donohill, they were driven to attack the stronghold by starvation. For the victors it meant a chance of filling their stomachs for the first time in days with something more substantial than grasses or roots.

While the motte remains as high as it ever was, almost all traces of the fort on its summit have gone. Only a few pieces of crumbling masonry lie on the grass beside the statue of the Sacred Heart. Just across the road on another hill is the shell of an ancient church in whose graveyard Dan Breen is buried. The man at the creamery told me that church and fort were linked by a secret passage; but he also told me wrongly the motte was built by the Danes.

"They carried up everything on their back!"

There was one more sharp engagement before O'Sullivan reached the shelter of the hills. The O'Dwyers and the O'Ryans made a half-hearted effort to block the trail, but when the men from Beare advanced, they retreated "stricken with fear".

At Annacarty stands the ruin of a small castellated structure which was once the R.I.C. barracks, before being blown up in the civil war. Tradition states this building was designed to be erected in India, but the plans got mixed up, and somewhere on the bare hills of the North-West Frontier there stands the correct Annacarty barracks. I would like to believe the story, but alas, I have heard it before about at least two other police stations—one at Ballyduff in Co. Waterford, the other between Killarney and Kenmare, both of which are wildly turreted and fortified against a siege from Pathan tribesmen. At Annacarty school, still a hotbed of O'Dwyers and Ryans, according to their teacher, I saw maps pinned on the classroom wall by the students, showing the two marches: that of O'Sullivan Beare

and that of Hugh O'Donnell coming the other way and veering
off towards Kinsale. The two routes intersected at Hollyford
some miles up the Slieve Felim.

The teacher's name was also O'Donnell. "My own family
absconded on the march and stayed down here." There were
other families hereabouts who were still known as *Ultacht*, or
Ulstermen, although it is open to question whether these
people with northern names are indeed descended from
O'Donnell's men. Some historians say that this tradition is as
false as the one about Connacht men being descended from
Armada survivors. But a name like O'Donnell . . .

From Annacarty the road began to climb into the hills; the
monotony of that monstrous plain changed quickly as grass
banks spotted with gorse took the place of the tall hedgerows,
streams crossed the winding road and each turn brought a new
mountain view. Among small thatched cottages and corrugated
sheds with roofs rusted golden, little roads swept up the mountains in a dizzy curve to meet the sky. At Ballysheeda there was
a substantial castle built with a round tower like a lighthouse,
belonging to the O'Dwyers, who first settled in this part of
Tipperary in 1297. The farmer I spoke to could tell me nothing
about it, beyond noting that the weed growing in its walls was
good for kidney complaints.

Some miles away from here a field called *Cluain an Ultaigh*,
the meadow of the Ulstermen, is supposed to be where
O'Donnell camped. Again, how reliable are such traditions?
One can only assume that an army passing and camping would
remain in folk memory for many generations, and observe how
often such places fit neatly into history. At Rath ui Bheara, for
example, the atmosphere and the circumstances seem exactly
right.

The road became an uneven brown thread that danced in
front of me over the hills. I sat on a bank and ate biscuits with
coffee, looking round at the patches of bog and rushes draining
off fields. Higher up, above abandoned farms the tops of the
hills were striped with forestry.

"I wouldn't consider those hills too low for your job," a
farmer said to me as he threw bundles of hay from the back of
his Volkswagen, and the cattle moved over.

By the time the road began to run downhill to Hollyford, a wind was rocking the tussocks of gorse, and the rain had begun. In a few minutes the ditches overflowed with muddy red water, sweeping down to Hollyford hidden in the downpour. This tiny village, with its houses, two bars and a sawmill squeezed into the narrow valley of the Multeen river, is supposed to be on the route taken by O'Donnell when he made his famous march from near Templemore to escape Carew. "For the nature of Slieve Felim, which in summer time is a good ground to pass over, was by reason of great rains so wet and boggy that no carriage or horse could pass it," Stafford wrote in *Pacata Hibernia*. "Having, as we thought by lodging where we did, prevented his passage, there happened a great frost, the like whereby hath been seldom seen in Ireland, and the enemy, being desirous to avoid us, taking advantage of the time, rose in the night and marched over the mountain aforesaid." A year and two months later O'Sullivan passed through here going the other way.

In Quirke's pub, the wife of the proprietor told me that her mother was another O'Donnell, descended from a northern fugitive who had settled here after the flight from Kinsale, having given up the struggle to find his way home. I met Paddy O'Brien, who in 1946 found in a bog near Barna a man believed to have been a follower of O'Sullivan Beare. Or rather, he did not find a man, but a suit of clothes, a greyish green coat with three ties, a balaclava helmet, felt boots and a shroud. The body had melted away under the influence of the bog water in which it lay steeped, so that nothing remained except a toenail in one of the boots. Mr O'Brien was given ten pounds for his "uniform", which is now in the National Museum. I have seen it there since; the tweed garments are more brown than green, just the colour of bogwater. The coat is slighty flared and loosely cut; the cap has two buttons fastening under the chin. The trousers were held up with a cord like modern pyjamas, and each leg has a slit up the sides which were fastened with a row of little buttons the way children's leggings used to be. Patches on the seat and hip suggest that these trousers were worn by a horseman. The suit, perfectly preserved, is a good example of the sort of clothing that a fairly prosperous native

Irishman would have worn in the sixteenth and seventeenth centuries. It could have belonged to a soldier, since soldiers didn't wear any sort of standard dress—to describe it as a "uniform" is incorrect. It is roughly contemporary with O'Sullivan Beare, but predates Sarsfield (he, too, came through Hollyford) by a considerable time.

The story of O'Sullivan Beare exerts strong impressions, and although Mr O'Brien and his neighbours instantly assumed that the dead and vanished man belonged to the chieftain's following, there is, of course, no proof whatsoever of this. However, he was wrapped in a shroud and buried in a bog. If he had died peacefully and had been a local man, the chances are that he would have been interred in consecrated ground. If he had been murdered and the body hidden, would it have got such tender treatment? Members of O'Donnell's army, marching at night in frost, would hardly have paused to chip away at the frozen bog to bury one of their numbers. The neatness of his clothes does not suggest that they belonged to a refugee fleeing from Kinsale; O'Sullivan's soldiers still marched in good order. He might well have been a member of Carew's army, or any of the countless bands of soldiers who crossed the Slieve Felim. But it is also faintly possible that he was a follower of O'Sullivan Beare.

Another descendant of Ulstermen who lived near Barna, where the suit was found, is Jim Armshaw, who told me that there used to be faction fights in the small villages of the Slieve Felim between the local Munstermen and the Ulstermen who claimed as forefathers the remnants of fleeing northern armies. He said that twenty years ago he found a saddle-tree buried under six feet of bog; the saddle itself had vanished, perhaps eaten away by bog acids. Unfortunately he had lost it. Impossible to say how far it resembled contemporary saddles such as Luke Gernon described in 1620. "The Irish saddle is called a pillyon and is made in this forme. The tree is as of an ordinary saddle, but the seate is a playne table of two foot longe, and a foote broad or larger, high mounted and covered with a piece of checkered blanketty. It is not tyed with girths, but is fastened with a breastplate before and a crupper behind, and a sursingle in the middle. The men ryde astryde with their leggs very farr extended towards the horse's neck. If the horse be dull, they spurreyeth him in the shoulder. It seemeth uneasy to us, but they affirm it to be an easy kind of ryding." "The peculiar seat" where the rider sat back without stirrups and extended his legs toward the horse's head, was of great antiquity and used both in Ireland and England.

I went to the tomb of the rapparee, Ned the Head. He was born Edward Ryan at Upperchurch, and was first a clerical student, and then a Jacobite officer until the dishonourable treaty of Limerick, when he became an outlaw, Ned of the Hills, and robbed the rich to pay the poor. He was captured for a reward of a hundred pounds, and beheaded, although a pardon was on the way. His body was buried in one place and his head in another, just to keep them apart and out of mischief. The sites of his graves were forgotten.

Nine years ago an American, who claimed descent from Ned of the Hills, arrived in Hollyford to put up a monument to his ancestor. He heard a local story about the head, that it was believed to be buried in a certain field under a thorn bush. He went to the field, found the thorn bush and dug a hole; there was Ned's skull grinning up at him. Later he had it reburied in a butterbox and put up a monument to him on the spot, which is rather in the shape of a lighthouse.

> Eamonn-an-Chnoic
> His spirit and song live in the
> hearts of his people.
> By Commander Ryan, U.S.N. Ret. 1963

"There's no danger an Irishman would do that," the farmer who showed it to me commented. He added that the field itself was where O'Donnell had been attacked before he went off and escaped the English army. I found myself thinking about the truth in tradition and also about gold in the Bog of Cullen.

CHAPTER TEN

Hollyford—Cloghjordan

They then took the route to Slieve Felim. Hunger pinching them bitterly, Thomas Burke and Daniel O'Malley, by O'Sullivan's order made a slight detour with sixty men to look for booty and food. These were suddenly attacked by the enemy, Daniel and twenty more being killed.

Philip O'Sullivan

IN SIXTEENTH-CENTURY Ireland traditional values of hospitality applied; it was a sacred duty and great importance was attached to its observation. Monasteries and religious houses, which formerly took in travellers, had been suppressed and outside towns inns were practically non-existent. But strangers were made welcome wherever they went, in the castles and houses of gentry or in humbler dwellings whose inhabitants considered that travellers who had taken off their brogues in the house were members of the family. An unknown visitor, writing in 1579 before famine and war had changed the face of the land, observed that "if you except the port towns, there are no hotels or lodging houses in the island. Every traveller sets up in the first house he meets, and there is provided with whatever he desires gratuitously."

In the twentieth century it was often rather more difficult to find accommodation. Small towns and villages lacked hotels and guest houses or they were closed for the winter. It was advisable to start looking well before dark. I was rather reluctant to startle householders by presenting myself at their door asking for somewhere to sleep, but in country villages when pressed, I could follow the sensible example of de Latocnaye in the late eighteenth century. "'Sir,' said I, 'I have not the honour of being known to you, and I have no letter for you, but I can assure you that I am very hungry, and that you will very much oblige me by giving me something to eat.' 'Faith,' answered he, 'you could not come in better time, for breakfast is on the table.'"

Since Hollyford did not have a guest house, I appealed to the good nature of the lady in Quin's bar. First she gave me a meal sitting in front of the fire, and then arranged for me to sleep in the parochial hall, empty except for a table and a couple of wooden pews. There was no light and the room was cold, but it was a lot better than sleeping out. In these circumstances I spent as much of the evening as possible around the town bars, which, rather to my surprise, were almost devoid of people. An old man screwed up in a corner drinking a solitary pint told me with a glory of pride that he had been to Dublin once. From somebody else I learned that Hollyford once had a coppermine with imported Cornish miners. They were able to tell there was a plentiful supply of copper around here by the condition of the fleece of the neighbourhood's sheep. Opened in 1832, the mine had a fitful existence, working during the famine years, and lingering on until its closure in 1866.

I rested over my stout at the turf fire, under a battery of merchandise hanging from the ceiling, until the last possible moment, before returning to the parochial hall. The chilly night in a sleeping bag on a concrete floor was compensated for by the ample breakfast served by the lady in Quin's who proudly brushed aside offers of payment before I set off on the road to Templederry. The sun pulled out from the clouds for a few minutes, then vanished again. The rain, never far off, gave a moist feeling to the countryside which was not allowed to dry out. Hedges were heavy with drops and a young rabbit picked its way reluctantly over wet grass. Bird noises were punctuated by the rasping cough of a cow. The hills curved gently from the valleys towards the brown heather-covered domes of Ring Hill and Knocklough with the soft sky behind them lit up in streaks of watery blue.

"Would it be about three miles to Upperchurch?" I asked a passing farmer.

"It would," he called back. "It would be five, anyhow."

I came out on the main Thurles road, which is still called after Lord Anglesea. His Lordship, caught in a storm somewhere in the region of Hollyford, was put up by the parish priest. In gratitude he built the road. "If it is not made with sovereigns flat, I'll make it with sovereigns on their edges," he told the priest. It is still called after him; no one has thought of changing the name.

At Upperchurch, with its wayside shrine, graveyard and large airy church full of Corinthian pillars, a bell was clanging the Angelus. After the exhilaration of the morning start, early afternoon was the time for thinking about comforts—and the knowledge that twelve o'clock had passed instantly set up a reflex so that I began plotting out the rest of the day—the next stop for coffee, the chances of getting somewhere to sleep, and above all else the prospects of the weather. Already mist was beginning to curl over the higher hills and the hillsides were in shadow.

"You're young and lively," called out an old woman in blue coat and boots as I passed her by. Sadly, I was neither.

It was in this part of the country that O'Sullivan, motivated once more by hunger, made the disastrous move of splitting up his soldiers and sending a force led by the two Connacht captains to forage for food. In the attack that followed, O'Malley and twenty men were killed, Thomas Burke was captured, and the rest of the expedition fled back to O'Sullivan who went in immediate pursuit of the enemy. On the way he met Burke hurrying towards him; he had broken his bonds and escaped, "his helmet on, but stripped of his sword, pike and dagger". The episode is curious. The enemy was admittedly attacking only a section of O'Sullivan's force, but it consisted of sixty experienced professional soldiers. Up until now no one of those who harrassed the O'Sullivans had been able to inflict such quick devastating havoc, or to turn his men in such a complete rout.

Burke's easy escape, and the fact that his enemies were unnamed, suggest that they were a group of local men gathered from one or more of the isolated mountain hamlets in this area. The attack may have taken place near Templederry where the mountains slope northwards towards the Nenagh plain, and the area was more heavily populated. The people who lived on the Slieve Felim had plenty of experience of passing armies, such as O'Donnell's, which plundered and burned as it went through. When O'Donnell's men returned after Kinsale the people of the countryside exacted a terrible revenge on them.

The Kilcommon Suit

St Odhran's Well, Latteragh

Lackeen Castle, near Shannon

There was no reason why they should meet O'Sullivan's soldiers with any less hostility. Burke and O'Malley with their soldiers, weakened by hunger, and careless in their need to find food, may have set out on the foraging expedition without carrying cumbersome firearms, and consequently had to fight with hand-to-hand weapons like those that Burke lost. If they were caught in a well organized ambush, they would have been at a grave disadvantage, and this may account for the sudden high toll of casualties.

In Kerry on the previous day O'Sullivan's friend, Owen MacEgan, the Bishop delegate of Ross, whom he had met at Ardea, was killed in battle. Even after O'Sullivan had vanished towards Leitrim, the fighting Bishop had stayed behind to hold out against the English. If he felt he was betrayed by O'Sullivan, Burke, Tyrell and the others, there is no mention of this, and it seems probable, since he appears to have been an unswerving optimist, that he still expected "the relief of men" from Spain.

Carew had a particular dislike of the Bishop, and there is some reason to believe that he thought MacEgan was aspiring to his position as Lord President of Munster. Equally he mistook his office of Vicar Apostolic for the equivalent of Papal Nuncio. The efforts of such energetic prelates and their bravery and persistence were largely responsible for keeping rebellion going. Abroad MacEgan had great influence; it was on his advice that Philip III had sent the army to Kinsale. Pope Clement VIII approved the plan, and in recognition of MacEgan's abilities conferred on him the livings in Munster and all ecclesiastical patronage. Carew accused the Bishop of being ruthless towards fellow Irishmen who opposed him, "for as soon as any prisoners were taken, though of his own country, birth and religion, yet if they served the Queen, he caused them first, in piety as he pretended, to be confessed and absolved, and instantly in his own sight would he cause them to be murdered, which religious tyranny in him was held for sanctity".

MacEgan joined up with a guerilla group under the command of the sons of Sir Owen MacCarthy, but without Spanish help it was only a question of time before this small force of four hundred men was cornered. Carew sent a force against them

F

under Captain Taaffe, which included Maurice Fitzgerald, the White Knight, whose people attacked O'Sullivan Beare outside Hospital. The Bishop was killed in an engagement on the north side of the Bandon river, when he was leading a counter attack to rescue a hundred captured cows. "Owen MacEgan, to put fresh heart into his men, with his sword drawn in one hand, and his porteus [breviary] and beads in the other, with a hundred men led by himself, came up boldly and maintained a hot skirmish until he was slain with a shot, whereupon his men broke." Legend has added that before he died the Bishop had time to remark about his enemies that "to me these unhappy people have brought life, for themselves they have earned death", while a halo appeared over his mouth and face.

"After this encounter," wrote Philip O'Sullivan, "the war in Munster ended." Carew was delighted about "the death of that traitorly priest" which, wrote Stafford, was "doubtless more beneficial to the state than to have got the most capital rebel in Munster".

The two highest mountains in the Slieve Felim, Mauherslieve the Mother Mountain (1,785 ft), and Keeper's Hill (2,278 ft), towered above the rest. Up until the nineteenth century eagles were supposed to have nested on their summits, and there is a tradition that treasure is hidden under their eyries. The Natural History Museum in Dublin has a magnificent specimen of the great white-tailed eagle, which is now extinct in Ireland, together with the golden eagle. Once they were common enough; Giraldus noted plenty. "You will see as many eagles here as you will kites elsewhere. The bird can look straight at the very rays of the sun with all its brightness, and so high does it soar in its flight, that its wings are scorched by the burning fires of the sun."

To the north-east down in a valley was the little village of Templederry. A roadworker advised me to take a back way into it, so that instead of walking along the valley, I would fly in more like a bird. "On a good day you can see a fierce distance," he said, "as far as Nenagh or Thurles." He was not far wrong. The view below me stretched across the roof tops of Templederry to another line of wooded hills where O'Sullivan spent his last night before making a dash to the Shannon.

Beyond them again the country rolled away in all its wildness towards a cold blanket of sky.

In Templederry I had the problem all over again of finding a place to sleep. Here were two pubs facing each other across the road, owned by rival brothers named Hogan. I talked to one Mrs Hogan, who told me that her husband was a descendant of the famous rapparee, Galloping Hogan. During daylight of 11th August, 1690, Sarsfield, with a body of six hundred cavalry, lay concealed on Keeper mountain, but that night they were guided by Galloping Hogan to Ballymeety, where those who were escorting the ammunition were encamped. I listened to Hogan's adventures, but I was really more concerned about my own immediate future, and asked Mrs Hogan if by any chance she had an empty floor. When she said she would think about it, I left the question open for about an hour. Before darkness fell there was time to go out and look at the ruins of Castle Otway.

"You wouldn't have been able to stand to look at it—and I know that," an old woman told me who could remember the place before its destruction in the civil war. A fine crumbling ruin survives with a Gothicized tower, line of stables and the façade of a Georgian house slipping into jungle. In the ghost of a parkland where deer used to graze, kept in by a haha, some monkey puzzles still linger, and a line of beeches goes up to the ruined front door.

According to the Downe survey, there was a castle here belonging to the O'Kennedys, but by 1684 John Otway had a certificate from the court of claims for his new estate at Templederry. "All erected into the manor of Otway with power to appoint Senseshals and other officers, to keep a prison, to have jurisdiction to the extent of £5 in all actions of debt."

In 1798 the family raised the Castle Otway Imperial Yeomanry with its own flag. An earlier head of the family, Thomas Otway, took some pains to exert the privileges of his position, as the ledger accounts for the estate of the years 1771 and 1772 indicate.

"October 30th, 1771. Thos. Otway gives notice to his tenants and workmen that he will punish each man who does not come to work. On any holy days (except Sunday) a shilling each time for the first time, two shillings for the second time and so forth—any person not satisfied with this law may provide for himself another place."

"April 13, 1771. Mick Bolan hired with Thomas Otway for three pounds a year."

"22nd May. Mick Bolan fined 3d for not having the dog's mess on time."

"1st June. Mick Bolan fined 1/–for not having the dog's mess on time."

"15th June. Mick Bolan fined 6d to suffering the pigs on the lawn."

"On the 14th of November, although he was owed one pound in wages, Michael Bolan ran away from his service."

A little down the road from the castle ruins is the small family church filled with memorials to the Otway family. Among them is one to Thomas Otway which states that he died "on the 26th day of June, 1786, in the 56th year of his age, sincerely regretted by his equals (superiors he had none), and followed to his tomb by thousands of labouring poor with tears and lamentations".

Thomas Davis spent much of his childhood in Templederry, where his aunt, Mrs Hastings-Atkins, was the wife of the rector. Davis claimed relationship on his mother's side to O'Sullivan Beare, and wrote an awful poem about Donal Cam's supposed return to collect his wife and child from Glengarriff.

> A baby in the mountain gap—
> Oh, wherefore bring it hither?
> Restore it to its mother's lap
> Or else twill surely wither.
> A baby near the eagle's nest!
> How should their talons spare it?
> Oh take it to some woman's breast,
> And she will kindly care it!

The Hogans whom I had approached not only ran a combined shop and bar, but also farmed. Their work schedule involved the long pub evening with its non-stop demand for

drinks, the family taking turns to fill up the glasses and con-
tribute to gossip and comment. The night grew long as they
waited for late drinkers to down the last pint and go off to bed.

"Is he still there?" Mrs Hogan would ask occasionally, the
sleep forming in her eyes at the antics of some lingering custo-
mer. After he finally trotted off, the place had to be brushed
out, glasses cleaned and numerous small jobs done in prepara-
tion for the rush of children who stopped at the shop on their
way to school. Then the house was locked for the night; "and
so to bed".

She had provided me with a mattress on the floor, which,
topped by the sleeping bag, was more comfortable than some
of the beds I had recently slept in. A cup of tea to the hand as I
opened my eyes, and news of the weather forecast. "Strong
gusty winds and rain spreading to all parts during the day."

I left Templederry on a deceptively clear morning. It had
frozen in the night so that the grass was bleached, the muddy
pools crinkled over with a film of ice, and the road was slippery
in every shady place. The country woke slowly with the sound
of rooks, the clatter of pails, and a smoker's cough from an open
doorway. I had breakfasted well at the Hogans', not as well,
however, as they used to in houses like Castle Otway on "eggs
and milk, brandy, sugar and nutmeg, a large loaf, fresh butter,
and a cold round of beef, red herrings, a dish of potatoes roasted
on the turf ashes, ale, whiskey and port . . .".

A side road took me down to the crossroads below Latteragh.
"What's the name of the river?" I asked the lady in the solitary
shop, pointing back to the bridge I had crossed. "God almighty,"
she replied, "there's no name to it at all. The Nenagh river is
all I've heard it called anyway."

On the sixth day from Glengarriff O'Sullivan Beare camped
at Latteragh in the vicinity of St Odhran's church and
monastery, a sixth-century foundation which was another place
of pilgrimage. St Odhran was believed to have been sent here
by St Ciaran of Saigher, and to have chosen this place at the
sign of the blowing of a candle. It was a signal that here he
would find solitude. He did not live all the rest of his life alone,
but is said to have presided over a community of three hundred
monks, a seat of learning in a mountain wilderness. He may

have died in 584. Like St Phocas the gardener, this is all, or rather more than all that is known about him.

When O'Sullivan arrived in Latteragh the ruined church of St Odhran was overlooked by a well garrisoned castle. This was a fortress belonging to the de Marisco family, who had built it in the thirteenth century, when one of their self-seeking relatives, Robert Travers, the Bishop of Killaloe, gave them the letting of the site. In 1602 the castle was still inhabited by de Mariscos who had no intention of being friendly towards O'Sullivan Beare. Incredibly, however, O'Sullivan, following his predilection for camping in holy places, chose to pitch his camp in the ruins of the church, well within musket range. Perhaps his choice was not so unreasonable as it first appears, even though "he was annoyed the whole night with firing and sallies of the garrison". Although it was "a rather mean small church" its enclosure offered a little protection from the weather, and could also be patrolled more easily than the environs of any camp out on the hillside. Eachros and Rath ui Bheara had been similarly attractive; in the desolation of the countryside, walls, however crumbling and ruinous, meant a welcoming shelter. O'Sullivan's enemies were everywhere, and would have sought him out, whether he camped just across from them or not. Even as his soldiers patrolled around St Odhran's church with their drawn swords and prepared muskets, they could hear through the darkness that another, larger band, quite independent of the garrison in the de Marisco fort, had mustered not far away. They waited for these newcomers to attack, but the expected assualt never came.

Ruins of church and castle survive, still the length of a musket shot from each other. The castle is topped by a large white crucifix; the church is represented by some ivy-covered walls and a straggling graveyard filled with rank brown grass and withered nettles. Nearby is the holy well where a few people still come on 15th August to be cured and to make the pattern. It is a circular pool, about four feet across, at the edge of the forest, a peaceful place with the sound of birds and the dark green forestry trees closing in. Holy wells are usually pre-Christian, and rituals here would have predated St Odhran. Modern tokens of pins, medals and buttons are pale shadows of the votive offerings of former times. When a pilgrim ties a rag to a tree, an international custom, it represents his prayer and the wish for it to go winging up to God.

The field above Mrs Pat Ryan's house was where the monks lived. She was over eighty, and she could remember many cures at the well . . . "a child that was cured of scruff at the third turn, another of ringworm", and so on. The well also had its strength. She remembered one time that there was dancing at the crossroads; and afterwards, they all went up to the well with the fiddler. But the fiddle went silent as they approached— not a note came from it, not a wrinkle. As for O'Sullivan Beare, he was meant to have slept everywhere. "The history of those times is worn out," she said.

From Latteragh O'Sullivan had to make his way down on to the Shannon plain and confront the great river, the most serious obstacle of the entire march. He started at dawn on 6th January, the Feast of the Epiphany. As the refugees picked up their baggage, loaded the animals and formed a column to move off, the garrison who watched from the castle sprang to life. "A storm of red hot balls blazed on O'Sullivan as he advanced. This was indeed, a daily salutation with which the enemy honoured him, a farewell as they drew off at night, a greeting as they turned up in the morning."

The road above Latteragh brought me to another turning point of the march. The Slieve Felim, which I had been crossing for two days, were behind me, and the view ahead was flanked by the curving shoulders of the Devil's Bit, Kilduff and Borrisnoe. From here I would be passing through country dominated by the course of the Shannon, and crossing the alluvial eskers with their flattened ridges and lumps of hills.

In the rain a farmer brought a cartload of hay to some cattle that rushed mooing across the fields. The wind rattled through dried fuchsia hedges as I came to Toomyvara, a grey deserted town on a main road, with the traffic splashing through and the only life in the bars. With my umbrella held high I sought out the remains of a fifteenth-century Augustine priory. Another saint, St Donnan, founded a monastery here in the seventh century. In the fifteenth century the O'Mearas, wardens of the priory, made it their burial ground and gave the town its name. One of the tombstones sticking out of the grass, like an ancient Maya head in the jungle, is a fine sculptured effigy of an ecclesiastic, his hands crossed. On a nearby stone there is an inscription in Hebrew which has been translated.

> William O'Meara of noble birth and fame
> Whose heroic actions and immortal name
> Have reached the skies,
> Yet in this marble work
> With his consort, Ellen Burke
> Entombed he lies.
> Whoever chance his eyes to rest on this
> May pray his travail to the saints in bliss.
>
> AD 1644.

I asked the time from a group of grave-diggers in a grave in the rain. "Twenty past eleven strong," one said leaning on his spade. He gave me a look. "A bit early for tourists." Another brought a bottle of whiskey out of his pocket. "Take a sip before you go." Digging graves in this weather was cold work. I thanked him and after a good pull set off down the deserted street.

North of Toomyvara I had my lunch sitting in the doorway of another castle. A tin of herrings in tomato sauce and biscuits as the rain poured down. Then bowling along the windswept road I hurried through the grey countryside, past empty cottages, an abandoned lodge, the well seasoned façade of a Georgian building with a misted fanlight and an avenue choked in sodden leaves. I was blown towards Castle Emmel which stood out above the fields like a towering black shadow. It was raining with an intensity that would have alarmed Noah. I stumbled towards a small church. The door was locked. Nearby was the rectory, and the canon and his wife insisted on providing me with a hot meal and drying off some of my waterlogged clothes.

O'Sullivan's route to the Shannon is speculative. He had to make his way to some place before the river empties into Lough Derg in order to find a crossing. His next objective from Latteragh seems to have been another shrine, Lackeen, which is

situated about five miles from the river. The Four Masters say
he camped there. He could have gone via Barna and Barriso-
kane, or alternatively via Barna and Knockshegowna. Barna,
which is a common name, means gap in Irish and usually is the
name of a place which is on a recognized road or route. This
Barna was a small hamlet, and in the weather I didn't try to
get to it, but instead went straight to Cloghjordan in search of
accommodation. After two nights sleeping on the floor, it came
as something of a miracle to find a small hotel there that was
open.

CHAPTER ELEVEN

Cloghjordan—Shannon

> At Shannon they were faced with a difficulty—the enemy
> had removed all boats. Moreover the soldiers were nervous
> from want. Every heart was hereupon filled with giant
> despair. In this critical state of things, my father Dermot
> O'Sullivan, announced that he would in a short time make a
> ship and put an end to the soldiers' hunger.
>
> Philip O'Sullivan

CLOGHJORDAN DID NOT exist until 1700, when a man named
Jordan came and chose its site to found a town for a colony of
disbanded Williamite soldiers. He had got his own name from
an ancestor who fought an engagement as a crusader on the
banks of the Jordan. Clogh derives from Irish *cloch*, a stone or a
stone structure, so that the name might be translated as Jordan's
Buildings. The town flourished, and by the early nineteenth
century there were 1,114 descendants of the original settlers, and
1,801 Catholics. Today there are still Protestant names like
Armitage, Gibson, and Hammell over the shopfronts.

A great open fire warmed the dining-room hung with ranks
of engravings and lamps which had not been used for thirty
years. I was the only guest. The commercial travellers come in
less as the little shops are replaced by supermarket chains. The
fair has gone, reducing the number of pubs, and people take
their cars to larger centres to do their shopping. Cloghjordan
lingers on as a kind of little dormitory town for Nenagh.

All night the rain fell and the wind rattled the windows.
I had been given a couple of hot-water bottles that slid about in
the wide bed with its piles of blankets and abundant eiderdown.
Next morning the forecast was hardly more encouraging and
included thunder.

A few yards up the street facing the green was the handsome
Church of Ireland with its tower placed in the centre of the
building. Some years ago there was talk that the tower might

have to be pulled down because of its shaky condition—a threat indignantly opposed by the few parishioners.

"If they do it, I'll never blacken the doors again," one lady told me, and since she represented quite a high percentage of the congregation, her threat had some significance. So far it remains; one hopes that it will not topple on to the varnished box pews one Sunday, and the little gallery running round the upper walls where church musicians once perched playing their violins and trombones.

A dog made a pass at my leg and I angrily booted it away. Then a long avenue of dripping trees, the rump of Knockanacree, and a mile or so further on the rain suddenly turned off as if by a tap.

In this flat sunken landscape leading to the banks of the Shannon, hills seemed like mountains. Knockshegowna, a little rise seven hundred feet high, looming out of the fields is Ireland's Olympus, traditionally the home of the fairies. When John Carr wrote his travels up in the eighteenth century, he could still say that "the common people also believe in fairies". Mary Carbury recorded that the country people round Lough Gur maintained a careful respect for little people. Not any longer, though. The Marian year was a particularly bad time for them, when the land became encrusted with grottoes and crosses rose on every hill. A cross was put up on Knockshegowna, which is illuminated on Sundays and has become a familiar landmark for the surrounding countryside.

"They took the castle out of it, when they put it up," said the old woman at the bottom of the hill, who lived in the shop. A short breathless climb took me up to the summit where a few yards away from the cross, draped in electric wires, are still some broken walls of the castle where the Munster fairies had danced and met before their last outpost was Christianized. People who tried to watch them usually vanished mysteriously, and others who disturbed the sacred soil by ploughing around the hill met with a similar fate. Una, the fairy Queen who lived here, was the traditional guardian of the O'Carroll family, Lords of Ormonde.

The land spread away from Knockshegowna, flat as paper, bounded by the silver glimmer of Lough Derg. I remembered the Turcoman plains in Persia which had the same feeling of infinite distance; only, the soil of the steppes had been an almost savage shade of orange, while the Shannon lands were a mixture of soft greens and browns—bogs, patches of trees, a few ridges, translated into the sort of scene that exiles remember of Ireland.

In 1650 Cromwell's guns boomed out around the hill, aimed at Ballingarry Castle, which was being defended by the O'Kennedys, who, in spite of a breach in the castle's south-west corner, managed to beat their attackers back to the hill. They were only subdued when they were starved into submission. Coming down I passed the walls of Ballingarry enclosing an apple orchard. On a tree near here, they say, Catholics were hanged in penal days. I came to a gatepost with a large handwritten notice saying POISON—nothing else—and a drive leading to the Gurteen Agricultural College, startlingly modern in its surroundings, a two-storey block of a building in plain international style, with tidy fields around it laid out like a textbook on farming. The college, interdenominational, accepting students from all walks of life, was opened in 1947 under the sponsorship of the Methodist Church. Today it is striving to bring students to terms with the exigencies demanded by farmers competing in the Common Market.

Beyond Gurteen the vision of the good life faded quickly into a vista of leathery brown bogs and old estate walls saddled with ivy. In this wasteland taken over by birch and alder I had my lunch—a nibble of biscuits and the usual thermos of coffee, and lay back under the shimmering trunks of birch trees. Turgenev wrote: "It seems that you are looking into a bottomless sea that is stretching out far and wide below you that the trees are not rising from the earth, but as if they were the roots of enormous plants. . . ." Down the road was a small Georgian house that had come down in the world to a plain farmhouse. The front door was painted a vivid turquoise, and a colony of ducks which had happily taken over a pool in the front, together with a bundle of hay which had a broomstick pushing out of the top, composed themselves into a detail that might have been painted by Breughel.

At Lackeen crossroads I drank in a dark pub under the trees

with a turf fire and prints round the walls with curled yellow edges of forgotten steeplechases. The silence of the place closed in like a church, as the only two other drinkers discussed farming prices in whispers and agreed that communists were waiting to take over the government. Cattle were ruinously expensive, and when the Common Market came there would be Dutch and Germans under every bush. "We'll be flooded out with foreigners." They shook their heads over their pints, evidently not graduates of Gurteen.

Beyond the pub the walls of Lackeen Castle rose out of the trees, facing the outline of Abbeyville, a neat Georgian toy house. Two different cultures, two modes of living, now merging into a similar rather battered compatibility with the Irish scene to which they both gave grace and meaning. Lackeen was the chief seat of the O'Kennedys, who, together with the O'Mearas and MacEgans, were the old rulers of this part of Ormonde and once owned eleven castles in two baronies extending from Lorrha to the banks of the Shannon. They kept their independence until 1553, when they acknowledged the overlordship of the Butlers. Then in the usual way they lost their possessions after joining with O'Neill in 1600, forfeiting their last vestiges of power to the Cromwellians. Donagh Kennedy of Lackeen, the son of the last chief of Lower Ormonde was reported in the Civil Survey of 1654 as residing "amidst the ruins of his father's greatness in the old ruined castle and bawne of Lackeen, the walls only standing and the mote of an orchard and garden, a mill standing in a little brook running through the said land, and six thatch houses . . .".

As castles go, it did not seem an altogether impossible dwelling place. There was an arched gateway, a sort of medieval enclosure, and the main structure, maintained by the Board of Works, still looked habitable. I must admit that my own interest was in searching for a place to stop the night. But it lacked immediate comfort; a farmer had used the main hall as a repository for rusty machinery, the passage was cold and draughty and I passed on.

In 1735 the Stowe Missal, written on vellum, dating back to the earliest period in the Irish church, was found here. It was wrapped in a dazzling metal shrine, refurbished by Philip

Kennedy, Lord of Ormonde, and his wife, Aine, between 1323 and 1350. The missal had once belonged to the abbey at Terryglass, but after Terryglass declined, it came to Lorrha monastery, which is about four miles from Lackeen. Later during some war it was hidden in one of the walls of the castle, and forgotten until its accidental rediscovery. Since it was believed that no local man could translate it properly, the job was given to a West Clare poet named Aindrias Mac Cruitín, who was paid with expense money, a new suit and a horse.

When O'Sullivan Beare brought his people to Lackeen, he again avoided the castle—which may not have been hostile, since the Kennedys who inhabited it had lately been allies of O'Neill. In any case no attempt was made to attack them, and once more they camped beside an ancient church. Their first duty before they made their camp would have been a religious one. Prayer exorcised some of their awareness of danger and gave hope. I reached the site just before nightfall, when the winter trees and a flight of pigeons were black against a red sunset. In 1603 the church was still standing; now it is a heap of stones in the middle of a thicket with one wall containing a little lancet window propped up by ivy, the sky shining through it like a bloodstain. Of all the ruins these small ancient churches are the most poignant. Rose Macaulay, that enthusiast of ruins, was depressed by Irish churches and abbeys "destroyed by Danes, by Normans, by Englishmen, by decay, by time, by poverty, vandalism and dissolution, their crumbling arches and portals and fragments of wall . . . in reproachful witness of the passing of a murdered culture".

I managed to put up in a farmhouse, another night of lying on a mattress beside a good turf fire. My hostess, who ran the farm with her nephew, did everything possible to make me welcome. A generously proportioned fry with slices of soda bread, heaped with butter, then television in the parlour with a bronze head of John Kennedy looking on from the dresser. "There would be no trouble in the North if he were here . . . but young Ted's speaking for us . . .".

By eight o'clock next morning she had already lit the stove and was preparing the day's bread from the flour kept in a large wooden bin.

"It's a caution," she greeted my bleary appearance at the door, as I tottered into the parlour, and she invited me to sit down to more bacon and eggs and strong tea. Her nephew, in spite of repeated knocking on his door, was still in bed. A wise man. He was a bachelor of thirty or thereabouts who during the evening had spent much time before and after television bemoaning the lack of opportunity for meeting members of the opposite sex, at the same time condemning marriage as disastrous. His attitude is said to be old fashioned; the modern farmer is ready to be wooed.

From Lackeen I went on to Lorrha, a small village with a tremendous heritage of Christian culture. St Patrick came here, and in the sixth century St Ruadan built his famous monastery which at one time contained his head preserved in a silver case, his holy bell, the Stowe Missal, and a "food-giving tree". I sheltered from the rain in the roofless nave of the monastery church, which had a nineteenth-century Church of Ireland built into its west end. It was Sunday and I could hear hymns through the wall, while outside four cars waited for the blessing and the papers to be picked up before the roast.

"This ancient parish church," the tourist guide said, "has an attached residence with a corbelled roof, and there are fifteenth century additions. The door on the West wall, the lower arch of which has a pelican vulny . . .". But it takes courage to hang around ruins with rain dripping down your neck. After a quick trample through the graveyard and a glance at the stumps of two early crosses spared by Cromwell's troops, I retreated by way of St Ruadan's abbey, founded after the monastery, whose most striking feature is an elegant window surmounted by a coiffured head. I reached the long shallow nave of the Dominican friary, erected by Walter de Burgo in 1269 to succeed the monastery. This stood beside the Catholic church which was now bursting with people. Local names, meaning the road to the Holy Women and well of the Holy Women, suggest that there was also a nunnery here at some time. If tradition were not so strong that O'Sullivan Beare spent the night at Lackeen, one might assume that he would find his way four miles further to Lorrha. However the small church at Lackeen must have very strong associations with the ecclesiastical stronghold at Lorrha. There are traces of foundations of two other buildings in the grass which were probably part of a sacristy of a house for monks. Lackeen was holy enough.

In the friary under a line of vaulted windows were some crested tombs of the O'Kennedys and MacEgans. The Mac-Egans were celebrated hereditary Brehons of the O'Kennedys and professors of the Brehon laws to all Ireland. Scholars, writers and teachers, Brehons had something like a Jesuitical education, which could take anything from twelve to twenty years and included learning a secret language of their own. In the fourteenth century a MacEgan compiled a manuscript with the delightful title of *Leabhar Breac*, the Speckled Book. By the sixteenth century their scholarly talents were becoming rather run down although the MacEgans still kept up some of the old traditions of learning. In 1602 they were supporters of the English. Possibly Lorrha was in their hands and this was one of the reasons why O'Sullivan preferred to stay at Lackeen.

From Lorrha I took the loop road to Ballymacegan and the Shannon. More torrential showers with the sun occasionally shining through and throwing coloured ribbons across the sky. "The climate of Ireland is more moist than that of any other part of Europe," the English traveller, Twiss, wrote in 1755. "It generally rains for four of five days in the week for a few hours at a time; one can see a rainbow almost daily." Afterwards I asked the meteorological office whether January, 1972, had been wetter than usual in western Ireland. No, nothing special, although in some counties the percentage of rainfall had been a bit higher all right. But in general the graphs did not differ too much from their normal winter patterns.

The modern Irish climate was formed some two thousand years ago. Before then it was warmer; the rain came just at the same time as the arrival of the Celtic people and has continued more or less ever since. "There is . . . such a plentiful supply of rain," wrote Giraldus, "such an ever-present overhanging of clouds, and fog, that you will scarcely see even in the summer consecutive days of really fine weather." Half Ireland can expect rain on two days out of every four. O'Sullivan seems to have experienced no rain during the first part of his march, but travelled on what seem to have been clear icy days. The rain was not to fall until after the Shannon crossing.

The district now called Redwood, once known as Kiltaroe, contained the old estate of the MacEgans. Their castle, "built with bullock's blood and water", I was told, stands on a de-nuded hillside overlooking the swamplands of the Shannon's shore. When O'Sullivan camped nearby it was a comparatively new building, having been erected in 1580. After the wars, the MacEgans, still following the old family traditions, used it as a school for teaching history and law. Its most distinguished scholar was Michael O'Clery, the main compiler of the *Annals of the Four Masters*. But by 1654 the Civil Survey described it as "an old ruined castle, the walls only standing, and two thatched houses". So the life of Redwood Castle was very short—just seventy years. Afterwards, in 1798 it became a refuge for an outlaw called James Meaney, known as The Bold Captain, who had fought with the United Irishmen. He hid in the ruin in a small cell which you can see, looked after by friends, until someone betrayed him.

In the last few years a descendant of the MacEgans has bought the place for £800 and is doing it up. The building is covered in ivy, its main floor, used by cattle, is a foot deep in cow dung the consistency of porridge, and altogether it looks a bit shook. But apparently it is sound enough. No country in Europe has so many small medieval castles as Ireland; if they haven't been bombarded or pulled down by ivy or vandals, they survive, because they are amazingly strong structurally. The timber goes, and roof, window frames and floors vanish; but the stone walls remain with chimney pieces hung above lost joists and staircases curved like a hunchback's spine. Yeats, shivering in the damp of Thor Ballylee, was perhaps one of the first people in modern times to start the vogue of adapting a castle as a residence. Placed strategically to command the area around them, for a castle's function is not defence but domina-tion, such buildings are often in very beautiful situations. Although the river is hidden by swamp and thickets, Redwood is a Shannon castle, and in 1602, before the present system of flood control it was a lot nearer its banks. From here the

MacEgans became aware of O'Sullivan Beare camped at the river's edge, and prepared the attack that made the crossing a tragedy.

For a while until you are quite close to it, there is no indication that you are approaching "that prince of Irish rivers". according to Barnabe Riche, "which sometimes narrow, sometimes broad by its many windings, washes many counties". The Shannon is secreted in brown swampland and screened by brushwood and the ragged edge of trees. There was a recognized ford further north at Shannon Bridge which O'Donnell and his armies had used twice—once in 1595 on a raid into Connacht when he was attacked by English soldiers and suffered a number of casualties and once in 1602 on his way south. Otherwise the river was crossed by ferries. O'Sullivan Beare sent scouts ahead who discovered that all boats and ferries had been removed, and the ferrymen in the district had received warnings and threats that the fugitives were not to be helped. The man responsible for closing off the Shannon passage to O'Sullivan was Donnchadh MacEgan, stationed at Redwood Castle, who was Queen's sheriff for this area.

Philip O'Sullivan wrote that the O'Sullivans hid themselves in "the thick and secure wood of Brosna". This was an extensive forest situated between the loop of the Brosna river and the Shannon. One strong local tradition claims Portland, a surviving wooded ridge towards the present bridge to Portumna, as the actual camping site. People point out a gap in the old woods where the refugees felled the trees. I prefer to believe that they camped much higher up the river, almost beside the MacEgan castle. O'Sullivan Beare was never intimidated by the proximity of his enemies. In Glengarriff the distance between the English and Irish camps was only two miles, and of course, down there, as in this region beside the Shannon, the dense woods would have offered them protection. At Latteragh he had not even the protection of trees when he camped within gunshot of the de Marisco castle.

A farmer led me down to a long field on the river's edge with a mound at one end and a pair of electricity pylons straddling both banks. Once this place was covered with forest. It is still called *Poll na Gcapall*, the field of the horses, and is supposed to be the place where O'Sullivan Beare's men killed and ate their horses and used the skins for making boats.

When they first came here they knew that they were cornered with their backs to the river, and sooner or later they would be trapped. They were on the verge of starvation. "Every heart was hereupon filled with giant despair," Philip O'Sullivan wrote. "In this critical state of things, my father, Dermot O'Sullivan, announced that he would in a short time make a ship and put an end to the soldiers' hunger."

Don Philip wrote up this episode in full, perhaps because his father had rather dwelt on it during his Spanish exile. Dermot of Dursey was seventy at the time of the march, and after going to Spain lived on to be a hundred; he is buried in Corunna.

He was the eldest of the sons of the Dermot O'Sullivan Beare who had been blown up by a gunpowder explosion in 1549. The other sons were Donal, who succeeded him as O'Sullivan Beare, and who was Donal Cam's father, Philip the Tanaiste, and Owen, who became Sir Owen O'Sullivan. While Dermot of Dursey's son, Philip the historian, is reticent about mentioning his father's relationship with the other O'Sullivans, it seems fairly certain that he was an illegitimate brother. In the Carew MSS. at Lambeth, there is a family tree clearly showing the three brothers, Donal, Owen and Philip, while Dermot is mentioned separately with a wavy line to denote illegitimacy. He is mentioned as marrying a daughter of McSwiney, and Philip tells us that his mother's name was Johanna McSwiney. This would explain why Dermot, who was the eldest brother, did not succeed to the chieftaincy, and was fobbed off with Dursey—a small inconsequential island. Writing in seventeenth-century Spain, where the purity of descent was considered important by the hidalgo class, Philip did not elucidate his murky origins.

Dermot of Dursey was a remarkable old man, a veteran of most types of warfare, who had taken a prominent part in the Elizabethan wars. He was at the siege of Youghal, and according to his son, "with immense valour, against immense difficulties, scaled the walls by ladders, the besieged in vain resisting". On another occasion, with his party of five retainers he beat off an encounter with the Queen's magistrates who were accompanied by fourteen soldiers. He survived, even though covered with wounds. He was also a seaman, and during the Desmond wars had been in a naval battle. His knowledge of the sea probably arose from his association with Dursey, where he had built the fort that was destroyed during the siege of Dunboy. He had plenty of experience of manœuvring boats across the treacherous currents of Dursey Sound. He knew the traditional type of boats which we have come to call currachs, and how to build them. Now he rallied his companions with the suggestion that the horses which they had brought with them to this point should be killed, their flesh eaten and their skins made into boats in which the Shannon could be crossed. Two vital problems of food and transport would be solved without further difficulty.

Philip O'Sullivan's account of the building of these boats is interesting, since it is the earliest in existence which gives a detailed description of the traditional method of constructing boats with osiers and wet skins. Two boats were built, one under the direction of Dermot of Dursey, which must have looked very like the long black currachs which are still seen today in the west of Ireland. The other was made under the direction of the O'Malleys, some of O'Sullivan Beare's Connacht mercenaries, who were members of a seafaring clan, and obstinately insisted on building a boat of their own. It seems to have been more like a coracle; even as it took shape the tubby little craft must have looked unstable for the purpose of crossing a wide swift-flowing river. Too small for Philip O'Sullivan to bother about giving its dimensions, it was "made of osier, without joinings, having a circular bottom like a shield, and sides much higher than the bottom suited. It was covered with the skin of one horse pulled across the bottom."

The currach was much more elaborate. "Two rows of osiers were planted opposite each other, the thickest end being stuck in the ground, and the other ends bent in to meet each other, to which they were fastened with cords. To this frame the solid planks were fixed, and seats and cross beams were fitted inside. Outside the skeleton of osier and timber was covered with the skins of eleven horses, and oars and dowels were fitted on. The keel was flat, both by the nature of the material, and also so that rocks and stones could be avoided. The boat was twenty-six feet long, six feet broad and five feet deep, but the prow was a little higher in order to stem the tide."

When most of the horses were slaughtered the refugees had their first proper meal since before the fight with Wilmot at Glengarriff. But O'Sullivan Beare, his uncle Dermot, and a man named Dermot O'Huallachain declined the unaccustomed meat. Their revulsion was more than that felt by the modern tourist on the Continent peering under the gilt horseheads of Bouchiers Chevalines at marble slabs loaded with petunia tinged steaks. Dislike of eating horseflesh is very ancient and widespread. In Ireland there was a definite taboo against it; an early Christian penitential decreed: "Anyone who eats the flesh of a horse or draws the blood or urine of an animal does penance for three years and a half." To avoid committing this sin, the sixth-century saint, Moling, on one occasion miraculously turned horse into mutton. He and his companions were guests at a house where "no food was found for them save that a horsesteak was put into the cauldron. Now the cleric blessed the house and the cauldron, for he knew that what was therein was the flesh of a horse. Now when the charge in the cauldron was turned, what was there was a quarter of mutton . . .".

O'Sullivan was a deeply religious man; it is possible, too, that the Anglicizing influences of his boyhood may have strengthened his prejudice even at a time when he must have been close to starvation. The ordinary Irishman, on the other hand, seems to have generally ignored this ancient interdict. Before the devastation of the wars horses had been plentiful, and often there must have been some to spare for slaughter. During O'Neill's retreat his troops had to eat their horses, but although this made their transport difficulties critical, it would have been no hardship if Fynes Moryson is correct. He reports that horsemeat was relished in Ireland. "Yea, (which is more contrary to nature) they will feed on horses dying of themselves, not only upon small want of flesh, but even for pleasure." He tells how Lord Mountjoy discovered the buttocks of a dead horse cut off, and suspected that some soldiers had been forced to eat it, because, as so often happened, they were not issued with their proper rations. But these recruits, who were English-

Irish and had acquired the habits of the country, had been giving themselves a treat. "Your Lordship," one of them informed him, "may please to eate pheasant and partridge, and much good doe it you that best like your taste; and I hope it is lawful for me without offense to eat the flesh that likes me better than beefe."

Both Derricke's *Image of Ireland* and contemporary descriptions show that on expeditions and out hunting meat was boiled in a piece of animal hide—a way of cooking that dated back hundreds of years. A book about Ireland published in 1585 with the strange title *Beware the Cat* describes a hunting party boiling meat in the traditional way. O'Sullivan's men may well have reserved one or two of the skins from boat building. "In the meanwhile after the Countrie fashion they did cut a piece of the hide and pricked it upon four stakes which they set about the fire and therein they set a piece of the cow for themselves, and with the rest of the hide they made each of them laps to wear about their feet, like brogues to keep their feet from hurt next day." Philip O'Sullivan does not mention shoes at this stage—only later on the journey does he specifically describe the making of brogues. But the left-over pieces of horse hides trimmed off the sides of the currach would have been very suitable for footwear.

The construction of the boat took two days. They worked within a palisade which they had made on a bank inside a ditch fortified with timber. Although they were hidden in the heart of the woodland, the activities of hundreds of people cutting down trees, building fires, slaughtering, skinning and cooking horses, could not have passed unnoticed, and it seems that Donnchadh MacEgan knew all about them Why did the Queen's Sheriff delay attacking them during this period? The camp at *Pol na Gcapall*, if it were pitched there, would have been very near to Redwood Castle. It is quite probable that MacEgan made a decision that O'Sullivan's people should be allowed to cross unmolested, and O'Sullivan Beare understood this. MacEgan had demonstrated his loyalty to the Crown clearly enough by preventing the Shannon ferrymen from using their boats to row them over. It would have been easy for him now to leave them well alone, and not to send his forces against his fellow

Irishmen. In any case, he may not have been interested in doing so, because he plainly did not consider his garrison strong enough to face O'Sullivan Beare's seasoned soldiers. He only moved against them when they were divided by the river.

Some casualties could be expected during the crossing. O'Neill, on his return, had lost two hundred troops at the Blackwater. You can throw a stone across the Blackwater, and the flooded Shannon would have been more than a quarter of a mile wide.

The first launching took place as secretly as possible on the night of 7th January under the dim light of the quarter moon. The two boats were carried down to the river on men's shoulders just as currachs are still brought down to the sea. Then the big boat began to ferry soldiers over, thirty at a time, while the surviving horses were drawn after them, swimming.

Disaster occurred with the little tub of the O'Malleys into which ten of them were crowded, trying to direct it with the paddles they had fashioned as it swirled and turned in the swift current. It overturned, and in the darkness they all drowned.

The currach did better. For the rest of the night it went back and forth taking its full load each time. By daybreak the majority of soldiers were over in Connacht. On the Munster bank the resourceful Thomas Burke, commanding about twenty pikemen and twenty musketeers, was detailed to look after the women, the non-combatants and the baggage (although some of them had probably already gone over). The motto of women and civilians last may seem unchivalrous, but it was merely a repetition of the way they moved throughout the march—vanguard, followed by non-combatants, followed by the rearguard. Over on the Connacht bank there were unpleasant surprises for the troops who had completed the crossing, since they would soon be attacked. The camp followers seemed to be in good hands guarded by Burke and his picked men.

At dawn, after the currach had made at least six or seven crossings, Burke was arranging another load consisting of civilians and baggage when MacEgan suddenly appeared with a small force. At first his men did not wish to inflict real harm on those left behind, merely to rob them and destroy their supplies, demonstrating their energy in the Queen's service. However, as they seized the packs, they found it too easy to kill the wretched sutlers who were guarding them and drive the shrieking women across the reeds into the river to drown.

Burke's hesitation to interfere with MacEgan strengthens the theory about the Sheriff's initial motives. When he tried to interfere and put a stop to what was happening it was too late; by that time the MacEgans were immersed in robbery and slaughter. So he attacked them, and his fine soldiers soon routed them. Fifteen MacEgans were killed, including Donnchadh MacEgan himself. The Four Masters, in their account of the crossing, felt that it was a tragedy that should not have happened, and that MacEgan brought his own death upon himself. "Donnchadh, son of Cairbre MacEgan, began boldly to attack and fire on O'Sullivan and his people, so that at length he was obliged to be slain . . .".

By this time the noise of firing had attracted hordes of people down to the river, partly to sightsee, partly to plunder anything that might come their way. Burke, now thoroughly rattled, herded his charges aboard the currach and pushed away as fast as he could. The boat was very much overloaded and sank almost immediately, luckily near enough to the bank to be in depth. A few of the men waded ashore; some may have been caught by the mob, but others went into hiding, although their subsequent fate has not been recorded. Some of the others performed the astonishing feat of swimming the icy river. The survivors were able to relaunch the boat and make the crossing safely, in what proportion of soldiers, women and non-combatants no one says.

It was a dreadful episode, but writers seem to go too far when they regard it as one of the most shameful of Irish history. They seek to justify MacEgan on the ground that his castle would have been forfeited if he had not proved himself an active Queen's man, and this is surely true. In addition the struggle to live was particularly hard that winter, and throughout O'Sullivan's march those who opposed him were under the constant threat of famine. MacEgan's men and those who came from the countryside around may well have hoped that O'Sullivan's supplies included food. Gleeson calls this episode "a pregnant sign of the changing times". I would have thought it the reverse. Irish society was tribal, and without drawing parallels, one can see similarities between the behaviour of MacEgan and people like him, and that of tribesmen during the feuds that have tormented modern Arabia. There is the same eagerness for leaders to keep all options open and the tendency to change sides as it suited the moment, since the choice between survival and honour is not an easy one.

When I was on the banks of the Shannon it was very quiet. There was a boat in a nest of reeds, a few thatched farmhouses, sunken fields, a flash of water and suddenly the great sweep of the river that broke the empty horizon in two.

I told the man who owned the boat that I wanted to cross at approximately the same place as O'Sullivan Beare.

"You're on the right track, but he was just a bit further down." The wind was rising. "I'll take you over from here, if you like." The sedgy brown current pulled us out into midstream past Ballymacegan Island where the wind tugged at our backs. About fifteen minutes of rowing, and I was brought across from Munster to Connacht.

CHAPTER TWELVE

Shannon—Aughrim

As O'Sullivan advanced from the banks of the river, he was
not given one single moment's rest from the attacks of the
enemy. O'Sullivan divided his famished troops into two parts
and reached Maheraherla before midday.

Philip O'Sullivan

A CONTEMPORARY DESCRIPTION of Ireland states that in
1601 Connacht of all provinces was "the most out of order",
and the general shortage of food was even more severe here
than elsewhere. "Her Majesty has to keep a force of 2,300 and
75 horse, and such is the waste and ruin, especially in grain, as
we are driven to victual most of these companies out of Her
Majesty's store."

On the west bank of the Shannon O'Sullivan Beare first gave
orders that the currach should be broken up so that it could not
be used again. Then he rallied his people to defend themselves
once more, for as they were assembling into some sort of formation on the river bank, trying to gather up the surviving remnants of their baggage, they were attacked by the O'Maddens.
These were people whose lands formed part of the old kingdom
of Ui Maine, bordering the massive territory of the Burkes.
The ruin of the O'Madden castle of Derryhiveney stands a few
miles from the crossing; it is interesting, because it was built in
1643, long after O'Sullivan's passage at a time when such tower
houses had become an anachronism.

The O'Sullivans fought their way inland from the river's
edge, across low lying swampy ground, backed by sallows,
birch and willow. The way to Aughrim was across Machaire-
an Iarla, the Earl's plain, where the gravel chain of eskers,
pushed by the ice age across the centre of Ireland, reaches its
southern limit. The tradition is that they spent the night in the
woods near Killimor, about eight miles beyond the Shannon.
This is plausible, since they would not have been capable of

more than a short march after their terrible experiences in crossing the river. They shook off the doggedly persistent O'Maddens with difficulty. Then the soldiers, or a group of them, chanced upon a little settlement, probably nothing more than a circle of straw huts. The inhabitants had fled, leaving them to seize whatever they could; their spoils consisted of sacks of wheat and barley and a quantity of beer. "This kind of food and drink seemed to their parched palates and hungry stomachs so much nectar and delicacies. Whatever other kind of food was in the village, the natives had removed." They had probably just had time to drive away their livestock. Philip O'Sullivan, identifying with his subject, expressed sympathy with this act of plunder, which must have left the villagers that much nearer starvation. Similarly the Four Masters gave their approval to O'Donnell's soldiers' raiding the countryside on their way south.

The next day the column was made up with eighty armed men forming the advance guard. As usual the baggage and surviving civilians were sandwiched between these and the rearguard, which consisted of two hundred men commanded by O'Sullivan Beare. A hundred and twenty soldiers had died or disappeared since the departure from Glengarriff, and the non-combatants must have been reduced in greater proportion. There was a shortage of transport horses now, since, in addition to those which had been slaughtered, other animals were left behind because they were worn out. This meant increased difficulties in carrying along the sick and wounded and some of them had to be abandoned, to almost certain death. It seems rather doubtful that many of the wounded survived the Shannon crossing, and there may have been new casualties who suffered from the attacks of the O'Maddens.

I did not go straight to Aughrim, but once again took a detour and stayed near the river. The rowing boat had landed me on a bank, a raised green dyke dating from the Shannon scheme begun in 1925, which stretched the whole way along the river from Portumna to Meelick. I had already made detours to see Kilcolman and Lough Gur; now on this calm winter's day I was tempted to walk between the plain and the river through a flat landscape dominated by the mood of the sky. Nowhere else had I been so aware of the sky, and of land, normally dominant, in retreat under the clouds. I watched rain fall on a distant range of hills, and nearer, where the clouds were white, they built up into crested peaks, changing shape and colour before dissolving in blue mist. The air was quite silent and motionless, except for the occasional patter of birds— flights of duck crossing overhead, a pair of swans mastering the current, and curlews circling and crying out. Every now and again I came upon herons, regularly placed on the river's edge like sentries. At Meelick weir the river became noisy, hemmed in by sluice gates. Listening to the roar and watching the thwarted brown flood water gathered off distant hills sweeping among the little islands of thickets and reeds, I thought of Joyce's phrase about dark mutinous Shannon waves. A few hundred yards up they were again silent, slipping past the old grey church and crooked gravestones of Mcclick, crowded with a fair-sized funeral. The troop of men bunched together in blue Sunday suits and hats moved ahead of creeping vehicles with a solid military compactness. They all turned their heads to watch me come plodding over the fields. Later the dead person was buried in the little tumbledown graveyard on the edge of the river, the mourners in a big blue silent group and the priest's voice blown away in the wind.

Before they filed in for the burial, one of the men pointed out to me a sally bush in the middle of the river, where, it is reputed three counties meet—Tipperary, Galway and Offaly. The islands that form a spine down this part of the river were important as stepping stones to Connacht. When Meelick Friary was threatened by Danish plunderers, Friar's Island was used to hide the church treasure. On Incherky the Keelogue batteries were built in 1798 among the overgrown willows, and later a Martello tower was added, in fear that the French might sail up the Shannon like the Danes used to do.

I turned inland along what was normally the most peaceful of country roads, but now the returning funeral cars were racing back along it and I had to walk for most of the time in the ditch. When I reached Eyrecourt they were all parked nose to tail in front of a hotel, while inside the blue-suited men were having their glasses filled as rapidly as the barman knew how.

I listened to the curiously different "western speech" of
Connacht for a time, before asking the landlord for a bed.
Above the hubbub he said that he wasn't prepared for winter
B and B's, and I should try elsewhere. I did a weary round of
going from one fine Georgian house to the next in search of a
bed, before returning to his place and persuading him to change
his mind and put me up.

My first views of Eyrecourt had been jaundiced, but now I
could appreciate the elegance of the village, which used to be a
manorial adjunct to the Eyre estate. The Eyres, originally
Cromwellians, settled here and established a wild-living line of
landlords each with a lavish life-style. Typical was John Eyre,
later Baron Eyre of Eyrecourt, visited by the English traveller,
John Carr, in 1768. In his "splendid but dilapidated house in
County Galway", he lived "with more hospitality than elegance.
For while his table groaned with abundance, the order and good
taste of arrangement was little thought of; the slaughtered ox
head was hung up whole, and the hungry servitor supplied
himself with his dole of flesh sliced off the carcass. Lord Eyre,
who had no books, and though fond of company, little taste for
conversation, sat most of the afternoon in his chair sipping
claret . . .".

Once the Eyre estate comprised 35,000 acres, stretching into
Galway, King's County, Tipperary and Kerry. An elaborate
series of ruins remains inside a little park. Beside the main
entrance gates are the walls of a seventeenth-century church,
built in 1667 by "John Eyre of Eyrecourt, knight . . . at his own
expense". They tried to save it in 1838 by putting on a new roof,
but only the shell remains with an inscription dimly seen
through nettles and dead grass, I KNOW THAT MY REDEEMER
LIVETH. In front of the vast stable, weighed down with ivy, a
grotesque old donkey was browsing, a swollen windpipe on her
patchy neck and hooves turned up like skis. George Eyre, the
prototype of Charles Lever's *Charles O'Malley*, who was Master
of the Galway Blazers, kept between thirty and forty horses
here, and more than seventy hounds. Their howling used to
disturb the worshippers in the church, but he did nothing to
stop it when they complained. He became M.P. for Galway,
spending £80,000 on a single election. Through the nineteenth

century when the Eyres' easy-going patterns of behaviour continued, they seem to have remained popular and retained a respectable reputation as landlords. All classes found something oddly attractive about their feckless ways, their continued obsession with horse-flesh. It was said that no man was ever turned away from the hospitable front door, beside which a plate of money used to be left for passing beggars to help themselves. Horsemanship, extravagance and generosity were attributes to be admired. When John Eyre, who also epitomized the Protestant with a Horse, died from a fall at the local hunt, the *Gentleman's Magazine* of 18th February, 1856, mourned dutifully. "It is today our melancholy duty to record the particulars of a painful accident which has deprived the county of Galway of the head of one of its most ancient families, and cast a woeful gloom over every shade of society throughout the neighbourhood." However, strangers and visitors did not always enjoy the unrestrained etiquette of rural Galway society which emulated the Eyres. John Maxwell found it intolerable. "In Connaught there was a laxity of form—a free and easy system of society that exceeded all belief . . . People on a half hour's acquaintance called you by your Christian name; and men whom you had never heard of rode to your door, and told you that they would stay a fortnight. . . ."

It seemed natural that the vast rectangular courtyard with its gallery of stables should dominate the overgrown approach to the house. Many of the abandoned places I saw in Connacht merely disfigured the countryside, but this graceful ruin, half hidden by the winter dusk, was very beautiful. The four fragile sides of the house remain, still containing rows of curved Gothic window frames, and the ivy, instead of crushing the brickwork like a boa constrictor, lightly holds it up like ivy in stage scenery. It has an air of drama and tragedy, rather belied by its horse-dominated history; while Churchtown suggested light opera, Eyrecourt is a setting for Verdi, for grand opera at its most strident and sad. It was built in the Dutch pattern with a wide-eaved roof; once there used to be a slab over the door which said "Welcome to the House of Liberty".

The beauty of the place is ephemeral because all the rows of pretty Gothic window frames and the rotting door jambs held between swaying walls will soon tumble into a pile of rubble. When I had tea with Mr and Mrs Hayes, who worked here in the last days of Eyrecourt, they described how the place passed into abrupt dissolution when the last Mrs Eyre to live here decided to go to England sometime after the First World War. Since she could not bear the thought of a stranger living here, she scuttled the house, together with the family church. The splendid oak staircase, unique in Ireland and specially constructed by imported Dutch craftsmen, with its carved acanthus leaves, ferocious masked faces and twenty-eight flowerpots topped with elaborate branches of wooden flowers which crowned each newel, is now in storage in the Detroit Institute of Arts.

Among the neat Georgian terraces of the town stands the old courthouse on the green, which later became a small theatre whose existence in a town of this size must be unique in Ireland. Before it was gutted by fire, the interior had a little railed gallery, and on the stage, among other strolling players, Percy French sang his songs.

In the main street the parish priest lives in a folly designed at the beginning of the nineteenth century by a retired nabob. The exuberance of its detail, emphasized by ecclesiastical silver paint, contrasts with the restraint of the neighbouring houses. Some stone pineapples, symbols of happiness and prosperity, balance above the front door flanked by silver eagles. Inside the priest lives under a series of ceilings painted with classical themes, mainly in lush blues and greens and flesh tints. The housekeeper guided me through the interior, deliberately darkened by the nabob, who suffered from some unspecified eastern disease and disliked sunlight; out to the back where he had built a miniature Hanging Garden of Babylon overlooked by a parapet wall and tower, and then back through the rooms where the P.P. dined, I think, under a draped Andromeda chained to a rock.

I went towards Clonfert past the shattered parkland of Eyrecourt. Outside a neat Shannon-style cottage thatched with straw instead of reeds from the river, a dog tried to squeeze through the wrought-iron gate to get at me, while a cat curled up on the ledge of the tiny window, its face turned to the sun

like a sunflower. Past another O'Madden castle called Brackloon, built in 1567, with a parapet topped by a pair of gabled chimneys taken over by a family of bickering jackdaws. Then a modern Catholic church, uninteresting from the outside, but containing Our Lady of Clonfert, a painted wooden statue of mother and child, dating from the fourteenth century and probably carved locally. She had a long rather flattened face with a recognizably Gaelic cast to it, for, like St Molaise and battered St Gobnat, she is one of the few surviving pieces of medieval statuary. Although she was not a cult figure, it was safer to hide her away and she was concealed in a tree in Cromwellian times, to be rediscovered and painted up comparatively recently.

Down the road is Clonfert Cathedral, first a tower jutting out of trees, then a tiny squat building, quite plain except for the arched Romanesque doorway at the east end, like a jewel in its head. With this arch surrounded by detailed carving it resembles a very elaborate forge. The cathedral was originally attached to a monastery founded by St Brendan in A.D. 1558 which over the years suffered even more than the usual ecclesiastical wear and tear, because it was plundered six times by the Danes. For the last four hundred years it has been a countrified Church of Ireland see, serving an ever decreasing congregation. As early as 1786 the enlightened Bishop despaired of acquiring a vigorous flock. "Unable to make the peasants around me good Protestants, I wish to make them good Catholics, good anything. I have therefore circulated amongst them some of the best of their own authors, whose writings contain much pure Christianity, useful, known and beloved sentiments."

Here was another church nearly ruined by neglect. Part of it was wrecked in 1541, and after that it was just left to disintegrate until, in 1882, Clonfert could be described as "the abode of the rat, the bat and the beetle. Noisome insects crawled all over the place, the walls were covered with ugly modern plaster and were reeking with damp, and the atmosphere of the cathedral resembled that of a charnel house." Some people consider that it has been over-restored, but the fact that it survives at all seems to be worth the zealous efforts of the

Crossing the Shannon

Clonfert Cathedral
Co. Galway (doorway)

Old whisky advertisement on wall

enthusiasts who saved it. They managed to retain much of its medieval simplicity. Survivals from the original fabric include a fifteenth-century font and a crisply carved smiling stone mermaid holding a comb and mirror, possibly an indirect reference to St Brendan's nautical adventures. The east Gothic window is there, admired by the archaeologist, George Petrie, as "exceedingly chaste and beautiful", and, of course, the doorway, as important a survival of monastic art as the *Book of Kells*.

No trace remains of the monastery school or the twelfth-century convent of the Canonesses Regular of St Augustine. The Bishop's Palace was one of the few seventeenth-century houses left intact in Ireland, but it was gutted by fire less than ten years ago. Its last owner was Oswald Mosley. From the palace an astonishing avenue of very ancient yews, laid out a thousand years ago in the shape of a cross, curves its old branches into a rickety darkened alley leading back to the cathedral. In spite of their firmly delineated Christian outline, the darkness they make seems to recreate their pagan significance and suggests a Druidical grove. Under them the old monks walked to mass, and later, after a few more feet of brown needles had been deposited along the cushioned passageway, the Anglican bishop hurried to morning service in his robes.

A few more houses, and that is about all that remains of St Brendan's foundation, which in the Middle Ages used to attract three thousand students at a time to a monastic education. At that time the cathedral was even more remote, hidden away in a place described by its name—*cluain* can mean a place of retreat, and *fert* a grave or trench. When St Brendan first chose this site, the area was naturally secluded, enclosed on one side by extensive forests and on the other by low-lying marshes which led down to the Shannon. The *cluains* of Connacht were bog islands, and when the river overflowed they must have been completely cut off. In ancient documents Clonfert is described as The Island called Clonfert. Islands and loneliness were part of a tradition of seclusion followed by Irish saints since the very first emulated the more austere desert fathers in conditions of extreme discomfort on the Skelligs.

Beyond Clonfert the old forests turned into an expanse of chocolate bog with a turf factory in the middle of it. One

moment I was walking among thorn bushes and scrub woodland, and the next I had emerged on to a glossy brown plain
dotted with big yellow machines with oversize wheels to stop
them sinking, turning out worms of peat to be covered with
crackling plastic as a protection against the weather.

I had hoped to walk along a branch of the Grand Canal
which was marked on my map as joining up with Ballinasloe.
But my map was old, and meanwhile the canal had been filled
in and turned into a small railway for carrying equipment in
and out of the factory. An engine went past carrying equipment
and two milk churns for the employees' tea. I followed the
towpath above the main stretch of bog towards Killimor bridge.
Although the canal had only gone for fifteen years, it seemed to
belong to a time remote as an old pilgrim route. There were
few signs of it along the ridge that swept above the bog; the
grooved stop post on which generations of barges once tied up,
the curved bridge at Killimor spanning a stretch of red and
black mud, and what was once the store and packet station for
generations of travellers in which a lock-keeper still lived with
his family. He told me that he had started on the canal in 1926,
and worked here until the last boat went down in June, 1956.
For most of his time the barges, which took forty to fifty tons,
had been mechanically propelled with a crew of four men,
including the greaser. The voyage from Dublin to Ballinasloe
took three days, and barges leaving Dublin on Monday reached
Ballinasloe on Wednesday evening. A team of horses in the old
days used to take a week. A pleasant enough life for a bargeman
back and forwards on the waterway. The packet station which
was his home had been built in the early nineteenth century, a
low two-storey structure with a cell behind it for locking up
unruly passengers. In times past passengers who became too
drunk were flung off the boats on to the bank—and there would
have been quite a few of them making excursions to Ballinasloe
Fair. (Mrs O'Dowd in *Vanity Fair*, sitting in a Belgian canal
boat in the Low Countries on her way to Waterloo, with a
cock's plume in her hat and very large "repether" on her
stomach, talked nostalgically about "Kenal boats, my dear! Ye
should see the kenal boats between Dublin and Ballinasloe.
It's there the rapid travelling is; and the beautiful cattle.")

After a cup of tea I continued walking in the direction of Aughrim along a road that skirted the side of the bog through a wide scrubland of birch and thorn. For a short time the scrub was broken by another ruined estate with denuded parkland and roofless lodge. It was called Lismanny House, said a man mending the road. He himself had taken part in the knocking when the Land Commission bought the place in 1937.

The ruins of Clontuskert Abbey, with the sun reflecting on the grey walls and making them shine, stood out among its gravestones. From here I took a series of little bylanes that soon had me completely lost. I walked about crossing fields, dodging out of thickets, with only the gleam of the distant Shannon to guide me on the flat wooded landscape.

"That road goes nowhere," a woman called out with an expressive gesture when I tried to find out where I was. "Go back the way you have come, and if you lose courage, ask someone." It wasn't so easy. I stumbled down lanes whose high briar hedges were like tunnels, past abandoned cottages and dark little fields also closeted by hedges, and never saw a soul. By the time I finally got on to the road to Aughrim it was getting dark, and the first drops of rain began to fall. Somewhere near here on the flat esker I caught up again with O'Sullivan Beare at a point where his weary soldiers would face the biggest battle of the march.

Above me was the distinctive rise of Aughrim called the Horse's Back. I walked in the pouring rain up past Bloody Hollow, named after that more famous battle of 1691, and heard through the trees the sweet sound of lorries on the main road. And soon with legs dropping off me and a devouring hunger I saw the neon blaze of the Aughrim Inn.

CHAPTER THIRTEEN

Aughrim—Ballygar

Aughrim was won by O'Sullivan against great odds,
mainly through his own valour, skills and presence of
mind . . .
                                        Standish O'Grady

It is scarcely credible that the like number of forces,
fatigued from long marching, and coming into the very
centre of their enemies, ever before achieved such a
victory in defence of life and renown, as they achieved
that day.
                                Annals of the Four Masters

AUGHRIM IS CUT off from the main road along which the
traffic flows endlessly between Dublin and Galway all day and
most of the night. For most travellers speeding past, the Horse's
Back—Aughrim is derived from *each druim*, the ridge of the
horse—along which the Irish battle line was drawn up in an
almost impregnable position on Sunday 12th July, 1691, is no
more than an inconsequential rise along the esker ridge from
Ballinasloe. The village, with its couple of petrol stations, road-
side café and two church spires, is a quickly passing blur on a
monotonous scene.

If General Ginkell and the Williamite army hadn't defeated
the Irish forces under the Frenchman, St Ruth, at Aughrim in
1691, there might be a chance that O'Sullivan Beare's victory
fought on the same battlefield a century before would be more
widely known. At least it was a victory. But people have forgotten that at Aughrim on 10th January, 1603, O'Sullivan
Beare routed a superior English force under the most adverse
circumstances. Guidebooks don't mention it, and poets, ranging
from Thomas Moore—"Forget not the Fields where they
perished"—and Emily Lawless to Richard Murphy, have con-
fined themselves to the depressing details of the second battle. I
have heard it said that the first battle is played down because
there is something contemptible in the spectacle of Irishmen

fighting Irishmen, for as usual the forces, which for convenience must be designated English, were largely composed of Queen's Irish. Of course, compared to General Ginkell's victory, the earlier battle was little more than a skirmish—only another incident along the march.

From Killimor, where O'Sullivan had camped on the night of 9th January, it would have been a good twelve miles' march to Aughrim; allowing for the terrain, the distance may have been longer. Even if he started out before dawn, he could not have reached Aughrim much before midday. There the English were waiting for him, having received news of his approach. They had assembled a large intercepting force under Captain Henry Malby, which consisted of five companies of foot, two troops of horse, and a nondescript local rabble. The Earl of Clanricarde's brother was there, confusingly bearing the same name as O'Sullivan Beare's captain, Burke; his Christian name was Thomas, and another Burke, named Richard, fought alongside him.

In an equally poised contest, O'Sullivan Beare's soldiers could expect to give a good account of themselves against the forces drawn up before them in conventional battle array with banners and drums. The men who fought for O'Sullivan would have been the best of fighting material, stimulated by constant fighting, and influenced by the genius of Hugh O'Neill's methods of reorganization and training troops. They were given regular pay and well armed. By now they fought as a unit, and were assembled more or less as a team; they would have been more efficient soldiers than their haphazardly gathered opponents. Irishmen had a flexible and mobile style of fighting, using their wide range of weapons as golfers change their clubs about. Hugh O'Donnell's soldiers had "plenty of broad shafted darts and broad green spears with strong handles of ash. They had straight keen swords and light shiny axes . . . the instruments of shooting . . . were darts of wood and elastic bows with sharp pointed arrows and locke guns." During the siege of Kinsale Mountjoy noted that "Irish fighting men, so far from being naked people as before times, were generally better armed than we, knew better their weapons than our men, and even exceedeth us on that discipline which was fittest for the advantage of the natural strength of the country".

In O'Sullivan's small army 280 soldiers had survived to fight at Aughrim. At Glengarriff they started with a small troop of cavalry, thirteen in all; presumably most of the horses had been slaughtered at the Shannon, since there is no mention of any fighting from horseback. Horsemen would never have made an important force on this march. The main body of soldiers was divided between gallowglasses and kern. Dymoke, in his treatise written in 1600, differentiates carefully between the two sorts of foot soldiers. The gallowglasses were "pycked and selected men of great and mighty bodies, crewell without compassion. The greatest force of battle consisteth in them. They were armed with shirte of mail, a skull and skeine [dagger]." The weapon he mentions them as using most is the battle-axe. However, developments in armoury were rapid, and even two years later Dymoke seems to have been out of date. The pike had largely taken over from the axe, and a number of O'Sullivan's men carried both pikes and spears. As many as were able had firearms.

Dymoke describes the kern as a "kind of footman, slight armed with a sword, a target of wood" (he meant a shield), "or a bow and a sheaf of arrows with barbed heads, or else three darts which they cast with wonderful facility. Within these years they have practised the musket . . .". Again it seems that Dymoke had not caught up with the times, since in addition to their hand weapons, as many footmen as possible had muskets. Firearms, expensive and cumbersome though they must have been, are the most frequently mentioned weapons in accounts of battles and skirmishes on O'Sullivan's march.

However, it is not possible to be at all dogmatic about weapons and about troop formations, since fighting was so flexible, and this was a transitional period with great changes in methods of warfare. Many soldiers must have preferred to keep to the old darts and spears, or else they lacked the means and opportunity of obtaining muskets. It is perhaps sufficient to say that O'Sullivan's men were picked and well armed. They represented the very best quality of Irish fighting soldiers, and up to now had amply displayed those military virtues of courage, stamina, resourcefulness and determination.

But they had been through a great deal, and at Aughrim they panicked. The first sight of the enemy spread out before them was too much. "The neighing of their horses, the sheen of their brilliant armour," wrote Philip O'Sullivan, "the braying of their trumpets, the sound of pipes, the beat of their drums, all joyously and proudly anticipating victory, unnerved the small band of Catholics and struck terror in their hearts." The vanguard of eighty soldiers marching before the baggage and other impedimenta turned and fled.

O'Sullivan, coming up with the remaining two hundred soldiers, must have felt the battle already lost, as he turned and exhorted all the rest of the men ranged behind him. Philip O'Sullivan relays his words, reported by his father in exile, and may have tidied them up. It may well have been one of the occasions when his accuracy as an historian was sacrificed to artistic effect. But this reported speech does reflect some of the despairing eloquence of O'Sullivan Beare's letters to his Spanish allies. He rallied his soldiers in the most effective way possible —by telling them the truth, that they had nothing to lose.

"Since on this day our desperate circumstances and unhappy fate have left us neither with wealth nor country nor children nor wives to fight for, but as on this instant the struggle with our enemies is for the life that alone remains to us, which of you, I ask in God's eternal name, will not rather fall fighting gloriously in battle and avenging your blood than like cattle, which have no sense of honour, perish unavenged in cowardly flight? . . . See the plain stretching far and wide without hindrance of bog, without thick woods, without any hiding place to which we could fly for concealment. The neighbouring people are no protection for us. There is no one to come to our aid. The enemy block the road and passes, and we, wearied with our long journey, are unable to run. Whatever chance we have is only in our own courage and strength of arms . . . remember that everywhere hitherto, enemies that attacked us were routed by the divine mercy. Victory is the gift of God. Let us think, then, that Christ our Lord will be with his servants in their dire need; and that it is for his name and holy faith that we are at issue with the heretics and those who cleave to them . . .".

Eighty-eight years and five months later St Ruth, exhorting

another Irish army in the same place, had a familiar theme, but
spoke with a different emphasis:

"I am assured by my spies that the Prince of Orange's
heretical army is resolved to give us battle, and you must see
them before you. . . It is now, therefore, if ever, that you must
endeavour to recover your lost honour, privilege, and forefathers' estates; you are not mercenary soldiers, you do not
fight for your pay, but for your lives, your wives, your children,
your liberties, your country, your estates. And to restore the
most pious of kings to his throne. But above all else for the
propagation of the Holy Faith and the subversion of
heresies. . . ."

St Ruth appeared to have a much better chance of victory
than O'Sullivan. The Catholics at the second battle of Aughrim
were about equal in number to Ginkell's forces, and although
they might be inferior in expertise and equipment, these
deficiencies were compensated for by their commanding position
on the hill. O'Sullivan Beare, on the other hand, caught in the
open with a smaller force on the verge of panic, seemed to face
inevitable annihilation. He was able to outwit the superior
force of the enemy and turn defeat into victory. It was a personal triumph, a demonstration of initiative and bravery.

After he had spoken to his soldiers, he moved off as rapidly as
the enemy advanced. He had to take up a defensive position as
quickly as possible and meet the charging companies of cavalry
in a less exposed place. Although he had told his people that
they had no chance to find cover or concealment, this was not
quite true; he was able to lead them through a patch of swamp
to a piece of woodland. The English reformed and tried to cut
them off, their musketeers assailing his rear and killing fourteen. The rest of the rearguard under William Burke was driven
back, and a few more of his soldiers broke and fled. At this
point O'Sullivan Beare suddenly wheeled his retreating men
around to face the main column of the enemy. It was one of his
favourite surprise tactics, and again proved effective when the
English, who had been charging forward in pursuit, hesitated
as they tried to deploy, throwing their front line into confusion.
They were now confronted, not by a fleeing rabble, but by men
preparing to make a determined assault. "Shortly before he

came within a spear's length of them, twenty marksmen whom
O'Sullivan had posted flanking his front ranks, shot down
eleven royalists." This was part of the familiar turn-about
manœuvre used at Ballyvourney and Liscarroll. O'Sullivan's
musketeers had deliberately held their fire until this moment.
They were well practised in the exercise, and could carry it out
at a word of command. The object was to achieve as much
effect as possible with one burst of gunfire, just as the enemy
had done a few minutes before. "High-sounding" massed
muskets fired at point-blank range were at their most effective,
producing a charge of red-hot shot described by one contemporary as "blood red spherical balls and leaden bullets from . . .
straight shooting sharp sighted guns". But in a battle of this
nature, after the one deadly volley there was no time to load up
again. Muskets had to be discarded and afterwards the con-
tenders had to resort to "bloody venomous javelins and other
missile weapons", before closing in to hand-to-hand fighting.

The effects of O'Sullivan's guns almost made the enemy
ranks break and flee; but they rallied. "The chief and bravest
held their ground against O'Sullivan. Forthwith the advance
lines of both parties fell to with drawn swords and couched
spears." The main targets for O'Sullivan's men were the
leaders, partly because it was expedient to cut them down,
partly because they felt a surge of pure hate. Three of them
rushed against Richard Burke. "First of all Captain Maurice
O'Sullivan closed with him, but as he had not firm ground he
was knocked down by Richard . . . he was not, however,
wounded, being protected by his coat of mail . . .". This is the
first indication that some of O'Sullivan's men wore armour.
"Donogh O'Hinguerdel, with a blow of his sword cut off
Richard's right hand as he was making a second thrust with his
pike, and Maurice, quickly getting up again, ran him through
with a spear, and Hugh O'Flynn finished him off with a sword
as he fell half dead."

Meanwhile O'Sullivan Beare was also using his sword; the
Four Masters describe how "O'Sullivan with rage, heroism,
fury and ferocity, rushed to the place where he saw the English,
for it was against them that he cherished most animosity and
hatred, and made no delay until he reached the place where he

saw the chief; so that he quickly and dexterously beheaded the noble Englishman, the son of Captain Malby". Beheading people during battle was standard practice; several contemporary woodcuts show the dripping heads of chiefs brought to triumph after the victory. One typical earlier battle described in the *Four Masters* tells how "O'Donnell's people returning back with the heads and arms of their enemies," after the battle of the Yellow Ford, "the soldiers and colones of the Irish army returned to strip the slain, and to behead those who lay severely wounded on the field". The custom was imported to America and taught to the Red Indians, who refined it; later by a curious historical switch scalping came to be accepted as proof of inherent Indian savagery. Defeated leaders were particularly prone to decapitation; the unfortunate young Malby shared the fate of Sir Conyers Clifford, beheaded by O'Donnell after the battle of the Curlews in 1599.

The loss of the enemy leaders gave O'Sullivan's men all the encouragement they needed, and soon the Royalists were in flight. "And now a heap was formed of bodies and arms, and the rest, not slowly, but pellmell, made for the adjoining fort at Aughrim. O'Connor, a peer of the bravest, shouted Victory! . . . And now those who had not dared to charge with O'Sullivan against the opposing force, were quick enough to fall on the routed enemy, abrogating to themselves with great blusterings the glory of the victory obtained by others, and anxious by a show of spirit to wipe out the abject disgrace of their ill-timed cowardice." They had also to deal with Malby's musketeers and a crowd of local men who had been annoying the noncombatants throughout the battle by throwing javelins at them and plundering their baggage. These were all safely put to flight.

"In the battle a hundred royalists fell, the flower of their forces, their general Malby, Richard Burke, three standard bearers, as many adjutants, more sergeants, and the rest were Irish, Anglo-Irish and English gentlemen. The conquerors lost fourteen." All O'Sullivan's casualties came early in the battle, when the English musketeers shot fourteen of the rearguard.

The morning brought rain and freezing wind. I had breakfast in the parlour, where the landlord, imbued with the martial spirit of the place, had hung the walls with Zulu spears, while underneath were a couple of cannon balls and a small silver button found locally.

I had hoped to explore the old battlegrounds and set off under a weeping sky. There was not much to find. A signpost on a pub indicated the place where St Ruth had his head blown off by a cannon ball; it was curious that the defeated leaders in both battles should lose their heads. Down the road stood a large Celtic cross. A postman watched me trying to struggle over a wall and some barbed wire to reach it, when I asked him if there were any further memorials or site indications about either battle, he confirmed that there were none.

"It's mad. We have thousands of tourists coming here every year looking for the sites."

The cross, carved from local limestone, has had a chequered history. It was made in 1891 to celebrate the bicentenary of the battle, but it was not put up until comparatively recently. At one time there was a suggestion that it should be erected in the Garden of Remembrance in Dublin. Now at last the really determined visitor can read the inscription on its base which is in three languages, French, English and Irish. "To the Memory of Lt. General Saint Ruth and those who fell at Aughrim, 1691." Unusual and just that both sides are commemorated.

Probably I would have seen very little more of Aughrim if I had not met Mr Joyce, the schoolmaster, who in addition to having an immense local knowledge of the area, has built up a collection of objects found in the neighbourhood of the village. He has a constant struggle to try and hold it together, as the best things, like the Somerset Hoard, which included rare examples of gold metalwork found nearby, have gone to the museum in Dublin. The exhibits that remain in Aughrim are displayed all over the school house, round the walls of the class-rooms and in the passageway. They include a fourteenth-century wooden carving of the Madonna from Kilconnell Abbey, rushlights, quern stones and drinking goblets. And there are many relics from the second battle of Aughrim.

The present village is built right in the middle of the battle-field, and hardly a year passes without something coming to light. Dead men, very often; casualties in 1698 were terribly high, so that the dogs in the neighbourhood got a liking for human flesh. A tree blew down recently near the Church of Ireland rectory which had skeletons entwined in the roots. On another occasion a schoolboy brought Mr Joyce, like old Kaspar, some poor fellow's skull with a bullet rattling inside. In the school there are cannon balls, horse shoes, a sword, pieces of gun metal from melted-down cannon, and a set of vestments presented to the parish priest of Aughrim by Napoleon which he wore while celebrating High Mass in honour of the Frenchmen who died here. But there was nothing that dated back to O'Sullivan Beare.

Mr Joyce brought me around the battlefield in the rain. For years the second battle of Aughrim has been his absorbing passion, and as he described each ploy and movement, he seemed to recreate the neigh of horses and rattle of drums in the rain that poured over Bloody Hollow. He believed that this field with grazing sheep, some pine-trees and bog stretching towards the heights might also have been the scene of the first battle, and that O'Sullivan might have made his stand here. Each phase of the second battle is known, but the site of the first battle has to be guessed. However, Bloody Hollow or thereabouts seems a logical choice for O'Sullivan's stand; coming from the direction of Killimor he would have passed very near to it, and could have taken refuge in the considerable bog that spread over much of the area, a part of which still exists.

After Aughrim he decided not to rest, but to make a night march deep into the heart of Connacht. Although he had put his enemies to flight, it was only a question of time before the others attacked him. There were always a few local stragglers following after his train looking for opportunities to harry him. His soldiers had been further depleted during the battle, and he must have felt that his only hope of reaching safety in the north was to travel at full speed. The non-combatants who looked to him as their leader would have to struggle along as best they could to keep up with him.

I thought that now was a good time to follow his example and try walking at night. A look at the map showed me that the road was extremely dull, and would probably be at its best in the darkness. A day's rest at Aughrim had refreshed me. But the rain was still spilling down, a steady drumbeat on the closed windows, a soporific muted feeling in the small bar with its television and bright coal fire. I sat with Mr Joyce and he told me of his plans to put up a garden round the Celtic cross and also something worthy to O'Sullivan Beare. Sometimes a figure would come in and greet him, a returned exile from England, an old schoolboy—everyone knew Mr Joyce. After he had left the lights went off at the eleven-thirty closing time. The clientèle shifted about a little, and one or two left, but the pints of stout were still being handed round in the dark, and the hard core seemed to have settled down for many hours yet. By twelve o'clock when the younger members of the landlord's family had gone to bed, I realized there was no point in further delay.

"How far are you going?" asked the landlord.

"Ballygar." It was about sixteen miles on.

"You had best have a double brandy. On the house."

I put on most of my clothing, two of everything, covering myself in the supposedly waterproof anorak and trousers, and opened the front door. Or rather it blew open in my face. After the brandy and making my intentions so publicly clear, I hadn't the strength of mind to step back inside. I lurched down the main street as the rain filled my screwed-up eyes and filtered down my neck. Out on the main road the distant lights of Ballinasloe stained the sky a dusty pink. Once I refused a lorry that pulled up on the road, its wipers beating a tattoo, its driver offering me a lift to Ahascragh. I listened to the disappearing hiss of wheels on water and thought of the pointlessness of the exercise.

Suddenly the rain stopped and all the clouds vanished leaving behind a sky pebbled with stars. Black trees became visible before the Great Bear, dark houses and the monstrous shape of a barn loomed up to the night sky. The silence was only broken by the movements of a rat or a bird in the hedge, the waning lament of a farm dog, and, always, regular hoarse gasps of cattle standing out day and night in their waterlogged pastures.

Coming into Ahascragh I was disagreeably surprised when a

police car stopped beside me and a guard asked me curtly what
I was doing. When I murmured about O'Sullivan Beare, his
eyes narrowed as he tried to sum me up . . . hippy, drunk,
trouble-maker from the North . . . happily I thought of Mr
Joyce and mentioned him. "That's all right then. Good luck."
He pulled up the window and drove away.

I walked uneasily through the main street of Ahascragh at
three-thirty. Only a telephone booth was lit up like a shrine.
Out on the other side there was more flat land; above the stars
were taking on an icy glitter and the air was becoming shiver-
ingly cold. I stamped my feet on the tarmac as I marched along.
Somewhere near here on the bog was Gowla farm, where bog
had been turned into pasture. It had long been the dream of
people in Ireland, like alchemy. "How many human beings,"
wrote the Reverend Sharkey, a native of Roscommon, "who
now languish in penury and drag out a listless life of inaction
and inutility, ending with the infirmities of premature old age,
might be employed in useful labour, and thereby rendered
comfortable and happy, if the bogs were once reduced to a
state of cultivation?" The most ambitious schemes for making
use of boglands were devised by Richard Pockrich, an eighteenth-century millionaire, known as Projecting Pock because
of all his projects. He had the idea of reclaiming all the bogs in
Ireland and planting them with vineyards; failing that,
bamboo. Another Irishman who had schemes to drain "the
bogs and morasses of Ireland" was the Duke of Wellington—
there is a note to the effect in the Irish State Papers. At Gowla
the Irish Sugar Company began a lavishly expensive experiment in 1961. Carrots, potatoes and celery have been grown
on the wasteland, and today eight hundred acres produce three
thousand tons of grass which is processed into meal for cattle.

The road was long, and I walked on hour after hour under
the beautiful chilled monotony of the sky. Then the dawn
came up behind me as the first lighted-up house appeared, a
startling landmark. Slowly the world changed as black objects
took on colour and dimensions; in this field there were sheep,
in that garden the two crazy-looking trees were monkey
puzzles, and so on. I was about five miles from Ballygar, too
close for comfort. I knew from past experience that nothing

much would open before nine o'clock and I would have to wait around. When I reached the Killian river I sat down to munch a few dates and drain the last of the coffee, but it was too cold to linger for long. My rucksack sparkled with frost. I was feeling pleasantly tired and none the worse for the night's drenching.

The stars had vanished to be replaced by a dun-coloured morning when a little after eight-thirty I reached the outskirts of Ballygar. The shops were grimly shut and the only sound came from the town's rookery. What do you do under such circumstances? I took off my rucksack and went down to the church, which was open. For a time I took an inconspicuous place in the back and sat half-dozing behind a few pious ladies and the soft glow of candles. Then I went outside and wandered about, stopping before the inscription to a famous local son. "Patrick Sarsfield Gilmore, Father of the Concert Band in America . . . this plaque was erected in 1969 by the Ballygar Memorial Committee." I read it and reread it until I knew it by heart, wondering about Mr Gilmore. Later when I had a chance of looking him up I found that he was the son of a monumental mason who emigrated to America in 1848 to become an imaginative impresario. He organized a series of giant concerts which featured orchestras with a thousand players and choruses running to several thousands. For his greatest efforts, the World's Peace Jubilee of 1872, he had a special building erected in Boston, Massachusetts, to accommodate a hundred thousand people. The monster orchestra (for whom he had Johann Strauss as a guest conductor) included some regiments of artillery firing guns, special chimes of bells, the band of the Coldstream Guards, the band of the Kaiser Franz Regiment from Berlin, and the Boston Fire Brigade which "played" a hundred anvils for the Anvil Chorus from *Il Trovatore*. Among the rewards he received for his pains were a goblet filled with gold, and a gold and ivory baton studded with diamonds. The boy from Ballygar did well.

By now some men were brushing down the main square after the cattle market the day before.

"Press the bell on the B.B.," one of them advised me. "It belongs to my sister."

Eventually a girl appeared rubbing the sleep out of her eyes.
I was tired too.

In the bedroom I took off my boots from which arose two
trickles of steam, like crude kettles. When I awoke it was midday, and I had the disorientated feeling of a long-distance air
traveller. I was lying fully clothed under a Sacred Heart on an
old-fashioned bedstead which swamped the small room. Outside in the square the same men were still sweeping away tufts
of manure.

In the dining-room a leg of the red plastic-topped table was
held up by a book, and some religious pictures lay piled on the
floor waiting to be hung. The staff seemed to consist of two
teenage girls, one of whom was in the kitchen preparing the
food for me and two young unmarried bank officials. The other
brought me in a giant steak, smothered with onions, and chips,
the best I have ever eaten.

"Did you enjoy it? If you didn't we'll cook you another!"

Ballygar was another town influenced by the patronage of
landlords, with a line of trees planted along the wide main
street, a market place and a diamond at one end with a fountain. At the opposite end was the gateway to the estate. The
landlords were O'Kellys, who belonged to an ancient Irish
family that became Anglicized. During the Elizabethan wars,
like so many other clans, they divided into two, the Queen's
O'Kellys and the rebel O'Kellys. An O'Kelly from Aughrim
marched with O'Donnell to Kinsale, while the head of the
family who lived at Castlekelly served as a captain of foot
under the Earl of Clanricarde against the disaffected Irish.

The last O'Kelly of Ballygar, who died in 1877, built himself
a fine castle. "Though a high Tory and a professed Orange-
man," wrote a friend, "he is the kindest and noblest soul I ever
met, a perfect Milesian gentleman, but softened by English
civilization and the lessons of St Paul." A few miles outside
Ballygar he commemorated his wives by building a round
tower on which there is an inscription: "Sacred to the memory
of the two wives of D. H. O'Kelly. Both Englishwomen, they
set themselves to the duties of their Irish house, and lived
beloved by high and low and died universally lamented." In
the same ragged graveyard beside the junction between the

rivers Shiveen and Suck, O'Kelly himself is buried in a vault which has been ransacked for its lead coffin. "He was chieftain of the Branch of the O'Kelly's of Screen and candidate for the Kingship of Hynamy. He was an earnest Christian and a kind friend."

The rivers form the county boundary between Galway and Roscommon, and the Suck at this point divides the old estates of the O'Kellys and the Talbots who were relations of the Earls of Shrewsbury. Their house, demolished by the last owner in the time of the civil war, made a heap of old bricks which did not rank very high in my estimate of Irish ruins. What atmosphere it lacked, however, was retained in the sad recently-closed Church of Ireland, where damp Bibles, torn prayer books and old hassocks still lay among torn-up floor-boards, thrown wildly round the pulpit. On the walls monuments to the O'Kellys and Talbots spelt out smug sentiments on clean white marble. But for how long, before the walls themselves crumbled? There are less than five hundred Church of Ireland parishioners in County Galway, which must work out at about one for each decayed church. Elsewhere in the country one church became a dance hall, another a restaurant, and so on. The Bishop of Killaloe, present when yet another was being turned into a folk museum, spoke sadly of how "they are hallowed by the prayers and worship of generations of good people. They are impregnated with the emotions of these people. Their children are baptized here, they are married here, and they began their last journey here. Because of this they tend to be careful about what happens to such buildings. They could be demolished or sold or left to become a ruin of doubtful charm."

> When churches fall completely out of use
> What shall we turn them into, if we shall keep
> A few cathedrals chronically on show,
> Their parchment, plate and pyx in locked cases,
> And let the rest rent-free to rain and sheep?
> Shall we avoid them as unlucky places?

CHAPTER FOURTEEN

Ballygar—Ballinlough

At dawn the following day O'Sullivan crossed Slieve Mary,
beat the drums and displayed the standards taken from the
English—pretending that his men were loyalists and
English, so that the food might not be hidden by the
inhabitants.

Philip O'Sullivan

THE MAIN STREET of Ballygar all the way down to the diamond was icy, and the school children were happily sliding on
it. Beyond the village the wrinkles in the ploughed fields were
filled in with snow, grass and dead fern stiffened and trees
glittered. I went over to the grounds of Aughrane Castle, the
old seat of the O'Kellys, who, according to an envious critic,
"swayed the sceptre for this district for generations; but the
downfall of Aughrim and Athlone put an end to their preten-
sions". In the nineteenth century, when they had abandoned
the old faith, they prospered on a smaller scale with a model
estate, an ornamental lake, a brand new castle, and acres of
rolling parkland which the same critic described as "stinking
with moors and marshes".

A few steps into the place I was approached by a thin chilled
man on a bike. Hopping off, he came straight over.

"I am looking for a cow that has escaped. Have you seen her?
No?" He paused. "Well, sir, I am skint and would be grateful
for the loan of a shilling." A shilling changed hands, and he
rode off at full speed, shouting "*Viva Inglaterra!*"

Rather narked at being taken for that rare species, the
English tourist, I inspected some frosty rubble. The castle was
burnt during the troubles, when a troop of British cavalry had
been sent over from neighbouring Mount Talbot and used the
place for storing hay and forage. An old man I met in Ballygar
told me that the local people set it alight with gusto. There was
bad feeling between them and the O'Kellys since the whole

estate was planted with trees a few years before that time. He could still remember the indignation this caused in an area where farming land was extremely scarce. The trees had been ripped up as soon as they were planted, and twenty men were sent off to Galway jail before the local parish priest was able to sort things out. The scheme went ahead remorselessly so that all the good land hereabouts is covered with trees except for one small piece that escaped the planter's zeal and survived as a football pitch. It took me a good hour to struggle out of the O'Kelly jungle on to a small byroad below Mount Mary, whose flanks were covered with yet more glum lines of firs, these ones the responsibility of the Forestry Commission. The sun was melting the snow and they dripped and wept, and water filled up the bursting drains. The site of an old abbey was marked on my map, but a farmer told me that the walls had been knocked down and made into a shed. I saw a huge ring-fort as big as a town looming out of alder and willow. Then I climbed the gentle slopes of the hill.

At one time Mount Mary, Slieve Fuire, was heavily popu-lated. "There was a weight of people here before the famine." Like Glendav, the old pasture and villages, the traces of old fields and the abandoned walls of cottages are all shrouded in firs. From the top, over the nest of woodlands, there is a good view northward over a tussocky brown landscape. The bogs are horizontal brown lines, the plantations bright green squares, and squeezed among them are a few pieces of arable land emerging from a film of melting snow. Bog seems to stretch ahead interminably towards Roscommon and Leitrim.

When O'Sullivan Beare passed over the summit of Mount Mary, having marched here from Aughrim without any dawdling around Ballygar, he did not pause but continued straight on. The mountain and surrounding countryside were deep in snow. It seems to have been the first time on the march that he experienced any other weather besides a succession of clear frosty days. I wondered what would have happened if there had been rain during the early part of the journey. Rain such as I had experienced might have put off many of those who attacked him and dampened their enthusiasm and gun-powder. But perhaps the refugees would have been trapped at the swollen Shannon. Now the cold was his greatest enemy. Irish people, like the Scots, were used to exposure in severe weather, and seem to have got through a good deal of cold and frost without wearing anything on their legs. The delightful description of Highland customs written by "John Elder" to Henry VIII in 1542 was almost certainly equally true of Ireland. "Please it your Majestie to understande that we of all people can tollerit, suffir and away best with colde, for boithe somer and wyntir (except when the froest is mooste vehemonte) goynge alwaies bair leggide and bair footide, our delite and pleisure is not only in huntynge of redd deir, wolves, foxes, and graies [badgers] wherof we abound and have great plentiie, but also in rynninge, leapinge, swymynge, shootynge and throwynge of dartis; therfor in so moche as we use and delite so to go alwaies, the tendir delicalt gentillmen of Scotland call us Redshankes."

But the cold that O'Sullivan now experienced was bitter, and from Mount Mary many of his followers, weakened by long hunger, would die from exposure. His soldiers had been halved since he set out, and he had about a hundred left. No one kept count of the civilians. The direct route from here to his destination in Leitrim would have been towards Elphin, but since he felt that at all costs he must avoid another confrontation with a well-armed enemy, he took his exhausted people on a wide detour to the north-west into the heart of Connacht. It was a route that meant many extra miles of marching over pathless territory covered with bog and scrub forest, deep in snow.

I went towards Glinsk, a landmark on his march, through a new and different countryside. Many of the dingy patches of brown and green visible from Mount Mary changed into numerous little hills and hollows with farms tucked into their sides linked by a system of untarred country lanes. When I took one at random, I found that walking through the mud and the long narrow puddles in the deep ruts was an unexpected pleasure. The old dirt road has an intimacy, an ageless sense of belonging to the scene, and nothing changes the whole tenor of rural life more quickly than a coating of tarmac. All the wild places are trimmed and neatened, and the smell of petrol drifts over the country; because of the ceaseless efforts of the County

Councils who are convinced that tarred roads must be among the basic needs of mankind, there are very few roads left like those Synge used to walk along. It seems unnecessary to tie down every remote section of the countryside with these bands of iron. I suppose one day when about five or six untarred roads are left they will be preserved as national monuments.

The sky disappeared again; a wind sprayed behind me and a long hayrick looked like a battleship against the storm clouds. I walked with a man leading a donkey cart containing a placid white sow which he was bringing to a neighbouring boar.

"This is the worst land in Ireland," he said as we walked along. "There is only one man in every house, and the rest are gone to England."

He pointed out the landmarks; a cottage with a field of rushes growing up to the main door where a widow lived; when she died it would be planted. Only five years ago there were twelve houses lived in, now there were five. The fir-trees, ranged and even as the crosses on a battlefield, were similar indications of death and failure. Later he cheered up, talking about the good price for donkeys. He kept a few, and had sold a piebald to an English dealer for a hundred pounds. A friend of his made a fortune during the summer months giving donkey rides on Galway strand.

We parted company when he turned down to a farm to take his plump passenger to her tryst. Near Glinsk, quite unexpectedly, and all the more beautiful for that, I came upon the ruined abbey and church of Ballynakill. There was a fine grim effigy of a knight on the wall of the church, dressed in armour with a helmet and a sword. This was William de Burgo, who was known as *Liam Garbh*, William the Rough, because of his uncouth ways. When his sister killed his infant son in a quarrel, he revenged himself by putting her astride a wild horse with weights tied to her feet, and in this position she remained until her body split in two. More to the point, this knight was probably a near ancestor of the MacDavitt Burkes who attacked O'Sullivan when he passed by. They had rounded up all the foodstuffs in the neighbourhood inside the castle, and O'Sullivan tried to get it from them by the simple ruse of disguising his force as royalists. Drums were beaten, his soldiers marched up to the castle gates in good order, displaying the banners they had captured at Aughrim as their own. But the MacDavitts, undeceived, kept their gates firmly shut and O'Sullivan's men had to retreat. They hurried on over the snow without further supplies, with some of the MacDavitts in pursuit.

Nothing remains of the old castle they approached, apart from a few bits of wall; but nearby is a magnificent fortress-like building, "a terrific roofless pile, haunted by a colony of rats", the ruin of a tower house built later in the mid-seventeenth century. Below the tower house of Glinsk stretched a slab of bogland and trees reaching down to the River Suck, the sort of territory marked on maps with little grassy eyebrows. When a foolish woman living nearby told me that there was a track across it, I made a half-baked decision to try to follow it. After about three hundred yards, the track gave up, and at the same time that I was treading through rich peaty brown water, a thunderous shower of rain broke over my back, blotting out the scenery. I reminded myself how bogs had been used as a means of escape by men like Brian O'Rourke in 1589 who "took to the bogs to escape from his distractors". Englishmen foundered, Irishmen skipped over them, although there were occasions when the Irish were successfully pursued over bog. By 1571 Sir John Perrot had attacked the rebels near Kilmallock across a bog. "The Lord President caused his men to light from their horses, to rip off their boots, and to leppe into the bogges, taking with them their petronels and lighthorsemen's staves, instead of pikes, after which they charged the enemy in the bogges, over-threw them and cut off fifty of their heads, the which they carried home with them unto Kilmallock, and put the heads around the market cross."

Two hundred years later Irishmen were still known as bog-trotters. Not only did they use turf for fuel, but the soft strands of bog cotton became material for stuffing mattresses, and bog beans and bog sorrel were eaten as blood purifiers and cures for heart trouble and other complaints. Even today one sixth of the country is still covered in bogs which are formed mainly from sphagnum moss growing and spreading in the damp like yeast. I waded in the slime, avoiding most of the worst spots, old cuttings well camouflaged with dead grass and ling. I have heard these called priest's holes and believed that men could drown in them, but the two or three that I investigated in error were only thigh level, and there was no danger, only the discomfort of being wetter than usual.

Just before dusk I reached a ridge of dry land and pulled myself out of the squelching water. A coquettish evening sun was shining on the village of Ballymoe, and I could lower my umbrella. My thoughts were of bacon and eggs.

The door of the guesthouse opened and there was a scuttle of children in the passage.

"What is it?" a voice called above the din of radio and babies.

"There's a strange man, Mammy."

When she saw me, I knew at once that my appearance was against me, even before I was given the hoary old excuse that the mother-in-law was staying and there wasn't room. She had every right to send me packing, but I stumped off down the road in a fury. Almost immediately I was saved from further fruitless searching by the friendly offer of a lift to another guesthouse a couple of miles out of town, a paradise where I could enjoy a bath and dry my clothes in front of a turf fire.

In the morning I went back to Ballymoe and across the County Bridge, underneath which the Suck appeared again, having looped around, still forming the county boundary. From here it flows southwards to where I saw it outside Ballygar, then on to Ballinasloe, ultimately joining up with the Shannon. At Ballymoe, it was a black line that wound through low-lying water meadows among banks of red osiers; it looked just like a snake, and later I read a Victorian writer who thought the same thing. Ballymoe, lying between the Suck and its tributary, the Island river, is supposed to be at least 140 years older than Dublin. Queen Maeve of Connacht built a fort, and Fionn MacCool sent his warriors here to look for game, but all they could find was some old scald crows. At one end of the street was another abandoned Church of Ireland growing fungi and weeds, and at the other an enormous long wooden hardware store, outside which on both sides of the road scores of old bath tubs formed a grand avenue into the village. They sold steadily to farmers as water troughs for cattle.

I walked into Roscommon, where the fields soon turned into rushes, another immense bog filled the distance, and a very straight road crossed it in the direction of Slieve O'Flynn. *Ros* meant a wooded or pleasant place, and *Comain* was a missionary who christianized it. By the side of the road some tinkers lived around a tarpaulin stretched on a wicker frame over an expanse of mud strewn with tins, splinters of orange crate, prams, puppies, bottles, and wet cardboard boxes. Rags had dropped on the hedge with the rain, and the red-headed children playing in the chill wind looked withered, like frost-bitten geraniums. There was a saying during the Famine about Ballymoe—"The day you go there, buy your own bread, or that day you will go hungry and fasting". The piebald horses nibbling at brambles could well end up being eaten like O'Sullivan's horses, since many itinerants breed them to be slaughtered for export.

Further down I paused to visit a solitary old man with a good knowledge of the neighbourhood. He lived in a thatched cottage in which nothing much had changed during the course of his lifetime. The dresser still faced an open fire which had a crane carrying a steaming black kettle, there was a rough deal table, a couple of chairs and the essential rudiments of comfort. Outside across the road he pointed out a small field where he used to grow corn and use the flail, but now it had reverted to bog.

His gentle old face relaxed in smiles as he sat down in front of the fire and gave me a cup of tea.

"Blast you, aren't you a great man doing the road?"

He told me about Ballymoe's staunch history of Republican-ism—how Ernie O'Mally had escaped from two members of the R.I.C. on 27th May, 1918. The barracks was the birthplace of Eamonn Ceannt, one of the leaders of the Rising who was shot, and is remembered by many people as the man who played martial music on bagpipes before the Pope. Another man they shot out in India, James J. Daly, the leader of the Connaught Rangers' mutiny, was also born here.

At its worst a bog is the "horrid wilderness" of eighteenth-century travellers, at its best it has the freedom and purity of a desert and the same feeling of limitless space. Bog air was believed to be healthy. "Our having remained so long free from plagues," wrote a Mr Parten in 1802, "might be attributed to the antiseptic and astringent nature of our bogs and marshes, whose exhalations must also be of that disposition." In the sixteenth century there was bog everywhere, much more so than forest. "But I must confess myself to have been deceived," Fynes Moryson wrote, "in the common fame that all Ireland is woody, having found in my long journey from Armagh to Kinsale few or no woods along the way, except the great woods of Offaly, and some low scrubby places which they called Glins." Most of the forest was in the western half of the country. But the bogs were everywhere. John Derricke described one in the doggerel under a fine woodcut: "a shakyng bogge, a forte of passying strength, from where a certain fire is drawne to sheeld from winter's colde".

Near Trien I fell in with a returned Irish-American in a red checked shirt and asked him how he felt to be back. "It's dead, there's no action here," he said. "But it's a good place for sleeping." Ahead was Slieve O'Flynn which had been a landmark for O'Sullivan Beare's exhausted people, who had now been marching from Aughrim without stopping for a distance of almost fifty miles. From Killimor eight miles beyond the Shannon's banks they had gone to Aughrim, fought a battle, and then come on all this way. The snow that covered the countryside must have been an unusual sight for those who had come from the coast of West Cork. The heroic quality of the earlier part of the retreat now changes to a narrative of utter misery. Over the miles, walking night and day, many men and women must have fallen out of the column to die in the snow. Then, at the approach to Slieve O'Flynn the snow turned to a torrent of rain which was so heavy "that they were scarce able to bear the weight of their soaked clothes". While they were trying to camp on the slope of the mountain under the trees, they were warned that the place was surrounded by the enemy. This warning, which seems to have come from a friendly local, was the first occasion that the party had received any sort of help from strangers during the whole journey. The enemy turned out to be the MacDavitts, who had kept on their trail all the way from Glinsk. Earlier on the march O'Sullivan might have prepared a fortified encampment and set about beating them off, but now he did not think that his soldiers were up to it. Instead he decided wearily to struggle on again through the most atrocious possible conditions and lose his pursuers. First he ordered huge fires to be lit to make it appear that the refugees were preparing to spend the night on the mountain slopes. Then in total darkness they forced their way through a wood which consisted of unusually dense undergrowth and brambles. They even managed to bring the surviving horses through it. The snow was an added impediment to their progress. "Quite tired out," wrote Philip O'Sullivan, "they sank into deep snow as if into pits, and when lifting one another were rather dragged down by their comrades, rather than the latter pulled out. Nor was darkness the least of their trials, for if any stars did shine, the boughs of the trees, interwoven with one another, formed an unbroken screen and shut out the light, so they moved almost as blind, following only the sound of familiar voices. And moreover, the winds rustling the branches made a louder sound than mere whistles, and made leaving difficult." In a recent book about Irish woodlands, this night journey is quoted to demonstrate how impenetrable an Irish wood could be.

Slieve O'Flynn seems hardly a hill at all; only the flatness of the surrounding bogland makes its gentle slope at all noticeable. A faint edge of bluish mist had begun to creep over the bog as I walked up through wet land gone wild, with a few inhabited cottages. Inside a window a diminutive Infant of Prague, still wrapped in a plastic drape, watched me pass. On the far side of the hill the firs began to impose their own brand of mediocrity once more. Below them, however, was the uneven outline of real trees, forming part of some old estate. Under oaks, elms and beeches was undergrowth which seemed to emulate the brambles through which O'Sullivan's people struggled. Clawing on hands and knees, I came out beyond it into the deserted yard of a Georgian house; shutters were drawn, gates boarded up, and the only signs of humanity I could find were some spent cartridge shells. But it is unwise to assume that every shuttered and ruinous place is deserted. Further on when I was nosing round an incredibly decrepit little house with curtains drawn and grass growing up to the front door, an indignant head peered out of one of the windows and asked me what the hell I was doing.

CHAPTER FIFTEEN

Ballinlough—Ballaghaderreen

The natives under MacDavitt . . . followed the track of
the fugitive and having come up with him about nine o'clock
attacked with missiles until he reached the top of a high
hill.

Philip O'Sullivan

IN BALLINLOUGH THE shops were painted light green and
Prussian blue and topped with old-fashioned gilt lettering,
while the curved panels of their windows were edged with
little Greek columns and pediments. The square was dominated
by an austere new memorial within an iron cage, put up by
American subscription to the men who were killed during an
attack on the R.I.C. barracks on 14th September, 1920.

> They started here a living flame
> That nothing can withstand.

The town was suffering from an epidemic of flu, and the
ashen-faced lady who served in the bar told me in a whisper
that she would have been glad to put me up at any other time,
except that only this morning she had got out of bed herself. I
began to feel disgustingly healthy and ashamed of myself, enjoying my pint as other drinkers coughed and spluttered around
me. I was lucky to find accommodation elsewhere, and went to
bed to the accompaniment of a *ceilidhe* band downstairs, where
a crowd was singing and dancing with the frantic enjoyment of
survivors of a plague. Sometime after ten a soloist sang "Mother
Mine" in a piercing tenor that made my bedroom light tremble;
I listened to the "Patriot Game" and "Men behind the Wire",
before, lulled by some jigs, I woke suddenly after midnight to
the final chorus of the "Soldiers' Song".

"Saturday is a quiet morning," the girl who served my ten
o'clock breakfast told me placidly, looking out on the postman's

van, a couple of sprawling dogs, and curtained windows pulled
tight shut. I took the road out of town, past a few stones that
remained of a MacEgan castle, a derelict landlord's house and
the dismembered railway station. Lough O'Flynn was a long
ovular depression fringed with reeds and sooty mud banks, the
source of the Suck. I thought of the sources of other rivers; in
Spain I had seen the mountain birthplace of the Guadalquivir
in a wood, bubbling from a fountain set in black rock. In 1894
Lord Curzon was the first European to visit the source of the
Oxus pouring out of two remote ice caverns with a ceaseless
tumult of grinding and crunching. The source of the Suck,
trickling from Lough O'Flynn through a drain scarring the soft
bogland, lacked the same heroic origins.

This country is associated with the Wills family to whom
Oscar Wilde was connected. It may not have been a blood
relationship, but the Wildes were proud of it and included
Wills among Oscar's many Christian names. The house I had
peered into the day before had once belonged to the Wills. The
original Wilde who settled in Connacht in 1759 married a
daughter of the O'Flynn of Lough O'Flynn whose brown
waters stretched before me.

Giraldus wrote of Ireland as "uneven, mountainous, soft,
woody, exposed to winds and so boggy that you might see the
water stagnating on the mountains". His geography was
sound, and it still remains a piercingly accurate description of
Roscommon. "This rather uninteresting country," as Hayward
called it, still has over 80,000 acres of bog. "It is rare," said a
Mr Weld, quoted by the Halls in their nineteenth-century
travel book, "to find four miles together without the occurrence
of bogs." Most of the morning I walked over the red-brown
waste, with nothing to break up the long road except the
occasional car whisking past, the odd cyclist and a postman
blowing his whistle as he pushed his bike along. "The children
will come out to me." A Pied Piper's progress among ditches
and watery fields saved him many extra journeys to isolated
farmhouses.

At midday I could see Lough Glinn with its trees, a line of
shiny black rooftops and church spire. The clang of the angelus
came over the bog from a great distance. It took a long time to

walk to the village and find the lake overlooked by the former residence of the Dillon family, which is a convent belonging to the Franciscan Missionaries of Mary. An active old nun, her face yellowed from living many years in the tropics, showed me around. The Norman founder of the Dillon family came to Ireland in 1185. Dillons changed religions as it suited them, and about thirty years after O'Sullivan Beare came here a Sir Lucas Dillon was offered the manor house and castle of Lough Glinn. A member of another branch of the family kept the old faith, went to France and created Dillon's Brigade. The Dillons at Lough Glinn built up their imposing mansion partly from the ruins of the old Fitzgerald castle on their grounds, dammed up the lake to make it more imposing as a pretty birthday present for a Lady Dillon, and finally, after the Act of Union, cleared out of Roscommon altogether to go and settle in less harsh surroundings at Ditchley Park in Oxfordshire. As absentees they sowed the usual dragon's teeth by appointing a string of agents to run their affairs in Ireland.

I followed the nun who skipped agilely along a bank above the lake to show me the castle on the far side. When it belonged to the Fitzgeralds it had been a substantial fortress with towers at every corner, and although it was quarried to build the house, as late as the eighteenth century there was enough left of it to house prisoners on their way to the county jail.

"They locked up priests here. Now it is dangerous and will have to be pulled down."

When I left her, she was thinking of Mandalay. From 1929 to 1966 she had been out east, first in Ceylon, then in Burma, never coming home on leave until the missionaries were ejected by the Burmese government. "If I had the chance I would pack my bags and go tonight." She had loved the people, the land, even the religion. "You're so good, sister, you should be a Bhuddist," they had told her. Coming back to Ireland and seeing Lough Glinn for the first time in forty-one years had been a cruel shock. Her family were long dead, the place utterly lonely and drained of people. The girls were gone who used to make the lace (a practice that must have been a little like recruiting children to make carpets in Persia). The convent had been famous for its lace, but today there were no young people to come and learn. Now that vocations had fallen off no new nuns came into the order, and the few left with herself had turned the place into a home for old women.

I retired to the least sad spot in Lough Glinn, a bar, naturally, a snug designed for shared intimacies or private reflection in the dark. It was of the Russian type, divided in two with the front half used as a shop, selling rashers in brown tissue paper and boots hanging from the ceiling. A potbellied stove kept us all warm, the women buying their provisions on one side, the silent old men drinking their pints away from the forlorn landscape that would break your heart.

When I left I asked the barman if he thought there might be accommodation in Frenchpark.

"It's a derelict old place; there's nothing to be seen."

"What about Lough Gara?"

"There's nothing there too. Except the scenery and it's a bit like a desert."

Furious driving rain lashed at my oilskin on the road to Frenchpark. "Showery weather!" called out a man wearing an old coat split up the back, a hat pulled over his eyes and nose revealing nothing but a richly stubbled chin. I trudged on to a bleak village grotesquely named Fairymount, where a few more tremors of blue appeared in the sky. On one side of the road, a badger clouted in the dark by a car lay in a bloody heap. Even though it was the middle of January there were flies on it. In the sixteenth century badgers were eaten as a luxury.

"The local Council should remove it," the man in the shop opposite kept saying. "That's what we pay them for."

This seems to be the most probable route of O'Sullivan Beare. In a way it may appear strange that, while on previous occasions he never feared meeting his enemies, he should now take such pains to avoid them. But his exhausted troops, reduced to little more than a fleeing rabble, were just about incapable of another battle, so much so that they had preferred to move on from Slieve O'Flynn after a forty-hour march, rather than stay to face the MacDavitts.

They would know that this countryside would be more friendly, or at least less dangerous, than elsewhere. Two years before the chiefs of the area had joined with O'Donnell in marching to Kinsale. After the battle most of them submitted, and technically speaking O'Sullivan was marching through royalist countryside, but he might well avoid conflict with them because of old loyalties. In this remote place there were less pressures on local people to take sides than there had been in Munster.

O'Sullivan wished to avoid going by Boyle to the east, where he would have had to pass close to a small garrison at Boyle Abbey held under Sir Oliver Lambert, the Lord President of Connacht. After the abbeys were suppressed many of them were taken over as military posts—Bantry Abbey, where Carew brought his men before Dunboy is another example of this process.

The English had established a chain of fortresses in Roscommon and Sligo which were constantly being attacked and changing hands. At this time, after Kinsale, most of them had surrendered to the crown, and several of them, like Boyle Abbey, were garrisoned by Queen's troops. But among them there was one to which O'Sullivan might have made his way. This was Ballymote, to the west in Sligo, which, after being in the hands of the English for thirteen years, had been recaptured and auctioned off by the Clann Donnaugh for four hundred pounds and three hundred sows. The purchaser was O'Donnell, who later set out from here on his march to relieve Kinsale. Ballymote did not surrender to the English until later in 1603. It seems to have been a good possibility for O'Sullivan. Although it was about a dozen miles westward from the direct route to Leitrim, it had the advantage of being on a route outside the Curlieu mountains. But there is no evidence that O'Sullivan considered making his way there; he was in strange country, and perhaps he was unsure of Ballymote's position, or more certain of a welcome from O'Rourke in Leitrim. He chose the more difficult undertaking to make for Leitrim across the Curlieus. In these mountains he would lose his way.

Before they reached the Curlieus his people rested and ate on a hill, somewhere beside Frenchpark. Philip O'Sullivan described this hill as "high", but he was wrong; there is nothing more than the very gentlest rise out of bog near Frenchpark. The refugees were still threatened by enemies, and in spite of their urgent need for rest, they found that they had to fight the battle they had tried to avoid. Their tormentors were still the MacDavitts, whom they had eluded at Slieve O'Flynn. When they discovered that the camp fires on the mountain were deserted, the MacDavitts had continued their pursuit, and managed to catch up, probably because they knew more about the countryside than the exhausted O'Sullivans floundering in the dark. After that endless march through snow there were now only about sixty soldiers left who were capable of fighting. "They swore they would rather hazard the worst in fighting the enemy than quit this spot before they had taken food or sleep." O'Sullivan, shouting encouragement, managed to push them together into some sort of battle order. In the event the attackers did not give much trouble, and they were driven off after a skirmish. Then at last the marchers could rest for the first time in fifty miles since they had camped on the west side of the Shannon at Killimor. They threw themselves down and slept for six hours.

When they awoke they killed two more horses for eating, probably the last. The skins were made up into emergency footwear. One can only speculate who had shoes and who had not. Most of the soldiers probably wore traditional brogues "single soled, more rudely sewed than a shoe but more strong, sharp at the toe, and a flap of leather at the heels to put them on". In earlier campaigns the kern had often gone barefoot, but in later pictures of the period they wore shoes; in spite of the exuberant behaviour of barefoot highlanders reported by "John Elder", it is difficult to imagine people making these forced marches without some sort of protection for their feet. In the normal way many of the women and servants would have gone barefoot; but at this stage of the journey the survivors must have wrapped their feet in rags at the very least. When it came to handing around the horsemeat, once again O'Sullivan, his cousin, old Dermot of Dursey, and Dermot O'Huallachain refused to eat it.

At Fairymount there was a view towards Lough Gara and the grey line of the Curlieus, the last mountains that O'Sullivan Beare had to cross. More of the badlands in the distance. When the sun came out, the bog would change to a bright gold, and

right:
View from
Kesh Caves,
Co. Sligo

left:
Tombstone
of knight,
Glinsk

Entrance to megalithic tomb, Carrowkeel

Monument commemorating
O'Sullivan Beare's march, Leitrim

ARMS OF O'SULLIVAN
HERE ON JANUARY 14TH 1603
BRIAN OG O'ROURKE WELCOMED
DONAL O'SULLIVAN BEARE
AND HIS FOLLOWERS
AFTER THEIR EPIC MARCH
FROM GLENGARRIFF IN 14 DAYS
THOUGH ONE THOUSAND STARTED WITH HIM
ONLY 35 THEN REMAINED
16 ARMED MEN 18 NON-COMBATANTS
AND ONE WOMAN,
THE WIFE OF THE CHIEF'S UNCLE
DERMOT O'SULLIVAN

around the cottages marooned in reeds there was a stirring of life and colour under the unexpected flash of light. Villages and church towers stood out like islands and lighthouses. Although this was Roscommon, the sky was a Connemara sky such as Paul Henry painted, bursting with fat cauliflower clouds against the blue edges of mountains and the empty road.

Frenchpark had a frontier atmosphere, since it was nearer to the lake and mountains, and the bog was coming to an end. Built around a crossroads, it used to thrive with its market house, monastery and lordly estate, but the usual things have blighted it. Nearby Charlestown, described by John Healy in *Death of an Irish Town* is much the same . . . "You named a dozen others in Barrack Street who were men when you were a boy, and they are gone, married and settled in England, America or Australia or Canada, wherever the English language is spoken. And you come back to Paddy Casey which has shut down . . . and you are forced to say, 'the town is really getting shook, isn't it?'" In Frenchpark there were peeling shopfronts and boarded up houses; an ancient enamel advertisement nailed to the wall referred to Raleigh, the All Steel Bicycle, and a solitary new building with Western Emporium Bargains Supermarket splashed across its front was shut down. The pubs were quite busy.

I was told that the estate used to belong to people called de Freyne, a name that jerked a memory. I had been at school with a de Freyne . . . something about holidays in Roscommon. And here was his place behind the old estate wall that bounded one side of the village. The ruined house abandoned in 1954, the walled garden with its withered apple orchard, the circular pigeon house overgrown with ivy and grass . . . that sort of thing was familiar enough. It was the dead trees that gave the park-land its particular atmosphere of desolation. They were like a fleet caught in a storm. Some had heeled over, others had fallen with their roots exposed, and the whitened branches, lying scattered everywhere among the splintered trunks, looked as if they had been kicked about. Landlord's trees. After the woods were cut, an act of 1698 made it compulsory to grow trees on new estates. For the first time beech, Spanish chestnut, lime, walnut and sycamore made their appearance in Ireland. Only

H

sycamores escaped out of the estate parks and into the hedges and hills; the rest of them, lining roads and avenues and grouped in planned woodlands, are literally planters' trees. Some of the older specimens may be among the first of their kind in the country; and when they are destroyed they may be the last.

"Lord de Freyne, of whom the public has heard so much," wrote Michael J. F. McCarthy in 1902 in his *Priests and People in Ireland*, "is, like myself and the denizens of the squalid country round his demesne, a Roman Catholic. He is the father of a young family; and he lives within the demesne wall in this un-lovable region all the year round. His existence becomes known to the villagers in Frenchpark, whose dwellings crouch beneath the twelve-foot wall and high beeches, by the occasional pop of the rifle when he shoots an unwary rabbit in the shrubbery. It would be impossible to see a resident landlord more utterly out of touch with the tenantry."

A mile away was a different ruin. Cloonshanville Abbey was founded in 1365 by MacDermot Roe and dedicated to the Holy Cross, although the name may derive from an Irish phrase meaning the retreat of the old leper. Perhaps the large solitary ancient cross a few fields behind it, bent forward like an old man, has some association with the name and dedication. The Abbey stood high above the bog and fields of rushes, a lonely ivy-covered tower, two carved doorways, pieces of wall and the dead. "O Almighty and eternal God, have mercy on the soul of Judy O'Connor . . . November 1790." Five years ago the main chancel window was still standing, a good example of Gothic tracery. It was knocked when the man who owned the land on which the Abbey stands decided that it might be dangerous and the best thing would be to pull it down.

I slept at the post office. In any post office where the exchange is not automatic, from eight o'clock in the morning to ten at night the family must respond to the peremptory summons of the telephone calling the household to duty. The baby, the sponge batter, the boiling milk, must be abandoned instantly to calls to and from Dublin, Tulsk, Castlerea, Boyle, Sligo, voices scratching on the wires, an old woman lying in a cottage, a date at a dance, a pregnant cow, a doctor, men discussing the price of sheep. All evening, at a time when most workers expect a bit of peace, the shrill rings dragged the postmistress out of her chair in front of the fire where she was trying to watch television. I began to find it hard to understand why, even with jobs so scarce, the position of post-master or -mistress is so highly sought after in a rural economy that its award can stir up much local bitterness. Feuds can develop even to the point of wires being cut and telephone poles toppled in the competition to be slave of the exchange.

It rained again next day, and holding my umbrella I walked out of Frenchpark past the punctured walls of the estate, past the rectory where Douglas Hyde spent his boyhood, his father being the clergyman. The church was locked, but in the church-yard I found the grave of the first President of Ireland marked with a Celtic cross. "He was selflessly devoted to the revival of the Irish language and to the collection of its folklore and songs . . .".

From here the rain-soaked tourist made his way towards Ratra House which had been subscribed to Douglas Hyde by the Gaelic League.

"Are you a Yank?" called out a blitzed figure with a sack over his head taking shelter under a tree. When I said that I wished to see the President's old house, he told me with glee that I would have to hurry. "They're after pulling most of it down."

I was only just in time. I made my way through dung-brown puddles over a quagmire across an empty field. The ruin was in the process of being demolished, but rain had stopped work, and enough remained for me to have a picnic under the windowsill, the last to enjoy a meal under its gaping roof. All the formal occasions that had taken place under the benevolent eye of the old President ended in the consumption of a few water-soaked biscuits and a thermos of coffee.

Walking back along the road, I met a farmer who was still indignant that the house had been deroofed by the Gaelic League in 1950.

"All of us around here have a grievance against them. If you meet any of them—tell them that!" So I will.

The cathedral spire of Ballaghaderreen loomed above the

flat countryside. The large bustling town, the main market centre for this part of Roscommon, is an ancient foundation. During the Elizabethan period it was an assize town for Connacht, together with Galway and Roscommon. It was laid out in its present form by an eccentric called Charles Strickland, an English Catholic who lived in the house at Lough Glynn as agent to the absent Viscount Dillon. He took to creating towns about the same time as the Famine. His first was Charlestown which he built purely to spite the Knox family whom he detested. The Knoxs owned the adjoining town of Bellaghy, and he was determined to make Charlestown as good as Bellaghy. In order to encourage people to build on what was virtually a bog, he offered one hundred acres to the first man who put a house together. Having succeeded with Charlestown, he turned his attention to Ballaghaderreen and modelled it on similar ideas, although not with the same motivation or frantic rush. He stipulated that all houses were to be of the same height, with lanes behind each one to give them a rear entrance. Both of Strickland's towns were said to have more pubs than any other of equivalent size in the country.

In Ballaghaderreen the present pub count is sixty-five. This is because the fair still thrives and the marts have not yet made headway here. The fair has always prospered in the town, which according to an advertisement in 1821, benefited from "its central position in the best grazing district of Roscommon", and was "peculiarly advantageous to the disposers and purchasers of cattle". Fairs have this advantage over marts, that when you sell your livestock in a mart, it takes the best part of a week to get your money. In a fair the payment is immediate and the pubs and shops benefit. The sombre monthly festival brings life into a town like Ballaghaderreen, when the streets overflow with cattle and the pubs stay open most of the night. From early morning the cattle are brought into the town, most in lorries, some herded in the old way by men in long coats and gumboots, thumping sticks in the rain. They are arranged facing the pavements in semi-circles like hands of cards for dealers to inspect their hindquarters; steam rises from their backs, and the rainwater running in the gutters and the square in front of the cathedral is bronzed with manure. Dealers' dogs and raw-faced farmers ignore the downpour and the bellowing, while money changes hands with the speed of batons passing in races.

But today was a quiet Sunday: church-going and papers, and groups of men on street corners waiting for the day to pass. I had a drink in a pub where behind frosted doors drinkers sweated with heat from the stove as they stood under a photograph of James Connolly looking like an opera star in bow tie and old-fashioned tail coat. Later in the hotel mini-skirted waitresses in white boots served soup, beef and fruit salad, while the radio, announcing the long vacuity of Sunday afternoon, replaced the chimes of the Westminster bells that had pealed out all morning from the massive cathedral tower. The cathedral that so dominates the town is a mediocre Gothic Revival structure, but its size gives it a sort of magnificence. In recent years the great Gothic interior has been modernized and outside some rather nice trees have been cut down to make room for an asphalt parking lot. Since Vatican II this desire for modernization is apparent all over the country. The interiors of many churches have been tidied up and changed, the altars turned round and pushed out, saints evicted or bundled together well out of prominence in a side aisle or even behind the main door. There is a zeal for simplicity which would have met with the approval of Puritan iconoclasts. Images are out; now they are not even allowed on the stained glass, and windows in new churches are usually blobs of colour.

CHAPTER SIXTEEN

Ballaghaderreen—Bricklieves

Here some of the Catholics got footsore from harsh weather
and long march. O'Connor was so bad that he could not
mount his horse. The highways and horsepaths were
here and there blocked by enemy.

Philip O'Sullivan

SNOW FURRED THE rooftops of Ballaghaderreen and filled the
streets with coffee-coloured slush. Outside the town, where
visibility was lowered to about twenty yards beyond my
umbrella, it had already covered up the bog and blotted out
the countryside between Lough Gara and the mountains. I
struck off a road to flounder across a field and view a curious
nest of four penal altars constructed by a man named Costello,
who also bankrupted himself by building a Gothic mansion
which later became the Bishop's palace. These altars, with their
small arched cavities, reminded me a little of the imitation
hermit cells at Gougane Barra, and had much the same air of
folly. But so, in its way, did the impressive Megalithic stone
fort that I found just behind an estate wall surrounded by a
park full of trees. I climbed around it and explored, noting a
souterrain; then I decided to have a look at the house to which
the trees belonged, and waded over some fields through the
snow, past some store cattle chewing mangels, to the door of a
nineteenth-century baronial manor. It was not in ruins, nor
boarded up, nor deserted nor occupied by nuns, and when I
knocked on the door, I was immediately made welcome. This
was Coolavin, and my host was The MacDermot.

MacDermots have always lived in this area, and once owned
great slabs of Sligo and Roscommon, from the Curlieus to
Elphin, and from Lough Gara to Carrick on Shannon. They
stayed on after the Elizabethan wars without changing their
religion, but adapting to the new conditions. In early 1601 the
MacDermot of the day, styled MacDermot of the Curlieus,

made his submission to Mountjoy. Much of the 30,000 acres of woodland and lake controlled by the family was lost during the confiscations of the seventeenth century, and the MacDermots were driven from their estates at Lough Key to settle in Cool-avin in a forest that was even more remote, and too wild to be desired by settlers. For a while it was a refuge for Irishmen and an exception to the general rules of confiscation; "the woods and bogs near the Corleas" were regarded as one of the fast-nesses of Connacht, but by the time Arthur Young toured, the MacDermots were reduced, and the Princes of Coolavin were living on "not above £700 a year". Still, they were full of consciousness of their rank and the antiquity of their family and their Celtic blood, while feeling contempt for the new settlers. One Prince would not allow his sons to sit down in his presence. When another received Lord Kingsborough, Mr Ponsonby, Mr O'Hara and Mr Sandford at Coolavin he greeted them as they deserved. "O'Hara, you are welcome; Sandford, I am glad to see your mother's son [his mother was an O'Brien]; as to the rest of ye, come in as you can . . .". The present Prince of Coolavin, less suspicious of planter stock, adhered to ancient laws of hospitality and offered me lunch.

Somewhere in the great forested area which stretched over the borders of Sligo and Roscommon, O'Sullivan Beare found himself in a place which was called *diambrach*, a word which can mean either mysterious or tangled. Philip O'Sullivan translated it as *solitudo*; anyway it was somehow even remoter and denser than the forests through which they had passed. Here, feeling themselves safe from any surprise attack, they threw themselves down to sleep; "scattering about without any order, bodies were stretched here and there, heedless of danger, each one resting until daybreak wherever he chanced to settle down." The weather must have lifted, causing a sharp rise in tempera-ture. O'Sullivan kept awake with a group of twelve com-panions, and he ordered a fire to be kindled so that when the stragglers woke they would see the blaze and gather around it.

At this stage of the march, during the long period of rest—or perhaps during the previous day's march—there were a number of desertions. Many of the surviving soldiers were near their homes or within reasonable distance of them. After crossing most of Ireland, they could assess how much in the past year since Kinsale the country had swung round to accept the inevitability of English rule. O'Sullivan himself must have felt increasingly that the chances were poor of O'Neill and his allies continuing the struggle without Spanish aid or the magnetic leadership of O'Donnell. It was understandable that the Connacht men among his soldiers should take the opportunity to slip away to their homes and families instead of following their leader to death or exile.

Even in this jungle their presence did not go unnoticed. For a second time they found a welcome from the local people. Earlier, on Slieve O'Flynn, friendly warnings had told them of the approach of the MacDavitts. Here in the Tangled Wood the natives of the district were attracted by the light of the fire and came to investigate. The Queen's allies did not have the same sort of control over the inhabitants of this remote region, who showed none of the customary hostility towards the outlawed refugees. Instead they not only brought O'Sullivan food, but arranged to deceive any spies attached to the garrison at Boyle who might see the smoke of their fires. They would spread the story that the fires had been lit by woodcutters gathering fuel. They so assured him that he felt safe enough to allow his people to rest for a whole day.

But soon there was news that Lambert had blocked the highways and horsepaths, setting sentinels to watch for him. Judging that he would have to make another night march, he aroused his people, telling them to prepare to move on again.

Suddenly the historian's account is unexpectedly broken by humour. The next passage in Philip O'Sullivan's narrative tells of O'Connor addressing his feet. Coming at the first point in the story that does not deal with disaster, it contributes a little light relief, but tends to make the reader distrust Don Philip's accuracy. There are a number of occasions when he embellishes his narrative for effect, and propaganda. Archbishop Ussher, with whom he had a long cantankerous doctrinal dispute, thought him "as egregious a liar as any (I verily believe) that this day breathed in Christendom". However, a modern historian like Cyril Falls, believes that he "was obviously a biased observer, but the details of the march—coming from the lips of his own father—have the ring of authenticity. Many of the incidents match up fairly well with Stafford."

This episode is the only occasion when he breaks off to be funny, and it would be pleasant to believe that it is founded on fact. It does a little to relieve the gloom of the post-Shannon stages of the march. Don Philip is talking about O'Connor Kerry, who, with old Dermot O'Sullivan, is one of the few figures on the march to emerge as a personality. O'Connor Kerry was a chief of Iraghticonnor in Kerry, whose main castle was at Carrigafoyle on the left bank of the Shannon near its mouth. (In the Desmond wars Carrigafoyle had undergone a siege of the ferocity of Dunboy, when the defenders had been driven upwards from floor to floor and hurled from the top down into the river beneath. The survivors at Carrigafoyle, like the survivors at Dunboy, were hanged after they had surrendered.) In 1600 O'Connor Kerry had handed over the castle to the crown, and became a Queen's man for a time. But when O'Donnell swept down through Ireland, O'Connor joined the final stages of the rebellion and fought at Kinsale before allying himself with O'Sullivan Beare. On this march he had suffered terribly; even before getting to the Shannon he had blistered feet that could hardly bear him, and all his body ached in agony. He had struggled on to take a prominent part in the battle at Aughrim, where he was "a peer of the bravest in the fight", the man who shouted "Victory!" when the English turned and fled. Somehow he managed the forced march that followed—probably while the horses survived, he was able to ride. Now he lay on the ground surveying his roughly bandaged feet. Sore feet were an inevitable result of trying to accommodate rough leather shoes to frost and snow. In 1592 Hugh O'Donnell himself on one of his campaigns suffered severe frostbite. According to the Four Masters he "sent for physicians to cure his feet; but they were not able to affect a cure until they had cut off both his great toes; and he was not perfectly well until the end of the year".

O'Connor addressed his feet with a heavy heroic humour. Did he really speak like this, or was perhaps Philip O'Sullivan influenced in his style of writing by Don Quixote? Cervantes'

masterpiece had been published in 1605, and by the time
Philip was grown up it had become a well-known work.

"'Feet! Have you not gone through the most difficult trials
these last three months? Why do you now shrink from the toils
of one night? Are not my head and the safety of my whole body
more precious to you, my most delicate feet? What does it avail
to have fled so far, if through your sloth we fall into the hands
of the enemy now? Surely feet, I will make sure that you shake
off this laziness.' Then with the utmost weight and effort of his
armour he struck his feet against the ground, and squeezing
out the matter, pus and blood, he got up and began to march
with the rest."

Just outside the gateway to Coolavin is the holy well of St
Attracta, surmounted by a seventeenth-century crucifixion and
eleven cursing stones. Recently the well has been tidied up and
surrounded by a concrete wall, while the stones themselves are
cemented in, all except for one smooth boulder which can still
be used for its proper function. There used to be thirteen. Their
origins predate Christianity, and so do their magical abilities to
heal and to throw curses. If your prayers had a benevolent
purpose, you turned the stones from right to left, but if you
wished to curse an enemy the direction was from left to right;
since they were instantly potent, like light switches, care had to
be taken before they were shifted. The victim could avert the
curse by putting three shovelfuls of clay on his head and reciting
certain rhymes.

St Attracta, to whom this well is dedicated, received the
veil and also the miraculous gift of the Celtic cross on the
occasion when St Patrick visited her church in Boyle. A golden
disc appeared over her head like a halo and rested on her
shoulders as she prayed. Later, when she placed it on the altar,
she found it to be a paten incised with a cross within a double
circle.

I walked with a man who talked about St Attracta as
if she was still a good friend. "She rested here before crossing
Lough Gara and going on to Boyle. . . . Did you ever hear
of the time when she was building a causeway over the
lake? Some fisherman came and disturbed her because he
wanted to have a good look at her ankles. She was a good-

looking girl, you see. She got so annoyed that she flung down the stones from her apron, and that causeway was never completed . . .".

"Every man, woman and child of Coolavin and the adjoining districts," wrote O'Rourke in 1890, "regards and reveres Attracta as one of the most favoured and privileged of all the saints in the service of God."

St Patrick used this route, travelling on to Croagh Patrick. We came out above Monasteraden from where there was a wide view across Lough Gara, snow and reeds surrounding a metallic glint of water. Monasteraden is a little village called after the shadowy St Auden whose reputation is completely eclipsed by the cult of St Attracta, and whose monastery is submerged beneath the present graveyard enclosed in a rath.

It began snowing again and I walked through a cloud of soft melting flakes past a commemorate cross sticking out of a drift which evoked the memory of Joseph Corcoran and Brian Flannery who were killed in a small tragic incident of the land war. "While defending with other brave and heroic men of this district their hearths and homes against landlord oppression," they were "shot and killed by the police and process server on April 2nd, 1881." During the nineteenth century Roscommon and Sligo were prone to the absence of their landlords. Perhaps it is hard to blame these gentlemen altogether for leaving such lonely places for cross-channel comforts. The tragedy commemorated by this monument resulted initially from an absentee being replaced by a zealous new landlord coming into the property, increasing the rents and putting up eviction notices. In the ensuing riot the police sergeant, Armstrong, with two constables panicked before a hostile crowd armed with sticks and stones. They shot the two men dead; afterwards Armstrong was lynched before his companions were rescued.

Before the crossroads of Monasteraden an isthmus cut off the upper and lower parts of Lough Gara which were surrounded by cushions of tawny reeds and scattered with swans. This is a lake jammed with crannógs; when a portion of it was drained in 1952, 308 were discovered. Fear of sudden attack and death induced men to construct these fragile little islands and make a permanent life on the windswept lake, rowing over daily to their farms on the shore in their boats of hollowed tree-trunks.

The four towers and large open quadrangle of Moygara Castle rose from a snowy field above the lake with the snow-covered dome of Keshcorran behind them. Once the castle is supposed to have had a pair of golden gates. ("Brass, more like!" a local cynic said when I told him this legend.) Before the MacDermots came and settled here, it was the O'Garas who were chieftains of the area, styled Lords of Moygara and Coolavin. By the time of O'Sullivan's retreat this castle was already a ruin—destroyed in 1581 by Scots mercenaries in the service and pay of Captain Malby, Governor of Connacht and father of young Malby, beheaded by O'Sullivan at Aughrim.

In 1637 a Fergal O'Gara still owned a great portion of the barony of Coolavin. He was important as the patron of Michael O'Clery, the chief compiler of the *Acta Sanctorum Hiberniae*, familiarly known as the *Annals of the Four Masters*. This was the same Michael O'Clery who was educated in the MacEgan castle beside the Shannon. The *Annals*, a massive compendium of information on Irish genealogical, military, social and literary history, were collected between 1632 and 1636 and were printed in Louvain where a press had been set up which used a proper Irish typeface. In his introduction Michael O'Clery acknowledged his debt to Fergal O'Gara. The O'Garas stayed on until the wars of 1690, when they supported James II with a locally raised O'Gara's infantry. Then they lost their lands and went into exile.

In this sort of weather it was difficult to walk quickly, and I dawdled around Lough Gara, since I had been given the name of an inn at the foot of the Curlieus. I had become used to chance and to relying on the good nature of landlords. But now I chased my luck too hard. Before closing the door on me, the lady at the inn told me very sensibly that there was nothing to prevent me from going a little further out of my way to Boyle, which was full of hotels. No, she could not give me the floor. She went to great trouble to send a boy to ask her neighbours, but they, too, had no floor space to spare.

With the choice of going ten miles or so through the dusk to Boyle and keeping to the direct route over the Curlieus to Ballinafad, I made up my mind to tackle the mountains and face another night in the open. The name Curlieu is supposed to mean the rough mountain. Mountain, however, is a rather exaggerated description of this heathery ridge, which is the result of a crumple in the earth's surface forcing up some old red sandstone.

In 1599 the Curlieus were the scene of the last notable Irish victory before Kinsale, when a superior force of English under Sir Conyers Clifford, Governor of Connacht, was decisively beaten by Hugh O'Donnell and Brian O'Rourke, Clifford himself dying with most of his men. This victory must have been fresh in O'Sullivan's mind as he struggled across the ridge. It was thickly wooded then, and according to Thomas Gainsford, "full of dangerous passages and especially when the Kern takes a stomach and pride to enter into action, as they term their rebellion and tumultuary insurrections".

Today the summit of the Curlieus have the plantations obligatory to mountainous Irish landscape, but their lower slopes are denuded, and the empty fields, squared off with stone walls, resemble parts of Connemara. I climbed into a lemon-coloured sky with banks of clouds massed above the Bricklieve range to the west. My map showed a fairly direct route into Ballinafad, but as I got into the hills, the road branched off into numerous small lanes that were choked with snow. The startled farmer I knocked up could direct me for several hundred yards. "You take the first on the right, then the first on the left . . . then if you are still dark, ask someone else . . .". Again I felt the exhilaration of walking by night, and did not mind being lost, jogging along in the silence under a full moon that lit up the snow.

O'Sullivan had also lost his way crossing the Curlieus by night. The usual way across them was by the Red Earl's Route, blazed by the Norman, Richard de Burgo, who in 1220 stormed his way through here to Sligo where he built a fortress. This route, from Boyle over the Curlieus Pass to Ballinafad and Sligo, is roughly followed by the present motor road. It is unlikely that O'Sullivan took it. It would have been too well guarded since the fortresses in the area, which had been built to confine O'Donnell and O'Neill in the north, could provide men to guard the passage of enemies from the south. Coming

from Lough Gara he may well have followed the same route
that I did, but struggling through forest, avoiding enemy out-
posts, he could not find his way towards the final stretch of flat
land to Leitrim about fifteen miles away. He needed a guide,
"and him God supplied", wrote Philip O'Sullivan.

Out of the darkness on the slopes of the Curlieus appeared a
figure unsuitably dressed for the January weather, in a garment
of linen, walking barefoot. His temples were bound with a white
wreath and in his hand he carried a long wand tipped with iron.

"I know you are Catholics," he is reported to have said,
"tried by divers misfortunes, fleeing from the tyranny of
heretics; that at Aughrim hill you routed the Queen's men and
now you are going to O'Rourke. He is fifteen miles distant. I
will be your guide."

What to make of him? A revenant figure from Irish mytho-
logy or hagiography? An apparition induced in many imagina-
tions by fatigue? A local druidical eccentric walking by night?
The only reason that the reader hesitates to dismiss him as a
vision is the fact that he accepted a fee of Spanish gold for his
services, "not as a reward, but in token of my good will to
you . . .". Also that even in their weariness they did not altogether trust him. He could be mad or an agent of the enemy.
But they were lost, and here he was, pushing across the mountains. He must have given them some sort of confidence as they
followed after him suspiciously groping through the darkness,
their feet slipping over the loose stones. From time to time they
fell into the snowdrifts heaped up on the windswept slopes.
O'Connor Kerry was in agony from the ulcers on his legs and
feet, and he was "only able to bear up because he suffered for
Jesus Christ". Then there was a rest period, as the survivors
came to a small mountain settlement where for the first time
they were able to buy food. There were pitiably few to provide
for now . . . less than fifty. They paused, lit camp fires, and were
able to eat and warm themselves.

When they resumed the march, O'Connor Kerry could not
stand. By this time all the horses were dead and the only way
they could get him along was for four men to carry him on their
shoulders. Towards morning someone managed to capture a
stray half-blind, half-starved horse that blundered across their

way, and O'Connor was set on this animal without saddle or bridle; its sharp backbone galled him. Some of his companions led it along, pulling it by the mane, others pushed it from behind. They made their way to the other side of the Curlieus, over the battle ground where O'Donnell had destroyed Clifford's army. At dawn their strange, spry old guide, who had led them on all night, felt that his task was completed. He "showed O'Sullivan O'Rourke's castle in the distance, and bade the rest farewell, assuring them that all danger was now past".

The forestry could not keep out of any empty mountain, and here it was once again on the plateau of the Curlieus which was covered with young trees like a Prussian haircut. They did not aid as direction finders. I pushed on a bit under the moon and came upon an empty cottage, where I thought I might spend the night. But it was not to be broken into, being locked with doors and windows securely boarded up. I went on and found another, equally inaccessible. At the third I decided to spend the night on the porch, out of the worst wind, and dressed in all my clothes, I laid out my sleeping bag on the cement floor and snatched a few hours of draughty sleep.

At dawn I woke shivering with a blast of cold air coming in at my feet. The snow had gone; across the even lines of the plantation I could see the gleam of Lough Arrow with the Bricklieve mountains beyond it. After a few undisciplined physical jerks to restore some circulation, I picked my way down to the nearest road. Once again, here was poor land on which many people had once tried to live, where the forestry had crept around their deserted homes. Later I met a man who asked me wasn't it a miracle they had all gone to England? They were happy over there with jobs. "What could they do with a few cows and empty divisions?" On one hillock he could remember twenty-five houses and a school full of children. The only man who lived there now was an Englishman who had fled the city life. "I'll give him three years," he cackled, "before he's off like the rest of them." He was an old fellow with drooping red-rimmed eyes like a spaniel and a jaw that had shifted round vanished teeth. His walk was arthritic, but active enough on this cold winter's morning. He seemed to be up and about exceptionally early, and I began to imagine what he would look like in a garment of fine linen with a white wreath round his brows.

At the foot of the Curlieus is Ballinafad, a small strategic village on the edge of Lough Arrow, which was once important because it guarded the way between the Curlieus and the Bricklieves. Here by the shores of Lough Arrow the two ranges almost meet; and here, on 2nd November, 1601, O'Donnell brought his army from his stronghold at Ballymote on the first stages of his journey down to Kinsale. Possibly on 14th January, 1603, O'Sullivan came through Ballinafad, but there is no way of knowing, since the last details of his march merge into a confusion that suggests no one had any idea where they were. Philip O'Sullivan's geography becomes totally vague at this point. A likely route would have been along the shores of Lough Key to Knockvicar and so to the refugees' destination at the fort of Leitrim.

The name Ballinafad derives from *beal an atha*, the Mouth of the Ford. The village was just about the first I had visited since leaving Glengarriff that was conscious of tourism. It had an exceptionally spick-and-span pub called the Mayfly Inn, some caravans and smartened cottages. I had arrived too soon for the shops to open, and I trailed around pursued by yet another unfriendly dog. Most of the snow had gone, but it was a cloudy sort of day, heavy with impending drizzle. I looked over the ruins of a neat little castle with two round buff towers—once there were four of them—a late fortress built in 1610 by Captain St John Barde. I walked down to the ruined monastery at the opposite end of the lagoon. A few ducks floated on the edge of the reeds, and the rain spluttered down. Nearby a woman came out of her cottage with a pail of slops.

"Could you tell me the name of the monastery?" I called out. But the door shut in my face. It was too early yet. I put on my rucksack again and marched out of Ballinafad, the dog following for three-quarters of a mile before it gave up. Almost immediately I regretted my decision as a heavy squall of rain descended and I was forced to take refuge in an abandoned estate, sheltering under the porch of a largish house whose deserted rooms were filled with musty papers, calendars and old photograph albums, scattered on the floor. It was a terrible shack, exuding a whiff of fungus, and after giving the ancient bell-pull a few lunges and listening to its faint squeaky ring, I was glad to make my way under the wet trees back to the road. Once again I was on a detour from O'Sullivan's route, following a road full of deserted cottages and small farms along the edge of the limestone terraces of the Bricklieves. Near the turn off for Castlebaldwin I skirted a little lake, an old church and graveyard, and another big empty house which a man I met said was haunted. I would have thought most of the places I had seen were stuffed with ghosts.

Later I found a farmhouse whose lady offered me a wonderful salty fry, eaten with thick slabs cut from her brown cake, and quantities of ox-blood tea. Sitting in the warmth of her kitchen, I felt the sort of dreamlike exaltation that comes from fatigue, a vague sense of well-being which blurred judgement. Seeing the rain ease off, I decided to spend the rest of the short winter's day climbing up the adjoining Bricklieves in search of megalithic graves at the bronze age cemetery of Carrowkeel.

The Bricklieves have similar origins to the Curlieus, but their limestone covering has remained, forming a far more definite high plateau squared off like giant steps, and interspersed with deep valleys. Behind the great terraces rises the high dome of Kesh. It is a very wild place, even for Roscommon, and I have heard people say that the range should be turned into a wilderness area after the American pattern. Limestone imparts an alien quality to the landscape, changing the flora so that everything has a slightly unfamiliar colouring; it also discourages the planting of fir-trees.

I reached the coves of Kesh, which consist of a line of caves high in the hill overlooking the road. I counted fifteen of them, although there are seventeen altogether, all with narrow slit entrances and grottoes inside full of dripping stalactites, ferns and moss. One is called the School Cave, another the Robber's Hole. The ground near the main cave was once a site for Lughnasa. According to the folklorist, Maire MacNeill, this almost forgotten festival was known as Garland Sunday, and took place on the last Sunday in July, a date that marked the end of the summer and the beginning of the harvest season. It was a leisurely excuse to go to the mountains and pick bilberries.

Perhaps the caves were slightly less damp when early man lived here. Excavations have produced bones and bits of twenty different animals, including reindeer, wolf, bear and arctic lemming, which had never previously been connected with Ireland. When the caves were first investigated sixty years ago, the only living occupant was "an enormous and ferocious species of spider".

The Carrowkeel cairns, in the heart of the hills, are hard to find, since they are unsignposted. With great difficulty, walking up and down the lonely valleys, I sought them out—and only found them by coming across a man who farmed on the lower limestone slopes of the Bricklieves. Even with his instructions I spent more time walking over the wet turf looking in vain for the flat tops of the passage graves. I found them more or less by accident, looking up and seeing the slight hump of a cairn in silhouette crowning one side of a steep escarpment. Up there, on top of the plateau were more graves, and then I saw that they were all around me on the summits of other hills. The place had the silence and seclusion of other chosen necropoli like Luxor. Bronze Age man chose these mountains for their isolation, and today there is still nothing to disturb the silence except sheep and the occasional hawk fluttering its wings.

Ireland has between a hundred and fifty and two hundred passage graves, of which thirteen are grouped in this cemetery at Carrowkeel on the highest point of the limestone sides of the Bricklieves. They were constructed when the mountain was bare of vegetation; later a blanket bog covered them to a large extent, and one known cairn and possibly others are still submerged in layers of peat. Those which are above the bog survived intact until 1911. Unfortunately they were opened up with far too much enthusiasm. Figuratively, the archaeologists employed the hammer, rather than the forceps, and their unskilled techniques were as destructive to proper scientific investigation as those of grave-robbers, so that the marvellous opportunity of discovering details about the tomb's builders was largely lost. We have Lloyd Praeger's tantalizing description of the opening of one of the cairns, and a regret that he lacked the pains and patience of a Howard Carter before the tomb of Tutankhamun . . . "I had the privilege of being the first to crawl down the narrow entrance, and did so with no little awe. I lit three candles and stood awhile to let my eyes accustom to the dim light. There was everything just as the last Bronze Age man had left it three or four thousand years before. A light brownish dust covered all. The central chamber was empty, but each of the three recesses opening from it contained much burnt bone debris, with flat stones on which evidently the bones had been carried in, after the bodies had been cremated in fires outside. There were also beads of stone, bone implements made from deer antlers, and many fragments of much decayed pottery. The little raised recesses in the wall were flat stones on which reposed the calcinated bones of children."

I, too, had brought a couple of candles with me and was able to climb into a grave, swept and tidy now. The pottery, the mushroom-headed bone pins, the stone hammer pendants that they took out are in the National Museum and called Carrowkeel ware. The shells which contained them remain the supreme technical achievement of megalithic man. The term megalithic is applied to people who built in slate or stone, or cut into rock surfaces. Of all the work they did, they put most skill into the passage graves, the chambers where they laid out the cremated bones of their dead.

Dusk and rain overtook me as I wandered from one cairn to the next. The rain fell in a fine spray. I was two or three hours away from any accommodation, and it looked like either a long soaking walk or another night out. The graves beside me were demonstrably water-tight. Again I ducked under a grey mound of stones standing out on its carpet of brown heather, and struggled through the narrow passage into the cruciform chamber with three little alcoves leading off it. A faint grey light seeped down behind me; the entrance was angled west-ward, and the last vestiges of daylight were struggling through the mist and rain. I had coffee and biscuits and prepared my tomb for the night. A few clothes scattered on the rough stone chippings, my sleeping bag on top, and I settled down. It was dry and warm like a cellar, without a trace of damp; infinitely more comfortable than my camp on the previous night. Probably the last people who were laid down here belonged to the late Stone Age. The tombs date back to 2500 BC, and were used for about a thousand years. My candle brilliantly lit up the interior, its light flickering beneath the patterned and plaited ceiling. I lay back and admired how the cairn had been built, tracing the eight monoliths that supported the roof, which was made of flat white stones, interwoven as closely as an upturned basket. It was a technique very similar to that used in dry-stone walls. I remembered uneasily that nothing was stuck together and it was all held up on balance, and reminded myself of the authority who declared that the megalithic Irish were some of the finest handlers of stone in the world.

CHAPTER SEVENTEEN

Bricklieves—Leitrim

> They reached Leitrim fort about eleven o'clock, being
> then reduced to 35, of whom 18 were armed, 16 sutlers and
> one was a woman. The others, who were over a thousand
> leaving Beare, had either perished or had deserted their
> leader or lingered on the road through weariness or wounds.
>
> Philip O'Sullivan

WHEN I MAPPED the route I had not foreseen how the country
that I would see fitted the theme of the story. Philip O'Sullivan
had not been in Ireland since he was a child, and he was
writing about it at second hand; in addition landscape had
completely changed. But some of the atmosphere remained, and
often I seemed to capture the defeated mood of the past.
Winter contributed with rain and wet snow over the bogs and
desolate fir forests and the chain of ruins from Glengarriff to
Leitrim. Most evenings I saw the television news, with smudged
pictures repeating ancient themes of violence and oppression.
I reached Leitrim on a Wednesday; the Sunday after was
Bloody Sunday.

But there were many stages on my walk where places of
exceptional beauty or mystery made exhilarating variations to
the succession of subdued pearly landscapes that seemed to hold
on tenaciously to bitter memories. The Bricklieves were one of
those, where traces of the past were so old that memory had
vanished. So was Lough Arrow, unexpectedly beautiful,
glimpsed occasionally through the mist after I had crawled out
of my cairn like a fox. Further down the misty mountainside, a
little more of it began to emerge like a photographer's print
taking shape in a bowl of developer. I made out the long curve
of the lake, and the dusty shapes of leafless trees. Just below me
a promontory of rock appeared out of billowing cloud, a rock
which bore traces of a Bronze Age village, probably the home of
the people who built the cairns. I paused to find the remains of

the circular huts, and then followed a winding road down to the flat land and the shuttered village of Castle Baldwin beside the lake.

The road around Lough Arrow passed another relic of the Bronze Age, the cairn of Heapstown, big as a gasworks, never excavated. A *cailleach* or hag threw it up in a night, and it used to be known as *fás-na-oiche* the growth of one night. Enchanted cats "as large as sheep", each having a nail at the end of its tail used to guard the interior. Any person unwise to pass by the cairn at night was pursued by these monsters' kittens. This part of the country was rich in beliefs of witches, giant's caves and magical lakes. Balor flourished round here. He kept his evil eye covered with ten sheepskins; it could destroy a man at a hundred yards if he took a few of them off, and a whole army if he completely uncovered it. The lakeside has traces of MacDonaghs, a castle, and ivy-covered Ballindoon Friary full of nettles and MacDonagh graves. One belongs to Terence MacDonagh, "the Great Councillor".

> Terence M'Donagh lyes within this grave,
> that says enough for all that's generous, brave
> fascetious, friendly witty just and good
> in this loud name is fully understood—
> for it includes whater'e we virtue call
> and is the Hieroglyphick of them all.
>
> 1737

I passed a crannóg, some flocks of widgeon settling on the water and Inishmore island with another ruined monastery. Then a short neck of land separated Lough Arrow from Lough Key, and here, in theory, I rejoined O'Sullivan Beare. This narrow division of the lakes, which is about a mile in extent, was a favourite route for O'Donnell when he made his sorties south- wards. In 1590 Sir Richard Bingham, the Governor of Connacht, built a small fortress here to try and contain invaders from the north. But it was a half-hearted sort of effort, no more than a couple of ramparts to control this stretch of frontier territory. It did little to stop O'Donnell. By the time that O'Sullivan passed between the lakes, it had either been flattened in successive raids or had reverted finally to the Irish or had been merely abandoned.

Arthur Young got very enthusiastic about Lough Key, calling it the Killarney of the West. "It is one of the most delicious scenes ever beheld—a lake of circular form, bounded very boldly by mountains." The islands on Lough Key are still wooded; in winter the rounded grey outline of trees gave them a look of so many mushrooms. Each has its own ruin, Castle Island, Trinity Island with its abbey where Sir Conyers Clifford's headless body is buried, and where the so-called *Annals of Boyle* were compiled, and so on. Most of the ruins are ecclesiastical, further evidence of clerical preference for protected seclusion. The ancient trees, which even the most rapacious of planters never got round to cutting, hovering round these ancient remains and concealing them, cannot have changed in appearance for four hundred years. In winter, that is—in summer the lake before them is streaked with speed-boats driven by joyful French and German vacationers.

At Knockvicar I found a guesthouse where I rested late in an ample Georgian-sized bedroom, recovering easily from two nights of exposure. The next day was the last of my walk, Wednesday 26th January, and it began typically with the sound of rain and the smell of fry. I lay savouring both, oddly regretting that there were only fifteen miles left to Leitrim, and wondering if I could sleep for another twenty minutes. For the first time I had caught the winter late-morning habit.

Knockvicar is a Shannon-side village with an old stone bridge, weir, and black river flowing between lines of trees. Beside the deserted pier I found a peeling charge list, made under the Conformation Act of 1804 in respect to Shannon navigation. This was another place where the marches of O'Donnell and O'Sullivan Beare converged. At Knockvicar O'Sullivan Beare's people rested for the last time and ate the rest of the food they had managed to purchase the day before. The kern, gallowglass and fragmented survivors and groomsmen then made their way through forests which were later replaced by the gracious planned expanses of Rockingham.

Here, it seemed, was the last ruined house I would see. It

had been a very fine one in its day. What Osbert Sitwell considered to be the best intact example of a Nash country house was accidentally burnt in 1957. A year later its owners, the King-Harmons, handed over the estate to the Forestry Department. The Department has gone to great lengths to finish what the fire began. The name "Rockingham" has been changed to the "Lough Key Forest Park," and the fact that the place was the careful creation of the King-Harmons is nowhere acknowledged. "The mansion, despite the fire, was nearly perfect," bewailed a recent correspondent in the *Irish Times*. "The church still had its pews, the lodges were in good fettle, the carved stone gateposts and the delightful balustraded bridges were in perfect shape. Under the Department's occupancy all of these have been pillaged; the wonderful red cedar walk near the house was piteously cut down." January seemed to be a good season for demolishing ruins, and as I passed they were painstakingly removing the last little bit of the old place. "There was a marble staircase, and you could drive up those stairs in the best Rolls-Royce," one of the workmen said, nudging a brick. The absence of even the shell of the building in a demesne of this nature—where, unlike Frenchpark, most of the trees have been carefully preserved—gives a curious slackness to the beautifully tailored landscape bordering the island-studded lake. The essential relationship between house and surroundings has been irretrievably broken, and the wooden buildings of the caravan park made inadequate substitutes for Nash's masterpiece. Only one little tower survives, a gazebo on a point overlooking the water, out of reach of the bulldozer.

From Knockvicar I set off along a cold wet road past a succession of reedy fields. Even when the reeds have been cleared, they soon show up sharp through the grass. Here were the borders of Leitrim, and an empty countryside, a morass from which people had fled. Between 1927 and 1970 the population of Roscommon fell by 37 per cent, and of Leitrim by 50 per cent. The land was not always bad, rather the contrary; it was once famous for its grass and cattle. "Champaign and very fruitful" was how the *Calendar of State Papers* described it; Barnabe Riche wrote in 1610 that "Leitrim consists entirely of mountains covered with luxuriant herbage. It feeds so many cattle that within its narrow compass it counted at one time above 120,000 head."

O'Sullivan made for O'Rourke's castle in the town of Leitrim because it still held out, and he knew that it was likely to resist surrender for as long as possible. The O'Rourkes, who were among the paramount chiefs in Ireland, at one time had land that stretched from the sea beyond Lough Allan to Carrick-on-Shannon to the borders of County Longford. Their kingdom was reduced, but enough remained for the current O'Rourke to continue the tradition of resisting the English, and maintaining their independence. Here in this corner of Leitrim, "the most champaign ground and the best of all", the old Gaelic pattern of life had remained unchanged. Some years before, in 1588, Brian O'Rourke, the father of Brian Oge O'Rourke, O'Sullivan Beare's host and saviour, had harboured another enemy of the Queen, the shipwrecked Spaniard Don Francisco de Cuellar. Or rather his wife did. "The chief was not there," wrote de Cuellar, "having gone away to defend a piece of his territory which the English had come to take from him. Although this chief is a savage, he is a good Christian, and an enemy of the heretics, and is always at war with them." On one occasion, according to the Four Masters, Brian O'Rourke "scornfully dragged the Queen's picture atte a horse-taile and disgracefully cut the same in pieces". His main enemy, with whom he had a deadly feud, was Sir Richard Bingham, the savage Governor of Connacht. He lost eventually, and driven out from his diminished kingdom, sought refuge with James VI of Scotland; that realist soon handed him over to the English authorities. On November 2nd, 1591, he was arraigned for High Treason by the Grand Jury of Middlesex. He refused to recognize the court. He would not plead for mercy, only asking to be hanged with a halter of withy as men were hanged in Ireland, rather than with English hemp. He died around Christmas time, 1591, scornfully repudiating the ministrations of the renegade Protestant Archbishop of Cashel, who tried to make him recant. "A prouder man walked not in his time," it was said of him. Sir Henry Sydney, the ex-Lord Deputy, considered him "the proudest man that he ever dealt with in Ireland. No one of his tribe excelled him in bounty, hospitality, in giving rewards, for panegyrical poems, and in sumptuousness in numerous troops, in comeliness, in firmness, in maintaining the field of battle . . .".

His son, Brian Oge, had actually been educated in England, where he was sent as a child along with Lord Clanricarde by Sir John Perrot. It was a colonial experience shared by Hugh O'Neill and repeated many centuries later by Rajahs' sons. The two "pretty, quick boys" were expected to benefit from a good cross-channel Renaissance education. It worked different ways; they fought on opposing sides at the Battle of Kinsale.

When his father was driven out of Leitrim, Brian Oge O'Rourke spoiled everything belonging to the English that he could lay his hands on. After the old man was hanged, however, he had a try at squaring the enemy and legally retaining his lands; in a letter to the Privy Council he told them that his father had justly been punished for his "fractiousness" and suggested that he should become his heir. When it became plain that his letter would be ignored, from that time on he sought revenge for old O'Rourke's death. In 1593 he attacked the unspeakable Bingham at Ballymote, burning Ballymote and some thirteen villages around it. In 1597 he joined O'Donnell and helped him to push back the English army which he was instrumental in defeating at the Battle of the Curlieus. He was at Kinsale. By the time O'Sullivan Beare sought his aid the O'Rourke clan was divided into contending factions with the Queen's O'Rourke in control of the main castle at Dromohair and Brian Oge holding out in Leitrim. At the end of 1602 "the Deputy kept Christmas at Galway, and there received the Flahertys, MacDermotts, O'Connor Roe and others, so that only the fickle and treacherous O'Rourke and Tyrone's Maguires and Tyrell persisted in the rebellion with the Earl of Tyrone". (Tyrell, of course, was O'Sullivan's old ally.)

I crossed a fine stone bridge over the infant Shannon with the weed-filled cutting of Lough Allen canal running parallel.

"Is this the way to Leitrim?" I asked a woman sheltering under the trees.

"The village, you mean?" She pointed to a signpost. A gust

of wind lifted the umbrella and the struts broke loose so that it hung over my head like a shot crow. "Leitrim one mile."

The name had meant much to me, and I had built the place up as something substantial. A dozen houses, a few shops and pubs. "You could spend a pound in it," the barman said, drawing a much needed pint, as I took off another layer of damp clothing and presented him with my broken umbrella. I had arrived thirteen days and two hours later than O'Sullivan, who is said to have finally reached O'Rourke's castle at eleven o'clock.

The surviving wall of the castle stood behind some shops and a line of washing. It was about twelve feet up, and on top a flat stone had been erected with the arms of O'Rourke on one side and O'Sullivan's wild boar on the other. To get up to see it you needed the agility of a monkey; not only does the wall have to be climbed, but you have to balance or sit astride it and read the inscription. "Here on January 14th, 1603, arrived Donal O'Sullivan Beare and his followers after the epic march from Glengarriff in 14 days. Though one thousand started with him, only 35 remained, 16 armed men, 18 non-combatants and one woman, the wife of the chief's uncle, Dermot O'Sullivan."

"I am astonished," wrote Philip O'Sullivan, "that Dermot O'Sullivan, my father, an old man near seventy, and the woman of delicate sex were able to go through these toils, which youths in the flower of their age and the height of their strength were unable to endure." Dermot O'Sullivan was a tough scarred veteran with another thirty years to live. One would like to know more about the woman of delicate sex. The writers of the inscription were wrong when they assumed that she was Dermot's wife and Philip O'Sullivan's mother; the historian states quite clearly that his mother stayed behind at Glengarriff with O'Sullivan Beare's wife to await a ship to take her to Spain. The woman who survived was not important enough to be named; perhaps she was a wife of one of the soldiers or one of the horseboys or body servants that had set out from Glengarriff. Probably most of the soldiers who came from Connacht and who deserted during the final stages of the march managed to make their way to their own homes. Some of those who ran away at the Shannon crossing or others who had fallen out wounded and exhausted may have managed to survive. But most of the people from Glengarriff must have died along the route. O'Sullivan Beare had given himself too great a task: to escort six hundred non-combatants with four hundred soldiers for two hundred miles in mid-winter over hostile territory was demonstrably impossible. That any were alive at the end of the journey made his march into a military epic.

Over the next few days a few other ragged and exhausted survivors staggered into Leitrim fort, where they were hospitably welcomed by Brian O'Rourke. Meanwhile O'Sullivan hardly paused to rest; his obsession to join with O'Neill and strengthen that remaining focus of resistance made him start immediately to collect another force together. Once again the Spanish gold, carefully nurtured all along the march, paid his allies. The three hundred men who made up this new expedition included a few who had survived the retreat from Glengarriff, and some of Tyrell's gallowglasses who had also made their way to Leitrim.

O'Sullivan joined with another resistance fighter, Brian Maguire, and set out for Lough Erne in modern Fermanagh, about thirty miles to the north-east of Leitrim. The lake and flooded fords of the Erne river, which flows from Lough Erne down to Lough Oughter, were in the hands of the Queen's Maguire. O'Sullivan brought his small army across the river above Belturbet and camped in the rear of the enemy. Even this small force brought its women and horseboys with it; on one occasion during the campaign, when O'Sullivan was left in camp with a reduced force, he was attacked by the enemy who arrived by water. He managed to frighten them off by arming the women and boys with staves that looked like spears.

With Brian Maguire he made a sudden attack on the Queen's people and utterly defeated them. Then, he took a terrible revenge for all his sufferings on the garrisons who held the islands on Lough Erne, visiting each one and annihilating it. His campaign was swift and successful; after the slaughter he continued eastward for fifty miles where he hoped to find O'Neill, who had been hiding out with his last sixty horseman and some infantry near Slieve Gallon in the north-east corner of Lough Neagh.

O'Sullivan and Maguire arrived early in March. But it was too late, and everything had been useless. Only a few days earlier O'Neill had gone to Mellifont, where, deceived, weary of defeat, "made a tennis ball of fortune", he submitted to Mountjoy. "Tyrone"—the English knew him as Earl of Tyrone —"being admitted to the Lord Deputy's chamber, kneeled at the door humbly on his knees for a long space, making his penitent submission to Her Majesty, and after being required to come nearer to the Lord Deputy, performed the same ceremonies in all the humbleness the pace of an hour or thereabouts". He had not been told that the Queen was already dead and that his humiliation, "one of the deplorablest sights that I ever saw", according to a witness, was the last public act of her reign.

O'Neill was given back his earldom, and continued as Earl of Tyrone for a few more years before going into exile in Italy. Most of those who were still in revolt hastened to follow his example and to go over to the English. Maguire, William Burke, Tyrell and others swiftly made their submission to the new King. Tyrell is said to have had an interview with King James, in which he offered to collect all the swordsmen in Ireland in a body and take them abroad out of trouble. (The refusal of this offer, in the opinion of Standish O'Grady, was the source of future bloodshed.) O'Connor Kerry travelled across the Irish sea to seek out the King, even before he had left Scotland for his new crown; the old rebel was honourably received, invited down to London and later reinstated in his own country.

Brian Oge O'Rourke, the son of the man who had been betrayed by James to his death, did not surrender and died almost exactly a year after he received O'Sullivan Beare, resisting to the last. He was besieged at Leitrim Castle by Sir Oliver Lambert, and died of a fever on 28th January, 1604. After that the castle was yielded. "A brave and protecting man," considered the Four Masters, " . . . a sedate and heroic man, kind to his friends, fierce to his foes . . . illustrious . . . for clemency, hospitality, nobleness, firmness and steadiness."

There is an unverified story that O'Sullivan Beare, like O'Connor Kerry, also went over to see the King and seek

pardon. If this is so he was refused; he was the one major Irish
rebel who was not given back his titles and lands. There was no
need to be magnanimous to a man who had caused so much
trouble. To restore him would have been awkward; everything was settling down nicely in Beare, where Sir Owen, who
had taken such pains to prove himself a Queen's man, was
granted the chieftaincy and held the surrounding land.

Even when Donal Cam had long been exiled to Spain, and
was in receipt of a pension from the Spanish King, he wrote to
King James promising obedience if his estate were restored.
But he was refused, and he spent the rest of his life in exile. His
family had all made their way to Spain, his wife and children,
uncle, aunt, cousins, and other close kinsmen and neighbours.
Many entered the service of the King of Spain; Philip the
historian served both as a soldier and a sailor; in 1618 two
O'Sullivans died in a naval battle against the Turks off the
Fortunate Islands, along with a number of other Munstermen,
a MacCarthy, an O'Driscoll, an O'Reilly and a Fitzgerald.

It was easy for Irishmen to live in Spain where they were
allowed to assume precedence over all other foreigners. Later
they intermarried with the Spanish nobility, took high positions
in the state, and their regiments were on a par with those of
Metropolitan Spain. As late as 1792 a resolution of the Spanish
Council of State approved that "the formalities of the oath, to
which all other nations have been accorded to submit, shall not
be exacted from the Irish, seeing that by the mere fact of settling
in Spain, the Irish are accounted Spaniards and enjoy the same
rights."

Donal Cam as a leading exiled chief was treated extremely
generously by the Spaniards. He was the first Irishman to be
knighted by the Spanish King, and he received a monthly
pension of three hundred ducats. (His old uncle, Dermot, got
fifty ducats.) He was awarded the cross of Santiago, one of the
most select military orders in Spain, which demanded a detailed
proof of nobility and genealogy requiring twenty-three witnesses. Later in 1617 he was made Count of Berehaven, much to
the indignation of King James. "His Majesty cannot chuse but
dislike that they should bestowe upon him any title or dignitary,"
one of the Ministers of State wrote to the English representative

at the Spanish Court, "which only properly belongeth unto him towards his own subjects; that therefore he would be glad that they would forbear to convey any such titulary honour upon any of his subjects without his privity." The protest was ignored and this title was inherited by his eldest son, Donal, who died as a result of an accident only a few months after Donal Cam's own death. Then the title passed to his second son, Derniseo O'Sullivan, who married a daughter of the Duke of Sesa and had one daughter, Doña Antonia O'Sullivan y Cordaba. In 1659 Derniseo O'Sullivan Beare died, leaving a fortune of 100,000 crowns to this twelve-year-old girl. She was married to her maternal uncle and died without issue in 1718. The Count of Berehaven's line became extinct and his fortune went to support the new College for Irish nobles in Salamanca.

Donal Cam himself had died in 1618. His end was violent, although his last years were spent in the corrosive tedium and peace of exile, where he sought increasingly the consolation of religion by attending two or three masses a day. He was conspicuously pious and generous to the poor and needy. Ironically the cause of his death was his cousin and biographer Philip O'Sullivan, the historian. On a stifling July day, Donal Cam was called away from reciting the rosary to settle a futile exiles' quarrel between Philip and a member of his own household, the sinister Anglo-Irishman, John Bath, who had previously played a long devious role in Irish affairs. Bath had referred to the Count of Berehaven in insulting terms and Philip insisted on a duel. Swords were drawn; when Donal Cam tried to interfere and stop the fight, Bath turned and stabbed him in the throat for his pains. He died carrying his gloves in one hand and his rosary in the other.

Philip took refuge from the civil authorities in the house of the French ambassador. Later he wrote an elegant letter to young Donal to console him on the tragic death of his father. The letter was considered "a masterpiece of language and style; the Latin is pure and the words breathe the most perfect resignation to the will of Providence in the heavy blow that has befallen Ireland". No one knows when or where Philip himself died; some say that he even returned to the country of his birth.

THE O'SULLIVANS OF BEARE AND BANTRY, 1549–1659

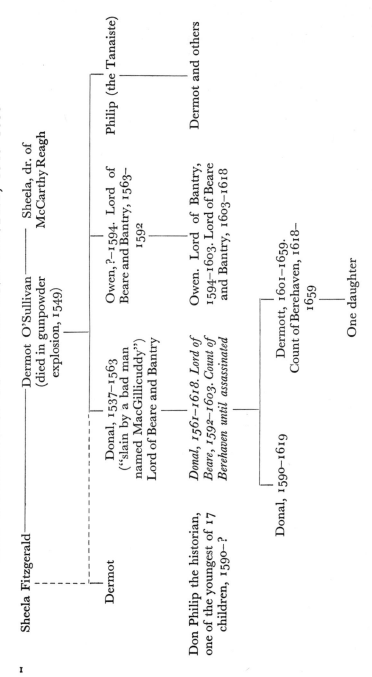

Copied from *Selections from the Zoilomastix of Philip O'Sullivan Beare* by T. J. O'Donnell. Dublin 1960.

BOOKS CONSULTED

The Retreat of O'Sullivan Beare.

AODH DE BLACAM, *O'Sullivan Bere*. The Capuchin Annual, 1946–47.

Annals of the Four Masters, trans. John O'Donovan. Hodges and Smith, Dublin, 1851.

THOMAS STAFFORD, *Pacata Hibernia*. Edited Standish O'Grady. Downey and Co, London, 1896.

PHILIP O'SULLIVAN, *Historial Catholicae Iberniae Compendium.* Translated as *Ireland under Elizabeth* by M. J. Byrne, Sealy, Bryers and Walker, Dublin, 1903.

Elizabethan Ireland

R. BAGWELL, *Ireland under the Tudors*. Holland Press, London, 1963.

W. T. BUTLER, *Gleanings from Irish History*. Longman, London, 1925.

JOHN DERRICKE, *The Image of Ireland*. Adam and Charles Black, Edinburgh, 1883.

CYRIL FALLS, *Elizabeth's Irish Wars*. Methuen, London, 1951.

E. HARDY, *Survivors of the Armada*. Constable, London, 1966.

G. HAYES McCOY, *Scots Mercenary Forces in Ireland*. Burns, Oates and Washbourne, London, 1937.

A. K. LONGFIELD, *Anglo-Irish Trade in the 16th century*. Routledge, London, 1929.

H. F. McCLINTOCK, *Old Irish and Highland Dress*. Dundalgan Press, Dundalk, 1951.

MARGARET MACCURTAIN, *Tudor and Stuart Ireland*. Gill and Macmillan, 1972.

EDWARD MacLYSAGHT, *Irish Life in the 17th Century*. Cork University Press, Cork, 1950.

EDWARD MacLYSAGHT, *The Kenmare Manuscripts*. Stationery Office, Dublin, 1942.

CONSTANTIA MAXWELL, *Irish History from Contemporary Sources, 1509–1610*. Allen and Unwin, London, 1923.

HENRY MORLEY, *Ireland under Elizabeth and James Ist*. George Routledge, London, 1890.

GRENFELL MORTON, *Elizabethan Ireland*. Longman, London, 1971.

FYNES MORYSON, *An Itinerary*. Reprinted, James MacLehose, Glasgow, 1907–8.

BARRY O'BRIEN, *Munster at War*. Mercier Press, Cork, 1971.

G. B. O'CONNOR, *Elizabethan Ireland*. Sealy Bryers and Walker, Dublin, 1896.

T. J. O'DONNELL, *Selections from the Zoilomastix of Philip O'Sullivan Beare*. Stationery Office, Dublin, 1960.

SEAN O'FAOLAIN, *The Great O'Neill*. Longman, London, 1942.

DAVID BEERS QUINN, *The Elizabethans and the Irish*. Cornell, 1966.
E. RYNNE, *North Munster Studies*. O'Gorman Ltd, Galway, 1967.
JOHN J. SILKE, *Kinsale*. Liverpool University Press, 1970.
M. WALSHE, *Spanish Knights of Irish Origin*. Stationery Office, Dublin, 1960.

General

MARY CARBERY, *The Farm on Lough Gur*. Longman, London, 1937.
J. C. COLEMAN, *The Caves of Ireland*. Anvil Books, Dublin, 1965.
J. C. COLEMAN, *Journey into Muskerry*. Dundalgan Press, Dundalk.
ERIC CROSS, *The Tailor and Anstey*. Chapman, London, 1942.
DE LATOCNAYE, *A Frenchman's Walk in Ireland, 1796–97*. Hodges Figgis; McCaw, Sado, London, 1917.
J. DOWD, *The County of Limerick*. McKern and Sons, Dublin, 1896.
T. W. FREEMAN, *Ireland*. Methuen, London, 1950.
J. ANTHONY GAUGHAN, *Doneraile*. Kamac Publications, 1970.
ROBERT GIBBINGS, *Lovely is the Lee*. Dent, London, 1945.
D. F. GLEESON, *The Last Lords of Ormonde*. Sheed and Ward, Dublin, 1938.
GROSE, *Antiquities of Ireland*. S. Hooper, London, 1791.
J. GROVE-WHITE, *Historical and Topographical Notes*. Guy and Co., London, 1911.
MR. and MRS. S. C. HALL, *Ireland, its Scenery and Character*. How and Parsons, London, 1841.
PETER HARBISON, *Guide to the National Monuments of Ireland*. Gill and Macmillan, Dublin, 1970.
R. HAYWARD, *Where the Shannon Flows*. Harrap, London, 1950.
JOHN HEALY, *Death of an Irish Town*. Mercier Press, Cork, 1967.
H. D. INGLIS, *Ireland in 1843*. Whittaker and Co., London, 1835.
H. D. INGLIS, *A Journey through Ireland*. Whittaker and Co., London, 1836.
SEAN JENNET, *Connacht*. Faber, London, 1970.
SEAN JENNET, *Munster*. Faber, London, 1969.
LORD KILLANIN and MICHAEL DUIGNAN, *Shell Guide to Ireland*. The Ebury Press, London, 1962.
ROSE MACAULAY, *The Pleasure of Ruins*. Weidenfeld and Nicolson, London, 1953.
CONSTANTIA MAXWELL, *The Stranger in Ireland*. J. Cape, London, 1954.
M. MCCARTHY, *Priests and People in Ireland*. Hodges and Figgis, Dublin, 1902.
EILEEN MCCRAKEN, *Irish Woods since Tudor Times*. David and Charles, Newton Abbot, 1971.

MAIRE MacNEIL, *The Festival of Lughnasa*. Oxford University Press, 1962.

W. H. MAXWELL, *Wild Sports of the West*. Gresham Publishing Co., Dublin, 1944.

JAMES MORRIS, *Pax Britannica: The Climax of an Empire*. Faber, London, 1968.

E. R. NORMAN & J. K. S. ST. JOSEPH, *The Early Development of Irish Society*. Cambridge University Press, 1969.

JOHN O'DONOVAN, *Customs and Tribes of Hynamy*. Irish Archaeological Society, Dublin, 1843.

SIR MICHAEL O'DWYER, *The O'Dwyers of Kilnamanagh*. John Murray, London, 1933.

CANON PETER O'LEARY. *My Story*. Translated from the Irish *Mo Sceal Fein*. Gill and Macmillan, Dublin, 1973.

SÉAN Ó RÍORDÁIN, *Antiquities of the Irish Countryside*. Methuen, London, 1942.

A. E. ORME, *The World's Landscapes*. Longman, London, 1970.

T. O'ROURKE, *History of Sligo*. Duffey and Co., Dublin, 1890.

CAESAR OTWAY, *Sketches in Ireland*. William Curry, Dublin, 1827.

R. L. PRAEGER, *The Way that I Went*. Hodges and Figgis Ltd., Dublin, 1947.

JOHN RICHARDSON, *The Great Folly, Superstition and Idolatry of Images in Ireland*. J. Hyde. Dublin, 1727.

SEYMOUR ST. J. D., *The Diocese of Emly*. Church of Ireland Publishing Co., Dublin, 1913.

P. A. SHARKEY, *The Heart of Ireland*. M. J. Ward, Dublin, 1927.

CHARLES SMITH, *State of the County and City of Cork*. A. Reilly, Dublin, 1774.

W. S. WOODMARTIN, *History of Sligo*. Hodges and Figgis, Dublin, 1882.

W. S. WOODMARTIN, *Pagan Ireland*. Longman, London, 1895.

ARTHUR YOUNG, *A Tour in Ireland*. Edited by Constantia Maxwell. Oxford University Press, 1925

CARLTON YOUNGER, *Ireland's Civil War*. Muller, London, 1968.

FRANK O'CONNOR, *Kings, Lords & Commons*, Irish poems from the seventh to the nineteenth century. Gill and Macmillan, Dublin, 1970.

PHILIP LARKIN, "Churchgoing" from *The Less Deceived*. Marvell, London, 1966.

Index

Compiled by H. E. Crowe

THE MARCH OF
O'SULLIVAN BEARE

IRELAND